BEYOND THE BASICS

A Guide *for* Advanced Users
of Family Tree Maker® 2011

BEYOND THE BASICS

A Guide *for* Advanced Users
of Family Tree Maker 2011

TANA L. PEDERSEN

ancestry publishing

Library of Congress Cataloging-in-Publication Data

Pedersen, Tana L., 1973–
    Beyond the basics : a guide for advanced users of Family Tree Maker 2011 /
Tana L. Pedersen.
        p. cm.
    Includes bibliographical references and index.
    ISBN 978-1-59331-335-7
    1. Family tree maker. 2. Genealogy—Computer programs. 3. Genealogy—Data
processing. I. Title.
    CS14.P424 2010
    929'.10285--dc22

                                                    2010047857

10 9 8 7 6 5 4 3 2 1
ISBN-978-1-59331-335-7

Printed in the United States of America.

Contents

Chapter 2: Defining Relationships 21

Chapter 8: Making the Software Work for You 221

Chapter 9: Using Family Tree Maker and Ancestry.com 233

Acknowledgments

This book has been a huge undertaking to which many people have directly contributed. I would like to thank Michelle Pfister for her kind words and confidence in me, Duff Wilson and Mark LeMonnier for their technical expertise and suggestions, the Customer Support staff at Ancestry.com for their willingness to help, the Alpha 8 group for their insights into the product, and Jana Lloyd Porter for being my go-to editor. I also want to express appreciation to Chris Trainor, Matthew Rayback, and Wendy Jessen.

I would also like to thank you, the Family Tree Maker user. Almost every day I receive e-mails from users who want to learn more or want to share successes they've had. It is because of you that I am inspired to try new things and find workarounds for the software's limitations. It would be hard to find a group of people more engaged than those who use Family Tree Maker; whether it's having spirited debates on the message boards and blog or holding monthly user groups, I am continually impressed at the generosity you show helping each other overcome obstacles and walking new users through basic tasks. I learn from you every day and I hope that this book will add to the conversation.

And as always, a special thanks to my son, Braden, and my family, without whom nothing would be possible.

Introduction

A few years ago I was entering several new generations into my Family Tree Maker database, and the same names seemed to be appearing over and over again. No surprise really—everyone in that branch of my tree seemed to be named Samuel, Benjamin, or Elizabeth. Then one day as I stared at the list of family names, I had an epiphany. The reason why all those people were so similar was because they *were* the same people. I hadn't recognized it before, but I had two ancestors who were cousins and married each other. I had faithfully entered the same branch of my family tree, twice.

I suspect that I'm not the only family historian who has dealt with this kind of situation. Whether it's your great-grandfather who appears to have married every young woman in the county or that elusive female you just can't prove is actually related to you, we've all struggled to figure out the best ways to record these types of genealogy puzzles.

And then, when the state of Utah put thousands of digital images of death records online, I was able to view the causes of death (and contributing health factors) for several of my ancestors and some collateral relatives. When I saw a pattern of coronary heart disease and stroke, I became interested in gathering even more medical information about my relatives and creating a family health history.

Because the *Companion Guide* covers every available feature in the software, I only have time to discuss the basic use of each component; I don't have much opportunity to discuss how you use the software to record "real" families. I wrote *Beyond the Basics* to fill in the gaps that the *Companion Guide* couldn't cover.

While each family tree has its own snags and unique challenges, there are some common dilemmas that most of us face at some time or another as we try to record our ancestors' lives. I have used examples from my own personal research and family tree to guide you through some of these real-life scenarios. I've also included some custom reports and decorative charts that I've found useful either for sharing my finds with other family members or tracking my research so I know where to look next. I hope you'll find them useful too.

This book is written with the advanced Family Tree Maker user in mind. I assume that readers are already proficient in basic Family Tree Maker skills such as adding individuals and facts, creating sources, working with media items, and making charts and reports. Some tasks don't include step-by-step instructions because the basics have already been covered in the *Companion Guide*. If you do need a refresher or more help, please consult the *Companion Guide* (it's available as a PDF from the Help menu). In addition, this guide doesn't need to be read from cover to cover. Feel free to jump from topic to topic and look over the subjects that are important to you.

As you read this book, you'll notice several features that provide you with useful information:

- **Tips** offer you timely hints about features and suggestions on the best way to complete tasks.

- **Notes** teach you additional ways of performing tasks.

- **Sidebars** give you additional information on a variety of family history topics, such as sources and Ancestry Member Trees.

- **Appendixes** at the back of the book list keyboard shortcuts for some common tasks and include information on source templates.

Best of luck with your family history search.

Chapter One

Filling Out Your Tree

As you enter names, dates, and places into Family Tree Maker, it's a good idea to consider what your ultimate goal is. Are you writing a family history book? Do you want to print wall charts and custom reports? Will you be sharing a GEDCOM of your tree with other family members? The way in which you enter your information today can affect how you access and use it in the future. This chapter explains a variety of conventions you can follow to keep your tree organized and your facts accurate and consistent.

In This Chapter
- Entering Names
- Entering Dates
- Entering Locations
- Entering Notes

Entering Names

Today most of us have a first name and a last name, and we spell them the same way every day. But not that long ago, our ancestors were a bit more flexible with the rules. Did it really matter if your surname was spelled Reed, Reid, or Rieth? Not to my Pennsylvania forefathers. Generally, when you record a name, you enter it exactly as it appears in the record or source. However, we all need help when we encounter challenging situations.

Alternate Names and Nicknames

Given name, legal name, everyday name, married name. Some of our family members like to keep us guessing about who they really are. So how do you decide whether a name is a nickname or an alternate name—and whether it should be recorded at all?

You will enter a "preferred" name for every individual in your tree. This could be the name that always appears in official records or it could be the name he or she was known by. It's up to you. After you've decided what the preferred name should be you can also enter nicknames and alternate names.

Adding an Alternate Name for an Individual

My great-grandfather's name was Michael John Reed, but he is almost always recorded as MJ Reed in records. I entered his "preferred" name (Michael John Reed) in the Name fact because this is the name he was given at birth, but I also wanted to document MJ Reed as an additional name. I had two options: I could add an alternate Name fact or enter the name in the Also Known As (AKA) fact.

It doesn't really matter whether you use multiple Name facts or the AKA fact; the main objective is to record names the same way for all people in your tree. The AKA fact does have some advantages however. Also Known As names can be listed as separate entries in the Index and can be included on charts and reports in addition to the preferred name—alternate Name facts cannot (fig. 1-1).

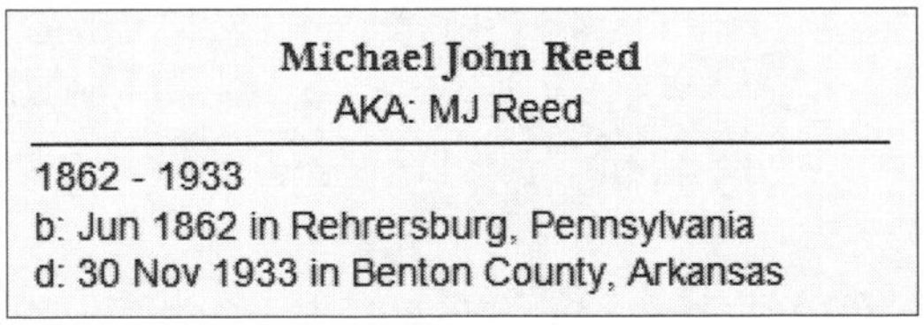

Figure 1-1

A chart can include a preferred name and an Also Known As name.

> **Michael John Reed**
> AKA: MJ Reed
>
> 1862 - 1933
> b: Jun 1862 in Rehrersburg, Pennsylvania
> d: 30 Nov 1933 in Benton County, Arkansas

To enter a name in the Also Known As fact

Go to the individual's Person tab on the People workspace. If necessary, click the **Facts** button. Right-click the workspace and select **Add Fact**. Select "Also

Known As" in the **Facts** list. In the editing panel, enter the alternate name in the **Description** field. Don't forget to add source information.

To add an alternate Name fact

Go to the individual's Person tab on the People workspace. If necessary, click the **Facts** button. Right-click the workspace and select **Add Fact**. Select "Name" in the **Facts** list. In the editing panel, enter the alternate name. Don't forget to add source information.

Adding a Nickname for an Individual

Growing up, I had always known one of my great-aunts as Tally. I naturally assumed that was her name—until I started searching for my family's history and couldn't find a mention of her anywhere. A quick call to my parents and I discovered her given name was actually Sarah Jane. Without this information I would have been stumped and unable to figure out why I couldn't find any records for her.

If one of your family members was known by a nickname rather than his or her given name, you'll want to enter this in your tree. If the nickname is a common one (for example, Tim for Timothy), this is not necessary. But, if the nickname is unconventional or uncommon, as it was with my great-aunt, you'll want to record it.

Some people like to indicate a nickname using quotation marks (for example, Sarah Jane "Tally" Gedge). If you follow this practice, be aware that Family Tree Maker considers quoted text in Name facts an error; you will need to change your warning preferences to accept quoted information. (To do this, choose **Tools>Options** and click the **Warning** tab. Then choose "Leave text in quotes" from the **Text in quotes in the name fact** drop-down list).

You can also record the nickname in the Also Known As fact (for instructions, see the previous task, "Adding an Alternate Name for an Individual").

Name Suffixes

Name suffixes such as Jr. (Junior), Sr. (Senior), and III (the Third) can be helpful in distinguishing between ancestors with the same or similar names.

To enter a suffix go to the individual's Person tab on the People workspace. In the editing panel, enter the individual's name in the **Name** field. After the surname, enter the suffix without a comma (for example, John Bobbitt Sr.).

> Note: Do not enter name suffixes such as "Jr." or "III" in the Title fact; it is reserved for appellations such as Doctor, Reverend, or Colonel (see "Titles" on page 7). Suffixes entered in the Title fact will be printed in front of the individual's name on reports (e.g., III George Hunt instead of George Hunt III, or Jr. George Hunt instead of George Hunt Jr.).

Surnames

You don't have to spend much time doing family history before you discover that surnames aren't as simple as they appear. Spelling variations, cultural traditions, and foreign languages can make it more complicated to record certain

Foreign Language Characters

Many of us have ancestors from foreign countries, and in our research we come across names and places that use special characters (such as ø, ú, ö, and ñ). Family Tree Maker has a tool to help you enter the most common characters. You can also use the language utility on your computer to choose from hundreds of characters and symbols.

Entering a Character Using Family Tree Maker
Place your cursor in the field where you want to insert the character. Then click **Edit>Insert Symbol**. Click the character you want to use; then click **Insert**.

Using Additional Characters Accessible in Windows
Place your cursor in the field where you want to insert the character. Open the Character Map (click the **Start** button on the Windows taskbar; then select **Programs>Accessories> System Tools>Character Map**). Use the scrollbar to find the character you want. Click the character; then click **Select**. The character will appear in the Characters to copy field. Click **Copy**. Then access your Family Tree Maker tree and place your cursor in the field where you want to insert the character. Click **Edit>Paste**.

names. Fortunately, Family Tree Maker can handle many types of unconventional surnames.

Duplicate Surnames

Occasionally, you may find a female ancestor whose last name at birth is the same as her husband's surname; in other words, her maiden name and her married name are the same. This happened quite often in certain areas such as Scandinavia, where patronymics were used for centuries. In my family, my Danish great-grandparents were both born Pedersens. To someone unfamiliar with my family tree, this name duplication might appear to be a mistake. To prevent any confusion, I have entered a personal note that explains why both surnames are the same.

Hyphenated Surnames

In recent decades, many women have forgone traditional name changes when they marry. Some women keep their maiden name and some choose to hyphenate their maiden name with their husband's surname. Although a woman is recorded in a tree with the name she received when she was born, you'll want to record any legal name changes, such as added hyphens. You'll want to record the surname as an alternate Name fact or in the Also Known As (AKA) fact (for instructions, see "Adding an Alternate Name for an Individual" on page 2).

Maiden Names

In genealogy, a woman is recorded using her maiden name, the surname she received at birth. Following this convention makes it easier to identify her parents. In addition, it is less likely people will misinterpret which family she belongs to. For each female, enter her maiden name in the Name fact.

Multi-Word Surnames

In some instances, a surname is made up of multiple words, such as "de Beaumont." In other cases, an individual may have two surnames, such as Pérez Mártinez—one inherited from his or her father and one from his or her mother. Although Family Tree Maker can recognize some common name prefixes such as Van or Von, you may need to identify multi-word surnames so they will be alphabetized and indexed correctly (fig. 1-2).

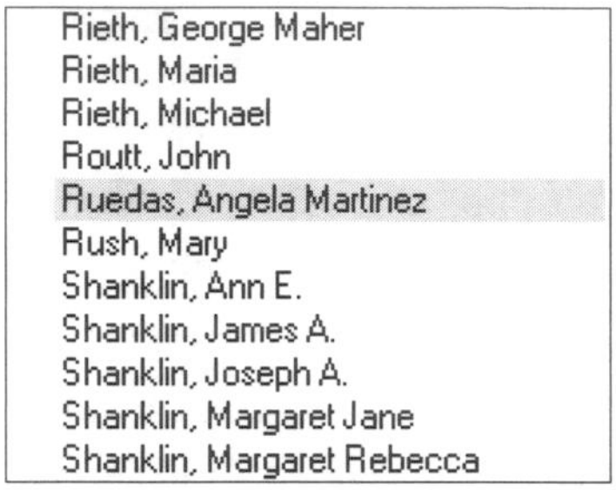

Figure 1-2

The surname Martinez Ruedas has been incorrectly indexed under Ruedas instead of Martinez.

```
Rieth, George Maher
Rieth, Maria
Rieth, Michael
Routt, John
Ruedas, Angela Martinez
Rush, Mary
Shanklin, Ann E.
Shanklin, James A.
Shanklin, Joseph A.
Shanklin, Margaret Jane
Shanklin, Margaret Rebecca
```

To identify a multi-word surname, you can use non-breaking spaces or backslashes; it doesn't matter which you choose. Some people find it easier to use backslashes because they don't have to remember a code; others find backslashes unattractive and choose to use non-breaking spaces.

To use non-breaking spaces

In the Name fact, enter the first name and a space. Then enter the first surname, a non-breaking space (hold down the **Alt** key and press "0160" using the number pad), and the second surname.

The name won't look any different than if you'd used regular spaces, but if you look at the Index, you'll notice that the name is indexed correctly.

To use backslashes

In the Name fact, enter the first name and a space. Then enter a backslash, the entire surname, and another backslash. For example, enter "Peter \Van der Voort\" or "Pierre \Bourbeau dit Lacourse\". Backslashes help the software index the name correctly; they won't print in reports or charts.

Note: You also need to use backslashes when entering a name for someone who does not have a last name, such as a person of Native American descent. For instance, if an individual's name is Running Bear you would enter the name as Running Bear\\. Without the backslashes, Family Tree Maker would read "Bear" as the individual's last name.

Soundex Calculator

Soundex is a term familiar to most family historians. It is a coding system that was used by the government to create indices of U.S. census records (and some passenger lists) based on how a surname sounds rather than how it is spelled. This was done to accommodate potential spelling and transcription errors. For example, "Smith" may be spelled "Smythe," "Smithe," or "Smyth." These "Smith" examples are all identified by the same Soundex code (S530). Family Tree Maker can determine the Soundex code for any surname. You can use this information to find other surnames that use that same code and then search for ancestors using all surname variations. (To see lists of surnames that use the same Soundex codes, go to <http://resources.rootsweb.ancestry.com/cgi-bin/soundexconverter>).

Click **Tools>Soundex Calculator**. Enter a surname in the Name field, or click **Index** to select a name from your tree. The Soundex number beneath the Name field changes automatically as you enter information in the field.

Surname Variations

Peterson, Pettersen, or Pedersen? Different branches of my father's family have chosen to spell our last name in a variety of ways. Over the years, the spelling of your surname may have changed too. In some cases this happens when a family immigrates to a new country and changes their name so it is easier to pronounce or spell. For others, names have been recorded phonetically—which can mean the surname is spelled differently on every record. Regardless of the reason, you'll want to search for (and record) your family members under all variations.

You can enter surname variations in a note. Or you can add the name in an alternate Name fact or in the Also Known As (AKA) fact (for instructions, see "Adding an Alternate Name for an Individual" on page 2).

Titles

Some of your family members may have titles such as Doctor, Reverend, or Colonel associated with them. These titles can be useful when trying to distinguish between ancestors with the same or similar names. In my maternal branch, I have five Samuel Haits—and that's just in my direct line. Luckily some of the records I've found include titles, so I can tell Captain Sam Hait from Deacon Samuel Hait.

Go to the individual's Person tab on the People workspace. If necessary, click the **Facts** button. Right-click the workspace and select **Add Fact**. Select "Title" in the **Facts** list. In the editing panel, enter the information in the **Title** field. Don't forget to add source information.

Unknown Names

Sometimes you will not be able to discover an individual's given name or surname (for example, you might know a woman's married name but not her maiden name). If you don't have a name for a person, you can indicate this in a variety of ways. It doesn't matter which method you use, but you should consider how your choice will affect the way in which these names will be sorted in the Index and displayed in charts. Here are some options commonly used by genealogists and how they would appear in the Index and a pedigree chart:

- Square brackets and hyphens (Margaret [--]).

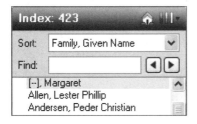

- Square brackets, a question mark, and hyphens (Margaret [--?--]).

- The term Unknown (Margaret Unknown or Unknown Reed).

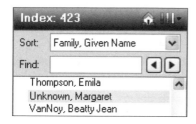
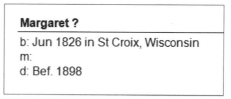

- A question mark (Margaret ? or ? Reed).

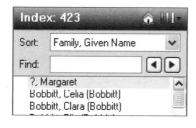

- A line created with the underscore key (Margaret _____).

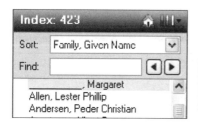
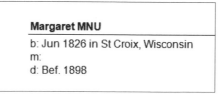

- The abbreviation MNU—Maiden Name Unknown—for women whose maiden names are unknown (Margaret MNU). If you don't know a woman's maiden name you can also enter her married name in parentheses, for example, Margaret (Bobbitt).

Unnamed Babies

Occasionally you find a record for a baby who died before being given a name. You may want to record this information differently than you do other unknown individuals. Here are some options:

- Infant Boy/Infant Girl
- Baby Boy/Baby Girl
- Male [Surname]/Female [Surname]
- Boy (unnamed)/Girl (unnamed)

Name Changes

What do you do if someone in your family decides to change their own name? When my grandfather and his family emigrated from Denmark, they chose to go by Peterson. However, when my grandfather returned to Denmark years later, he discovered that his surname was originally spelled Pedersen. When he returned to America, he decided to switch his name to the "original." To record this change in Family Tree Maker, I created a custom fact named "Name Change." Then I entered the date and the reason why my grandfather started using a different surname. If you have individuals in your family who officially—or unofficially—changed their name, you should record this information. You can create a custom fact, enter the information in a note, or enter it as an alternate name.

Entering Dates

Dates are pretty straightforward, right? Seven days in a week. Twelve months in a year. One hundred years in a century. How hard could it be? Anyone who has tried to document their family history can tell you, it's not as easy as it seems. Calendar systems change, countries use different date formats, and records include only partial dates. Fortunately, Family Tree Maker can handle the unique situations you encounter.

Date Formats Used in Different Countries

An understanding of how dates are recorded in different countries (and different time periods) can help you interpret dates correctly and help you communicate your family history more effectively. Not only do regions write dates in different orders, but they also use a variety of punctuation marks (or separators).

- **Australia.** Uses "day month year" with slashes as separators (for example, 26/9/1900).
- **Canada.** Officially uses "year month day" with hyphens as separators (for example, 1900-9-26). However, the UK standard format is used often.
- **Germany.** Uses "day month year" with periods (or full stops) as separators (for example, 26.9.1900).
- **United Kingdom.** Uses what is generally considered the European standard, that is "day month year," with slashes as separators (for example, 26/9/1900). Written out, this date would be 26 September 1900, the genealogical standard.
- **United States.** Uses "month day year" with slashes as separators (for example, 9/26/1900).

Setting Up the Entry Format for Dates

Family Tree Maker interprets dates you've entered based on the format you've chosen: day/month/year or month/day/year. For example, if you enter "6/7/2011" Family Tree Maker can read this as 7 June 2011 or 6 July 2011.

To change the format, open the options window by clicking **Tools>Options**. Then click the **Names/Dates/Places** tab. In **Date input format**, choose **Day Month Year** or **Month Day Year**.

Setting Up the Display Format for Dates

You don't have to display dates in charts and reports in the same format that you enter them. The default display format is the genealogical standard: day month year. However, you may want to change dates to a format that is more familiar to family members or that is appropriate for the country you live in.

To change the format open the options window by clicking **Tools>Options**. Then click the **Names/Dates/Places** tab. In **Date display format**, select **Day Month Year** to display the day before the month (e.g., 07 January 2011); select **Month Day Year** to display the month before the day (e.g., January 07, 2011). Then use the drop-down lists to choose different formats for days, the months, and separators (see table 1-1 for help).

Table 1-1

Display formats for dates.

Day		Month	
Number	6	Full name	September
Number with leading zero	06	Abbreviation	Sept
Number with period	6.	Number	9
Number with leading zero and period	06.	Number with leading zero	09

Separator	
Spaces	6 Sept 2011
Forward slash	6/Sept/2011
Bullet	6•9•2011
Period (or full stop)	6.9.2011

In the option window you can also specify the label used for approximate dates in the software and charts and reports. In the Fact labels field, enter your preferred label, such as Abt. for About or ca. for circa.

Note: When you change a label, dates that have already been entered using a different label will be updated.

Using Keywords Instead of Dates

You may encounter situations where a standard date isn't available for a specific fact or event. For example, you may find a record that says a child died as an infant or you may figure out an approximate death date for an individual based on when his or her will was probated. Family Tree Maker lets you enter special keywords to indicate these types of dates. Table 1-2 shows the keywords you can enter and how Family Tree Maker will display them in the software and on reports and charts.

Keyword	What Is Displayed	Date Example
About, ABT, or A	Abt.	Abt. 26 April 1900
AD	AD	100 AD
After or AFT	Aft.	Aft. 26 April 1900
Ante	Bef.	Bef. 26 April 1900
Before, BEF, or B	Bef.	Bef. 26 April 1900
Between or BET	Bet.	Bet. 10 March - 26 April 1900
BC	BC	100 BC
Calculated	Cal.	Cal. 26 April 1900
Child	Child	Child
Circa, Cir, or C	Abt.	Abt. 26 April 1900
Dead	Dead	Dead
Deceased	Deceased	Deceased
Estimated or EST	Abt.	Abt. 26 April 1900
From. . . to	Bet.	Bet. 10 March - 26 April 1900
Infant	Infant	Infant

Table 1-2

Date keywords.

Keyword	What Is Displayed	Date Example
Never Married	Never Married	Never Married
Post	Aft.	Aft. 26 April 1900
Stillborn	Stillborn	Stillborn
Unknown	Unknown	Unknown
Young	Young	Young
?	Unknown	Unknown

Estimating Dates

As you search for your family, you may come across a document or artifact that doesn't specify a date but gives you clues as to when an event occurred. For example, I have discovered several family tombstones that include death dates and ages at death: years, months, and days. I can enter this information in the Date Calculator and calculate the individual's birth date. You can access the Date Calculator from the Tools menu, but a faster option is to place your cursor in the Date field and when the calculator icon appears, click it.

Perpetual Calenders

A few years ago I found an obituary for my great-grandfather in a newspaper clipping. The only problem? It didn't include a death date; the paper simply said that he "died at his home on Sunday." Fortunately, the clipping included the date of the paper: August 11, 1942. Using a perpetual calendar I discovered that the previous Sunday was the 9th of August. Now I had an exact date to work with. If you find a church record that says an infant was christened on Easter Sunday 1789 or you locate a letter that says your grandparents were married in 1890 on the second Saturday in May, you can use a perpetual calendar to identify the actual date. You can find perpetual calendars on many websites; here's one I like to use: <www.searchforancestors.com/utility/perpetualcalendar.html>.

Entering Locations

Recording locations consistently and completely is an important part of organizing your family history. Generally, when entering a place, you will record the location from the smallest to largest division. For example, in the United States, you would enter city or town, county, state, country (Haddam, Washington, Kansas, United States). For most European locations, you would enter city or town, parish or district, province, country (Birmingham, West Midlands, England). You may choose to not enter a country for a location if it is the country in which you live and where most of your ancestors lived. If you do leave off country information, include this fact somewhere in your tree.

You can abbreviate place names if you want. However, make sure you use the standard abbreviations that will be recognized by others who might want to look at your research. Also, be consistent; don't spell out some place names and abbreviate others. Table 1-3 shows some common place abbreviations:

Location	Abbreviation
Township	Twp.
County	Co.
District	Dist.
Parish	Par.
Province	Prov.

Table 1-3

Common abbreviations for locations.

Entering a Short Display Name for a Location

Recording locations in a complete and consistent manner is an important part of creating a quality family history. Unfortunately, those long location names can become unwieldy and clutter your reports and charts. Family Tree Maker lets you enter your own shortened or abbreviated display names that can be used in charts and reports. For example, if you enter Heidelberg,

Baden-Württemberg, Germany, as a birthplace, you can enter Heidelberg, Germany, as the short display name (fig. 1-3).

Figure 1-3

Place name options in a pedigree chart.

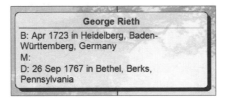

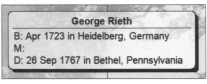

Go to the Places workspace. In the **Places** panel choose "Place" from the **List by** drop-down list. Select the location you want to change. In the **Short** field enter a display name.

GPS (Global Positioning System) Coordinates

Although the online mapping feature in Family Tree Maker is able to recognize millions of locations, there are times when it won't be able to identify the exact location of a place you've entered. Perhaps your relatives are buried in a rural cemetery that doesn't appear on the map. Or perhaps census records show that your family lived in a township that no longer exists. You can set the exact position for the location using GPS (Global Positioning System) coordinates.

To enter GPS coordinates click the **Places** button on the main toolbar. In the Places panel, click the name of the location to which you want to add GPS coordinates. Then place the cursor in the **Location** field and click the **Location calculator** button that appears. Enter the coordinates for the location and click **OK**.

GPS receivers can display a location's coordinates in a variety of formats. Although Family Tree Maker uses the Decimal Degrees (DD) format, it contains a Location Calculator that will convert other latitude and longitude coordinates to the default format. This example shows what the coordinates for Trafalgar Square in London, England, look like in the formats used by Family Tree Maker.

- Degrees:Minutes:Seconds (DMS)—51° 30′ 28″ N, 0° 7′ 41″ W
- Degrees:Decimal Minutes (DM)—51° 30.468′ N, 0° 7.686′ W
- Decimal Degrees (DD)—51.507778, -0.128056

Entering Notes

Recently my parents moved, and when my mother was going through her family history files she found a loose scrap of paper where she'd jotted down some memories of her grandmother—my great-grandmother. To me, these little glimpses into the past are what family history is all about. Whether you have research ideas jotted down on the back of a telephone bill or a notebook full of records you transcribed at the local library, it's important to get this information into your tree. And that's where notes come in.

I like to think of notes as little Post-its® all over my tree. I can add research tips, stories, source commentary—just about anything. Notes vary from a one-sentence physical description to lengthy analysis of a source. Fortunately, Family Tree Maker notes have an advantage over paper sticky notes; their text is available in searches and they can be included in reports and Smart Stories.

Person Notes

A person note like the one shown in figure 1-4 is useful for preserving stories, including historical details, keeping track of name variations and

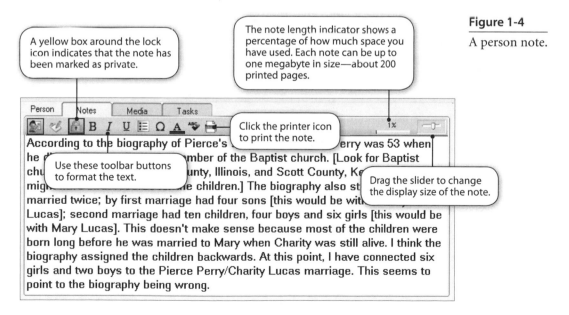

Figure 1-4

A person note.

misspellings, and much more. I also consider this an all purpose area for organizing my ideas and thoughts.

> Note: Person notes can be included in Ahnentafels, descendant reports, family group sheets, Individual reports, and custom reports.

To enter a person note, go to the individual's Person tab on the People workspace. Click the **Notes** tab at the bottom of the window and click the **Person note** icon.

TIP

Your notes may include information that you do not want to share with other family members or researchers. You can make any note in your tree private so you can choose whether or not to include it in reports or when you export your tree.

Research Notes

Many times when you find a record or learn a new fact about someone in your tree, you will discover clues that can help you learn more about your family. You can create research notes to remind you of the next steps you want to take.

Don't forget to spell out your ideas and use language that is easy to understand. You don't want to come back months later and wonder what the note meant (something I've done multiple times).

> Note: Research notes can be included in Ahnentafels, descendant reports, family group sheets, Individual reports, custom reports, and the Research Note report.

To enter a research note, go to the individual's Person tab on the People workspace. Click the **Notes** tab at the bottom of the window and click the **Research note** icon.

Fact Notes

If you're concerned that important bits of information will get lost in a long person note, you might consider using fact notes. For example, a description of the family homestead can be added to a note for a census or residence fact; specifics about the church a family attended might go with a christening fact.

> Note: Fact notes can be included in Ahnentafels, descendant reports, family group sheets, Individual reports, and custom reports.

To enter a fact note, go to the individual's Person tab on the People workspace. Click the **Facts** button and select the fact you want. In the editing panel on the right side of the window, click the **Notes** tab.

Relationship Notes

You might want to use relationship notes to record conflicting information about marriage dates, details about who the marriage was performed by, or even to enter information about why a couple never married. You can also include general information about a family.

> Note: Relationship notes can be included in Ahnentafels, descendant reports, family group sheets, Individual reports, and custom reports.

To enter a relationship note, go to the individual's Person tab on the People workspace. Click the **Marriage to** button in the editing panel. Click the **Notes** tab.

Source Citation Notes

I use source citation notes a lot. They're convenient for transcribing documents, translating foreign records, explaining how I came to certain conclusions, or stating the value of a particular source.

> Note: Source notes can be included only in the Source Usage report.

To enter a source citation note, go to the Source workspace. Select the source citation you want. At the bottom of the window click the **Notes** tab.

Media Notes

When I have additional information about a media item that won't fit in the Description field, I like to add this to its notes. If it's an old photograph, I may add background information about the studio or time period. It it's a scan of an heirloom, I may include details about how I came into possession of the item and who originally owned it.

To enter a media note, go to the Media workspace. Double-click the media item you want to add a note to and click the **Notes** tab.

TIP

To delete a note, simply select all of the text by pressing **CTRL+A**. Then press the **Delete** or **Backspace** key.

Chapter Two

Defining Relationships

When I look at my family tree, I see a pair of sisters who married a pair of brothers, grandparents who adopted their grandchildren, multiple stepfamilies, and even a polygamist. You might have a similar tangled family history that includes stepbrothers and stepsisters who marry, families with multiple sets of twins, or an individual who marries over and over.

As your tree grows you'll find that keeping relationships straight can become a job in itself. Family Tree Maker has various tools to help you clarify and define the diverse families you'll come across.

Multiple Spouses

You may need to add more than one spouse for an individual—for example, if a widower or divorcée remarries. After you've entered both spouses, you'll need to choose a "preferred" spouse. Usually this is the spouse whose children are in your direct line. This preferred spouse will be the default spouse displayed in the family group view, pedigree view, and in charts and reports.

Adding an Additional Spouse

1. Go to the **Family** tab on the People workspace.

2. In the pedigree view or Index select the individual you want to add a second spouse to.

3. In the family group view, click the **Spouse** button next to the individual for whom you want to add an additional spouse. From the drop-down list, you have the choice of accessing the information for an existing spouse or adding a new spouse.

4. Choose **Add Spouse** from the drop-down list. Then enter the spouse's name in the blank field and click **OK**. Family Tree Maker displays a new family group view, including the new spouse.

    You'll now need to choose which is the "preferred" spouse.

Choosing a Preferred Spouse

If you enter more than one spouse for an individual, you need to indicate who is the preferred spouse. Usually this is the spouse whose children are in your direct line. Once you make someone the preferred spouse, he or she will be the default spouse displayed in the family group view, pedigree view, and in charts and reports.

1. Go to the **Family** tab on the People workspace.

2. Make sure the individual with multiple spouses is the focus of the pedigree view and family group view.

3. Click the **Person** tab and then click the **Relationships** button. You should see two names listed under the Spouses heading.

4. In the Spouses list, select the individual you want to become the preferred spouse. Then click the **Preferred spouse** checkbox in the editing panel.

Choosing the Sort Order of Spouses

If an individual has more than one spouse, you can choose the order in which they will be displayed in the Family and Person tabs and also in reports and charts. By default, the preferred spouse is listed first and then others are listed in order of marriage date.

1. Go to the **Family** tab on the People workspace.

2. Make sure the individual with multiple spouses is the focus of the pedigree view and family group view.

3. Click the **Spouse** button next to the individual and choose **Set Spouse Order** from the drop-down list.

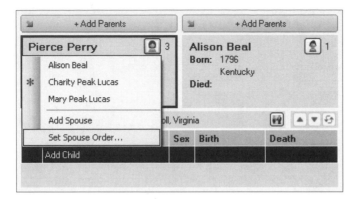

4. Click a spouse and do one of these options:

    •   Click the **Move up** and **Move down** buttons to move a spouse to a specific place in the order.

    •   Click the **Reset** button to display spouses in the default order.

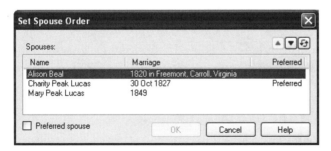

5. Click **OK**.

Switching Between Multiple Spouses

You can view the information and children of only one spouse at a time, so you may need to switch between multiple spouses when you want to work with a specific family. You will also need to switch spouses if you want to add information about that particular marriage.

1. Go to the **Family** tab on the People workspace.

2. Make sure the individual with multiple spouses is the focus of the pedigree view and family group view.

3. In the family group view, click the **Spouse** button next to the individual. From the drop-down list, choose the other spouse.

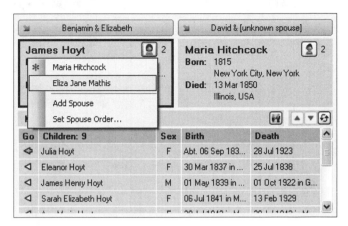

The family group view now displays the individual and the alternate spouse you have selected. After making any necessary edits to this alternate spouse, click the **Spouse** button again to choose the preferred spouse.

Multiple Marriages to the Same Person

One of my uncles—I won't mention any names—married and divorced the same woman twice, in addition to marrying two other times. Sometimes it's difficult to choose which wife is "preferred" and document the duplicate marriages without making it seem like you've made a mistake. And it's even more complicated if children are involved. Fortunately, Family Tree Maker makes it fairly simple to record multiple marriages that involve the same individuals. This task assumes that you've already entered one marriage for the couple.

1. Go to the **Family** tab on the People workspace.

2. In the pedigree view or Index select one of the individuals.

3. Click the **Person** tab; then click the **Facts** button. You should see the name of the husband or wife next to the Shared Facts heading.

4. Right-click the Individual and Shared Facts workspace and choose **Add Fact** from the drop-down list.

5. In the Add Fact window, select "Marriage" and click **OK**.

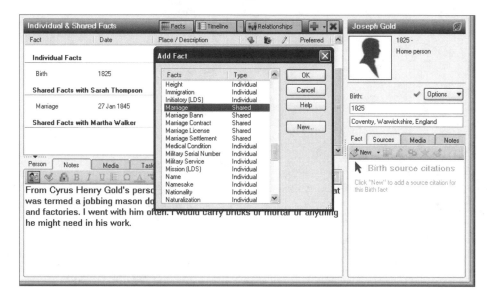

6. In the editing panel, enter the marriage's date and location. Then choose the name of the spouse in the drop-down list.

   Both marriages now appear on the Individual and Shared Facts workspace.

Marriage Between Cousins

If your family history search takes you back very many years, you're bound to find at least one set of cousins who married each other. This wasn't unusual hundreds of years ago when people were born and lived in the same place their entire lives and marriage options were limited. Unfortunately, we usually don't realize that two people are cousins until we've entered the exact same family and duplicate individuals in two separate ancestral lines.

If you have entered duplicate family lines in your tree, there is no easy fix to join the two branches together. The best workaround is to merge the duplicate individuals.

But if you know individuals are cousins before you add them to your tree, the key to keeping them straight is to use the "Attach" menu options.

1. Go to the **Family** tab on the People workspace.

2. In the pedigree view or Index select one of the individuals. Do not click "Add Spouse" to enter the spouse.

3. Choose **Person>Attach/Detach Person>Attach Spouse**. The Select the Spouse to Attach window opens.

4. Select the spouse in the list and click **OK**. The Attach Spouse window opens.

5. Select which family the spouse will be attached to (an existing family with children or a new family).

6. Click **OK**. The cousins are now shown as a couple in the pedigree view and family group view.

Relationship Calculator

The Relationship Calculator helps you identify the relationship between any two individuals in your tree, shows an individual's nearest common relatives, and gives his or her canon and civil numbers.

Note: Canon and civil numbers indicate the degree of relationship between individuals. Canon laws (used in the United States) measure the number of steps back to a common ancestor. Civil degree measures the total number of steps from one family member to another. (For more information see the sidebar on page 166.)

To open the Relationship Calculator, click **Tools>Relationship Calculator**. The first field contains the name of the home person. The second field contains the name of the individual who is the current focus of your tree. To change the individuals whose relationship you are calculating, click the **Person from people index** button next to a name (the button with an index card). In the Index of Individuals window, select a new person and click **OK**.

The individuals' relationship is listed in the "Relationship" section. If they have multiple connections (for example when cousins marry), you can click the drop-down list to see each relationship. You can also see how the individuals are related in the "Path" section.

Same-Sex Relationships

Family Tree Maker is flexible enough to show different types of nontraditional relationships. If you have a couple in your tree who are in a same-sex relationship, you can indicate this in your tree.

Add the two individuals as you would any other couple. Then specify a relationship type. Go to the **Person** tab for either individual and click the **Relationships** button. Under "Spouses" select the appropriate individual. In the editing panel, choose a relationship type from the **Relationship** drop-down list (for example, spouse or partner). You can also choose a status for the relationship from the **Status** drop-down list.

Divorce

Divorce can strain family relationships and bonds. You may be reluctant to include information about these marriages, especially if the union didn't produce any children. However, each detail you learn about a person can lead you to new records and new information. Also, these events complete the picture of what your ancestor's life was really like. If you are concerned about this information appearing in reports and charts, remember that you can choose to include or exclude people and facts in many of these. Also, when you export your files, you can choose to exclude facts you've marked as private.

Changing a Relationship Status to Divorced

If a marriage ends in divorce, you'll want to record this change in your tree.

> Note: This task shows you how to change the status of a marriage that has already been entered in your tree. If you haven't already, you'll need to add the couple to your tree and record their marriage information.

1. Go to the **Family** tab on the People workspace. Select the individual whose marital status you want to change.

2. Click the **Person** tab; then click the **Relationships** button.

3. Select the spouse in the Relationships workspace; then choose "Divorced" from the **Status** drop-down list in the editing panel.

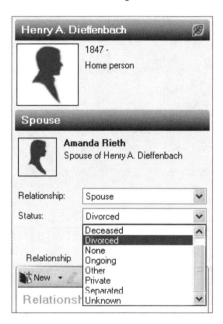

Entering Information About a Divorce

If you have court records, divorce decrees, or other records pertaining to an individual's divorce, you'll want to enter these details into your tree.

Go to the individual's Person tab on the People workspace. If necessary, click the **Facts** button. Right-click the workspace and choose **Add Fact**. Select "Divorce" in the **Facts** list. In the editing panel, select the divorced spouse and enter any dates and places associated with the divorce in the necessary fields. Don't forget to add source information.

Dissolving a Marriage

You may find that you've entered a marriage for the wrong couple. You'll need to delete any marriage facts you've entered and also detach the individuals from each other.

1. Go to the **Family** tab on the People workspace.

2. Make sure the couple you want to remove a marriage from is the focus of the family group view.

3. Click the **Person** tab for one of the individuals. Then right-click the Marriage fact and choose **Delete Fact.** A message asks you if you want to delete this fact (and associated notes) from both individuals. Click **Yes.**

    Note: If you don't delete the Marriage fact, the individual will still be considered married but to an unknown person.

4. Now you will need to unlink the couple. Select one of the individuals. Then choose **Person>Attach/Detach Person>Detach Selected Person**. Select the family with the incorrect spouse and click **OK**.

    Any children associated with the marriage will remain attached to the remaining spouse.

> **TIP**
>
> If you accidentally create an "unknown" spouse when removing a marriage, see "Removing an Unknown Spouse" on page 266.

Blended Families

If you want to start a lively debate, ask a family historian whether genealogy is for tracking blood lines or family relationships. Differences of opinion occur in what should be recorded but also how software should handle the information.

Your blended family may include a combination of stepchildren, adopted and biological children, half-brothers and half-sisters, or even children raised by family members other than their parents. Before you begin recording these types of relationships, it is important to understand how Family Tree Maker stores and displays these family connections.

Stepfamilies

When a child's parent remarries (or enters a new relationship), the new spouse is considered the child's stepparent. Family Tree Maker figures out this relationship automatically, and if you run a Kinship Report or plug the individuals into the Relationship Calculator the appropriate relationship type is displayed. In many situations, this simple designation may be an adequate way to handle the stepparent relationship. However, if you want a stepchild to be included in charts or reports with his or her biological parent and stepparent you will have to add two sets of parents for the child: biological/biological and biological/step (for instructions, see "Adding Two Sets of Parents for an Individual" on page 34).

In my opinion it is best to add two sets of parents for a stepchild only if you are going to designate the biological/step couple as the preferred parents who appear in charts and reports. Here's why. Family Tree Maker treats both sets of parents as if they are indistinguishable. For example, the child will be included on the family group view with his or her biological parents and the family group view for his or her biological/step parents—without any labels to point out the actual relationship (fig. 2-1).

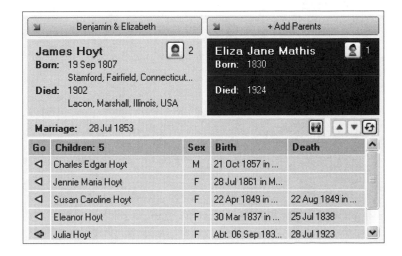

Figure 2-1

The family group view includes two biological children and three stepchildren. The relationship types are not labeled in this view.

In addition, Family Tree Maker will duplicate relationships in charts and reports. For example, in the Outline Descendant Report, the child (and all his or her descendants) will appear once under his or her biological parents and then again under his or her biological/step parents (fig. 2-2).

Figure 2-2

An Outline Descendant Report. *Above,* Julia Hoyt is listed beneath her biological parents; *below,* Julia is listed again beneath her biological/step parents.

Outline Descendant Report for James Hoyt

1 James Hoyt b: 19 Sep 1807 in Stamford, Fairfield, Connecticut, USA, d: 1902 in Lacon, Marshall, Illinois, USA
...... + Maria Hitchcock b: 1815 in New York City, New York, m: 19 Sep 1833, d: 13 Mar 1850 in Illinois, USA
...........2 Julia Hoyt b: Abt. 06 Sep 1834 in Chillicothe, Ross, Ohio, USA, d: 28 Jul 1923
.... + John W. Bobbitt b: 09 Jun 1832 in Kentucky, USA, m: 18 Oct 1852, d: 24 Aug 1909 in Dawson, Richardson, Nebraska, USA
................3 Seymour Bobbitt b: Mar 1853 in Illinois, USA
.... + Clara (Bobbitt) b: Feb 1851 in Illinois, USA
....................4 Daisy E Bobbitt b: Sep 1887 in Nebraska, USA
....................4 Evelyn Bobbitt b: Oct 1890 in Nebraska, USA
................3 Cornelia O. Bobbitt b: Mar 1857 in Illinois, USA
.... + Hermon P. Shier m: 02 Feb 1873 in Varna, Marshall, Illinois, USA
....................4 Verner H. Shier
....................4 Venetta O. Shier
....................4 Nettie O. Shier
....................4 Mabel F. Shier
................3 Willis R. Bobbitt b: Dec 1860 in Illinois, USA
.... + Ella M. (Bobbitt) b: Jun 1853 in Pennsylvania, USA
....................4 Ovanda R Bobbitt b: Jan 1888 in Nebraska, USA
....................4 Julia O Bobbitt b: Oct 1889 in Nebraska, USA
....................4 Opal J Bobbitt b: 1890 in Nebraska, USA

...... + Eliza Jane Mathis b: 1830, m: 28 Jul 1853, d: 1924
...........2 Charles Edgar Hoyt b: 21 Oct 1857 in Marshall County, Illinois, USA
...........2 Jennie Maria Hoyt b: 28 Jul 1861 in Marshall County, Illinois, USA
...........2 Susan Caroline Hoyt b: 22 Apr 1849 in Marshall County, Illinois, USA, d: 22 Aug 1849 in Marshall County, Illinois, USA
...........2 Eleanor Hoyt b: 30 Mar 1837 in Chillicothe, Ross, Ohio, USA, d: 25 Jul 1838
...........2 Julia Hoyt b: Abt. 06 Sep 1834 in Chillicothe, Ross, Ohio, USA, d: 28 Jul 1923
.... + John W. Bobbitt b: 09 Jun 1832 in Kentucky, USA, m: 18 Oct 1852, d: 24 Aug 1909 in Dawson, Richardson, Nebraska, USA
................3 Seymour Bobbitt b: Mar 1853 in Illinois, USA
.... + Clara (Bobbitt) b: Feb 1851 in Illinois, USA
....................4 Daisy E Bobbitt b: Sep 1887 in Nebraska, USA
....................4 Evelyn Bobbitt b: Oct 1890 in Nebraska, USA

Half-Brothers and Half-Sisters

In Family Tree Maker half-sibling relationships work much like stepfamily relationships. When a child's biological parent has a child with another individual Family Tree Maker figures out this relationship automatically, and the relationship type can be viewed in the Relationship Calculator.

If you want half-siblings to be included in each others Relationship view, you will have to add two sets of parents for each child: biological/biological and biological/step (for instructions, see "Adding Two Sets of Parents for an Individual" on page 34). Be aware that Family Tree Maker doesn't distinguish between full siblings and half siblings; all siblings are listed as simply brother or sister (fig. 2-3).

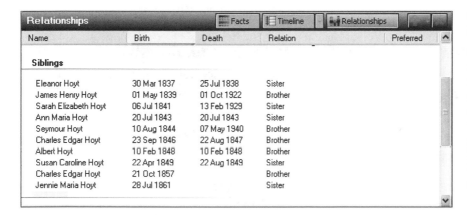

Figure 2-3

The Relationships view includes eight full siblings and two half-siblings, but the relationship types are labeled only brother or sister.

Adopted and Foster Children

Traditionally, genealogy is used to track direct bloodlines. So how do adopted or foster family members fit in? In most families, these children are as much a part of the family as any biological children and you'll want to include them in your family trees. If you do include adopted children or foster children, make sure you clearly identify them as such. That way others who view your tree will have a clear picture of your family.

You will need to add two sets of parents for the child: biological and adopted (for instructions, see "Adding Two Sets of Parents for an Individual" on page 34). Then once you've entered both sets of parents for the adopted individual, you should choose the "preferred parents"—the parents you want displayed in charts, reports, and software views. Usually this would be the individual's blood relatives; however, with adopted children you may choose to display their legal parents.

Entering Information About an Adoption

If you have adoption or court records pertaining to a family member's adoption, you'll want to enter these details into your tree.

Go to the individual's Person tab on the People workspace. If necessary, click the **Facts** button. Right-click the workspace and choose **Add Fact**. Select "Adoption" in the **Facts** list. In the editing panel, enter any dates and places associated with the adoption. Don't forget to add source information.

Adding Two Sets of Parents for an Individual

You may need to add two sets of parents for an individual—for example, when you add an adopted or foster child to your tree or you want to display stepfamily relationships.

Adding Biological Parents

1. Go to the **Family** tab on the People workspace. Enter the child in the pedigree view or family group view.

2. Use the **Add Father** and **Add Mother** buttons in the pedigree view to enter the biological father and mother.

3. Select the child again in the pedigree view or family group view. Then click the **Person** tab.

4. Click the **Relationships** button. In the editing panel, make sure "Biological" is displayed in the **Relationship** drop-down list.

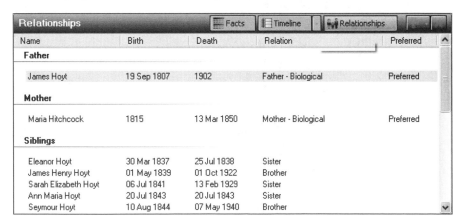

Adding a Second Set of Parents

1. Go to the **Family** tab on the People workspace. Select the child in the pedigree view or family group view.

   Because you've already entered biological parents for the individual, you'll need to use the add person options in the Person menu to add an additional set of parents.

2. Choose **Person>Add Person>Add Father**. Enter the father's name and click **OK**. (If the father already exists in your tree, choose **Person>Attach/ Detach Person>Attach Father**.)

3. In the mini pedigree tree above the workspace, click the **Add Spouse** button next to the father you just added. Enter the mother's name and click **OK**. (If the mother already exists in your tree, choose **Person>Attach/ Detach Person>Attach Mother**.)

4. In the editing panel on the Relationships workspace, choose "Adopted," "Step," etc. from the **Relationship** drop-down list. If necessary, repeat this step for the other parent.

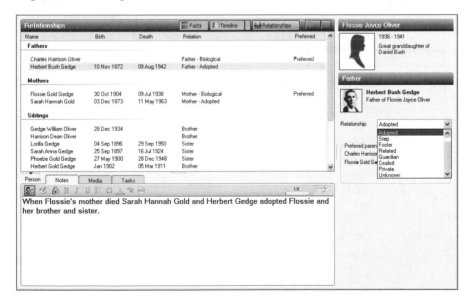

Once you've entered both sets of parents, you should choose the "preferred parents"—the parents you want displayed in charts, reports, and software views.

Choosing a Preferred Set of Parents

If you have entered two sets of parents for an individual, you can choose which parents are the preferred parents, the parents who will be displayed in reports and charts.

1. Go to the **Family** tab on the People workspace. In the pedigree view or Index select the individual with two sets of parents.

2. Click the **Person** tab; then click the **Relationships** button. Under the "Fathers" and "Mothers" headings, you should see two sets of names: the biological parents and the alternate parents.

3. Select one of the individuals you want to be displayed as the preferred parent; it doesn't matter whether you choose the father or the mother.

4. In the editing panel, click the **Preferred parent** checkbox. The Preferred Parents window opens.

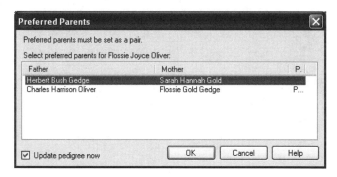

5. Select a set of parents and click **OK**.

Illegitimate Children

As you search for your family you may uncover some potentially painful and unnerving family facts—and one of the biggest can be illegitimate births. Even though I know the value of recording these types of facts and understand the importance of portraying an accurate picture of my ancestors' lives, I too felt reluctant to enter the facts about an illegitimate birth that occurred in my family.

If your family tree is for your personal use only, you can record an illegitimate birth in any way that makes sense to you. However, if you plan on putting your tree online, printing charts, or sharing your trees with others, you will want to be careful in how you approach this relationship. This section shows a variety of ways that you can enter information about a child born out of wedlock, depending on the details you have discovered.

Entering a Private Note About a Birth

You can easily put information about an illegitimate birth in a person note, either for the specific individual or the mother or father.

1. Go to the **Family** tab on the People workspace. Select the individual you want to add a note to in the pedigree view or family group view.

2. Click the **Person** tab; then click the **Notes** tab at the bottom of the window.

3. Click the **Person note** button in the notes toolbar and enter the text you want to include for the individual.

4. If you want to be able to exclude this note when you create reports or export your tree, click the **Mark as private** button in the notes toolbar.

Adding an Illegitimate Child to Your Tree

I chose to add an illegitimate child to my tree instead of entering a note about the birth. That way, I can enter facts about him, source my information, and keep track of what research I still need to do.

The way in which you'll add the illegitimate child depends on the details you've been able to gather and how the individual fits into your tree. For example, you may know the mother's identity but not the father's. I prefer to add the child as an unrelated individual and then link them to the appropriate parents; you may need to adapt these steps to your family's specific circumstances.

1. Go to the People workspace. Choose **Person>Add Person>Add Unrelated Person**.

2. If you know the child's name, enter it in the appropriate field. Then choose a gender from the drop-down list and click **OK**.

   You can now connect the child to a father or mother.

3. Do one of these options:

   • If the father or mother already exists in your tree, choose **Person>Attach/Detach Person>Attach Father/Mother**. Select the parent and click **OK**. If necessary select the family to attach the child to and click **OK**.

   • If you are adding a new individual to your tree, choose **Person> Add Person>Add Father/Mother**. Enter his or her information and click **OK**.

4. If necessary repeat step 3 to attach or add the other parent.

5. On the Person tab click the **Facts** button. You can enter any details, such as birth and death dates, that you have for the individual.

TIP

As you add facts for an illegitimate child, you might want to mark each fact as private so you can exclude them from charts and reports.

Choosing a Relationship Type for Unmarried Parents

When you add parents for an illegitimate child, Family Tree Maker automatically classifies the couple's relationship type as "Spouses." But you can indicate that the two were never married and clarify the type of relationship they had.

1. Go to the **Family** tab on the People workspace.

2. In the pedigree view or Index select the child's father or mother.

3. Click the **Person** tab; then click the **Relationships** button.

4. Select the other parent under the "Spouse" heading.

5. In the editing panel, choose "Partner," "Other," or whatever is appropriate from the **Relationship** drop-down list.

Twins and Multiple Births

If you have a family member who is a twin, triplet, or part of a multiple birth, you'll want to indicate this in your tree. This information could lead to additional birth certificates or family facts that you might not find otherwise.

A 1910 census record for my maternal great-grandparents indicated that my great-grandmother had given birth to twelve children—nine of whom were living. I had information—and photos—for the nine children. But who were the missing ones? Luckily I knew that my grandmother had a twin who had died when she was only thirteen months old. That left only two unaccounted-for children. I soon found information about them on a family plaque that memorialized these two who had died young. If I hadn't known my grandmother had a twin who died young, I could have spent months or years looking for a child who wasn't really missing.

You can include this type of birth information in a personal note; or, if you want to be able to see this at a glance, you might want to include this information in the Name fact. Simply enter the name followed by a comma and the individual's birth information (for example, enter "Maurine Bobbitt, twin"). If you choose this last option, make sure you record this convention somewhere in your tree so people don't accidentally think that "twin" is a name suffix.

Individuals Without Children

If you determine that an individual or couple in your family tree never had children you might want to record this fact somewhere in your tree. This helpful tidbit can save other family researchers (and you!) from spending time on fruitless searches for nonexistent children and records.

I have two maiden aunts who lived together their entire lives, never marrying or having children. One option was to record this information by simply entering it in a person note for each aunt. Although this would have been an adequate solution, I decided to create a custom "No descendants" fact. Facts give you an advantage because they allow you to include source information and you don't have to worry that the information will get lost at the bottom of a note. In addition, you can include facts on any reports or charts you create.

Once you have created a fact, you can use it for anyone in your family tree if you discover he or she has no offspring. To learn how to create a custom "No descendants" fact, see "Creating a Custom Fact" on page 225.

Unrelated Individuals

In your searches, you may come across an individual who might be related to you but you're unable to determine a connection. You don't want to connect this individual to anyone in your tree until you're certain they're family, but you don't want to lose his or her information in case you discover a relationship with the person at a later time. In these cases, you'll want to add the individual to your tree without linking them with anyone.

I found a death index entry for an infant that bore the fairly unique surname of my great-grandfather. I wasn't sure whether this was one of his children, but I added the individual to my tree "just in case." Months later when I was able to view the actual death certificate, I learned that this baby was indeed one of his children. Because I had already added this person to my tree, it was easy to simply link her to her parents.

Click the **People** button on the main toolbar. Then choose **Person>Add Person>Add Unrelated Person**. Enter the name of the individual, select a gender, and click **OK**.

Note: To attach this person to someone in your tree at a later time, select the individual in the People workspace and choose **Person>Attach/Detach Person>Attach Father/Mother/Spouse**.

Chapter Three
Working More Efficiently

When your family tree is small and only contains a few hundred people, it's not too difficult to keep track of individuals. But the larger your tree is the more time-consuming it can be to navigate to specific individuals. Family Tree Maker simplifies the process by letting you access a variety of methods to help you search your tree and locate people.

In addition, the flexible nature of Family Tree Maker means that you can edit information and add new family members from just about anywhere. This chapter discusses the many ways you can make your data entry more efficient.

In This Chapter

- Using the Index
- Selecting a Group of Individuals
- Searching Your Tree for Specific Individuals
- Editing an Individual
- Adding Family Members

Using the Index

The People workspace is where you will spend most of your time in Family Tree Maker. And the Index on its Family tab (see fig. 3-1 on the following page) is your key to displaying the individuals and family lines you want to focus on. By default the Index lists all individuals alphabetically by last name. However, you can add dates, change the sort order, and filter the list.

Figure 3-1

The Index on the
Family tab.

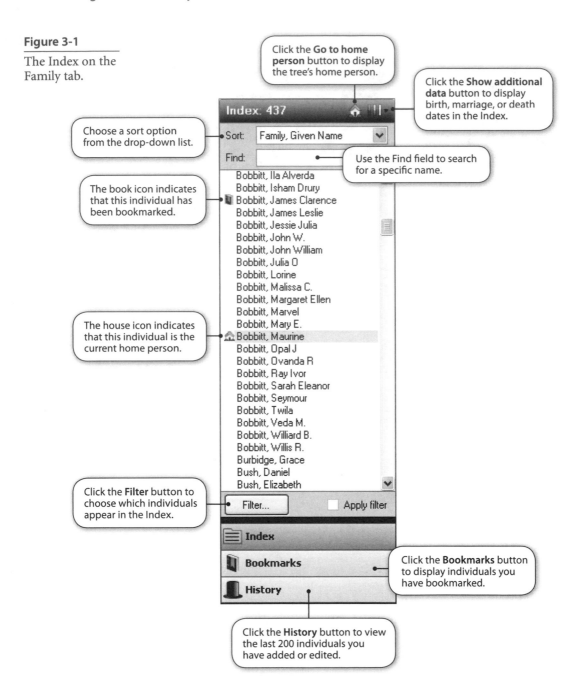

Click the **Go to home person** button to display the tree's home person.

Click the **Show additional data** button to display birth, marriage, or death dates in the Index.

Choose a sort option from the drop-down list.

Use the Find field to search for a specific name.

The book icon indicates that this individual has been bookmarked.

The house icon indicates that this individual is the current home person.

Click the **Filter** button to choose which individuals appear in the Index.

Click the **Bookmarks** button to display individuals you have bookmarked.

Click the **History** button to view the last 200 individuals you have added or edited.

Displaying Alternate Names in the Index

Family Tree Maker lets you determine how names are displayed in the Index. You can include titles, alternate names, and married names for females.

From the **Tools** menu, choose **Options**. Click the **Names/Dates/Places** tab. Change these options as necessary:

- **Use AKA if available after middle name.** Select this checkbox to include the Also Known As name with the preferred name (for example, Mary Eliza "Mollie" Bobbitt).

- **Use AKA if available as an additional entry.** Select this checkbox to include the Also Known As name as its own entry in the Index (for example, Hannah Shepherd and Anna Shepherd).

- **Use titles if available.** Select this checkbox to include titles with the preferred name (for example, Captain Samuel Hait).

- **Use married names for females.** Select this checkbox to include a woman's married name in addition to her maiden name (for example, Maria Hitchcock Hoyt).

Displaying Dates in the Index

If, like me, you have a tree full of Sams, Elizabeths, and Marys (all with the same surname, of course) you might want to display birth, death, or marriage dates in the Index so that it's easier to distinguish between them (fig. 3-2).

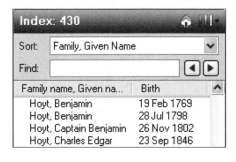

Figure 3-2
The Index displaying birth dates for each individual.

Go to the Family tab on the People workspace. Click the **Show additional data** button in the upper-right corner of the panel. From the drop-down list, choose birth, marriage, or death dates.

Changing the Sort Order in the Index

Names in the Index can be sorted alphabetically by name (given or surname) and by date (birth, marriage, and death) (fig. 3-3).

Figure 3-3

The Index sorted by birth dates.

Go to the Family tab on the People workspace. From the **Sort** drop-down list, choose how you want to sort the names. If you choose to sort by date, you will see sub-headings grouping the names together.

Filtering the Index

If you have a large tree with thousands of individuals, you might find the Index more useful if you filter it to display only those individuals or family branches you are currently working on.

Go to the Family tab on the People workspace. Click the **Filter** button beneath the Index. For instructions on filtering the list, see "Selecting a Group of Individuals" on page 46.

> Note: This filter affects *only* the Index on the People workspace. You can still navigate to any individual in your tree using the mini pedigree tree or the Index of Individuals.

Reviewing Your Work History

You're probably familiar with the History list on the People workspace, where you can see the last 200 individuals you've edited or added to your tree. But did you know that you can also see a summary of the changes you've made to each person on the History list? Simply move the pointer over the individual you're interested in and a pop-up shows what you've changed—and when (fig. 3-4).

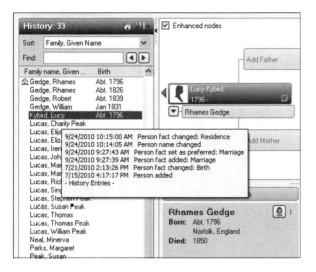

Figure 3-4

A history of changes for an individual.

Using Bookmarks

Bookmarks help you quickly access the people you work on most frequently. I also like to bookmark individuals who help orient me within a tree. For example, I always bookmark me, my grandparents, and my great-grandparents. That way if I get lost in my tree, I can select one of these bookmarked individuals and know right where I am again. You can access the list of bookmarked individuals (fig. 3-5) by clicking the **Bookmarks** button on the Index.

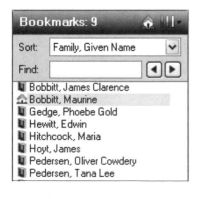

Figure 3-5

A list of bookmarked people.

Bookmarked individuals can also be accessed on the Index of Individuals by clicking the bookmark icon (fig. 3-6).

Figure 3-6

Selecting a bookmarked individual on the Index of Individuals.

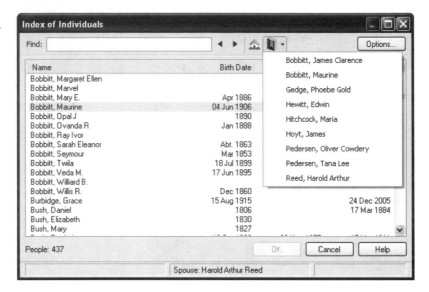

Adding a Bookmark

Go to the Family tab on the People workspace. In the Index right-click an individual and choose **Add Bookmark**. (You can also choose **Person>Add Bookmark**.)

Deleting a Bookmark

Go to the Family tab on the People workspace. In the Index right-click a bookmarked individual and choose **Delete Bookmark**. (You can also choose **Person>Delete Bookmark**.)

Selecting a Group of Individuals

Almost every time I use Family Tree Maker I find a need to select a specific group of people: one day it is because I'm uploading a tree to Ancestry, the next because I want to filter the Index to display a specific family line. To me, the ability to divide, categorize, and create subsets of people in my tree is one of the most powerful—and useful—features of Family Tree Maker.

Although this task explains how to use the filtering tool in the Index, you can use these steps to select a group of individuals when you're exporting or merging files, deleting a branch of your tree, or creating charts and custom reports (for example, I can create a custom report that displays people who are buried in a certain cemetery, or I can select all people with the same surname who were born in a certain city or state or county). If you haven't been using the filter tool to its full potential, I hope this will encourage you to give it a try.

1. Go to the **Family** tab on the People workspace; then click the **Filter** button beneath the Index. The Filter Individuals window opens. Every individual in your tree is listed on the left side of the window.

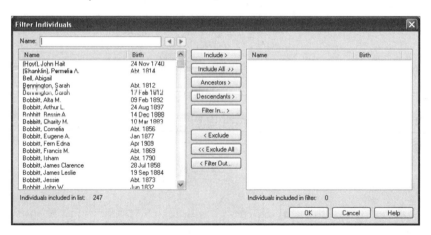

2. Use this chart to select individuals you want to include in the group:

To do this	Do this
Include a specific individual	Select an individual and click **Include**.
	Note: Click **Include All** to include everyone in your tree.

To do this	Do this
Include an individual's direct ancestors	Select an individual and click **Ancestors**. The Ancestors window opens.
	• Click **Include all parents** to include all parents in the list of ancestors; click **Include only preferred parents** to include only parents who have been marked as preferred.
	• Click **Include all spouses** to include all spouses in the list of ancestors; click **Include only preferred spouse** to include only spouses who have been marked as preferred.
	Note: If you choose to include your ancestors' descendants, this option applies to the spouses of descendants too.
	• Select the **Include ancestors' descendants** checkbox to include the descendants of your ancestors. Then choose the number of generations to include (1 generation would be each ancestor's children; 2 would be each ancestor's children and grandchildren, and so on).
Include an individual's descendants	Select an individual and click **Descendants**.

If you want, use the Filter In and Filter Out options to further define which individuals are included in the group. For example, you may want to exclude individuals who were born in a specific location or before a particular date.

3. Click **Filter In** or **Filter Out** depending on whether you want to add more individuals to the group or exclude people from the existing group.

4. Select a search type:

   - Select **Vital facts** to filter by names; genders; and birth, marriage, or death information.

   - Select **All facts** to filter by any fact, including custom facts you've created.

   - Select **Other** to filter by all facts, media details and notes, source details and notes, or relationship types and statuses.

5. Use this chart to define the search criteria:

Option	Description
Search where	Choose the fact or property you want to use from the drop-down list (for example, you could choose the Emigration fact or relationship status).
	Note: Depending on the type of fact you've selected, you may see another drop-down list, where you can specify whether to search in the Date, Place, or Description fields (or all).
	Then choose a requirement for the value from the drop-down list. You can choose from "Equals," "Does not equal," "Is before," "Is after," "Is blank," or "Is not blank."
Value	Enter a date, name, or keyword that you want the selected fact to match.
	Note: Click **Match all values** if the date, name, or keyword has to match the fact exactly; click **Match any value** if the date, name, or keyword can match any of the words in the fact.
Secondary facts	When filtering by facts, you can select this checkbox to include all facts in the search (preferred and otherwise). If this checkbox is not selected, only preferred facts are searched.

Searching Your Tree for Specific Individuals

Family Tree Maker lets you add thousands (or hundreds of thousands) of individuals to your tree. And the larger your tree gets, the more difficult it can be to locate a specific individual. Sometimes I can't remember an individual's name, but I can recall the cemetery they're buried in or where they were born. Instead of scrolling through the Index endlessly looking for the right person, I use the Find Individual tool to help me quickly navigate to an individual.

You can use any of the facts in your tree (such as occupation, immigration, burial, or a custom fact) to locate either a specific individual or a group of individuals who fit specific criteria.

1. Choose **Edit>Find Individual** and choose the type of fact you want to search for from the drop-down list. Then enter a search term and click **Find**. The window displays the individuals who match your search criteria.

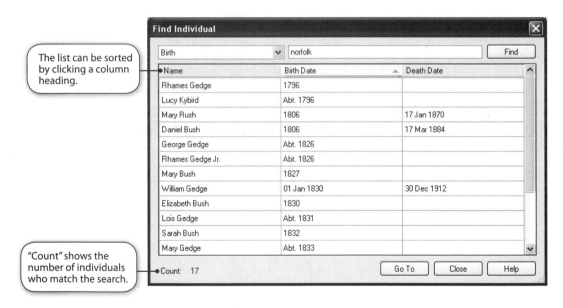

The list can be sorted by clicking a column heading.

"Count" shows the number of individuals who match the search.

Note: Keep in mind that search results include preferred facts only. If you think an individual belongs on the list but he or she is not included, it may be because the information is in an alternate fact not the preferred fact.

> **TIP**
>
> If you don't enter a search term, the search results will display every individual who has data entered for the selected fact. For example, I can see all individuals who have a recorded cause of death by selecting the Cause of Death fact and leaving the search term field blank, or I can enter "heart failure" and display the individuals who have that specific cause of death.

2. Select an individual in the search results and click **Go To** to open the individual's Person tab.

Editing an Individual

Has this has happened to you? You're viewing a pedigree chart and realize that you've reversed your grandfather's birth date and month, or perhaps as you're viewing your uncle's migration path you notice a location is missing. Instead of leaving the area where you're working, Family Tree Maker has the flexibility to let you edit facts, write notes, and add media items from every workspace.

To edit an individual in the Places workspace

Choose "Person" from the **List by** drop-down list. Then right-click an individual and choose **Edit Person**.

To edit an individual in the Media workspace

Choose "Person" from the **List by** drop-down list. Then right-click an individual and choose **Edit Person**.

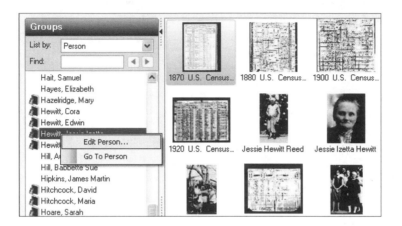

To edit an individual in the Sources workspace

Right-click an individual on the Links tab at the bottom of the window and choose **Edit Person**.

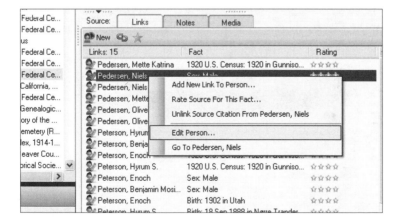

To edit an individual in the Publish workspace

When a chart or report is open, right-click an individual in the mini pedigree tree below the main toolbar and choose **Edit Person**.

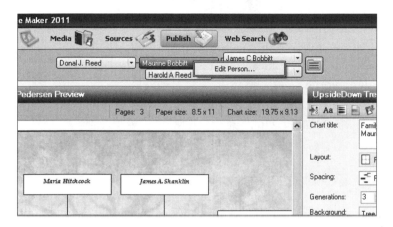

TIP

When making a chart, you can also double-click an individual to edit his or her information.

To edit an individual in the Web Search workspace

Right-click an individual name in the mini pedigree tree below the main toolbar and choose **Edit Person**.

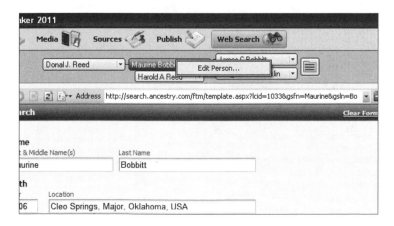

Adding Family Members

Because everyone uses Family Tree Maker a little differently, the software includes a number of ways to add family members. You can choose the option(s) that works best for you.

Adding a Spouse

To add a spouse in the pedigree view

Go to the Family tab on the People workspace. In the pedigree view, click **Add Spouse** underneath the primary individual.

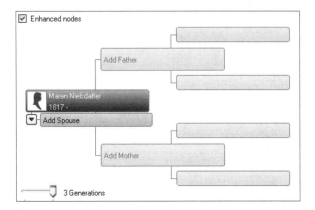

To add a spouse in the family group view

Go to the Family tab on the People workspace. In the family group view, click **Add Spouse**.

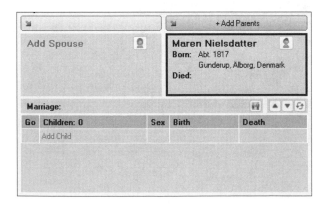

To add a spouse using the Marriage to button

Go to the Family tab on the People workspace. Click the **Marriage to** button in the editing panel.

To add a spouse using the Add button

Click the **Add** button beneath the main toolbar and choose **Add Spouse**.

To add a spouse from the Person menu

Go to the People workspace. Choose **Person>Add Person>Add Spouse**. (If the child already exists in the tree, choose **Person>Attach/Detach Person>Attach Spouse** to link the spouse to a family.)

Adding a Child to a Family

To add a child from the Person menu

Go to the People workspace. Choose **Person>Add Person>Add Child**. (If the child already exists in the tree, choose **Person>Attach/Detach Person>Attach Child** to link the child to a family.)

To add a child in the pedigree view

Go to the Family tab on the People workspace. In the pedigree view, click the down arrow underneath the primary individual and choose **Add Child**.

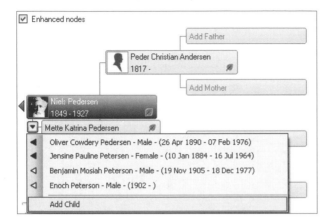

To add a child in the family group view

Go to the Family tab on the People workspace. In the family group view, click the **Add Child** link.

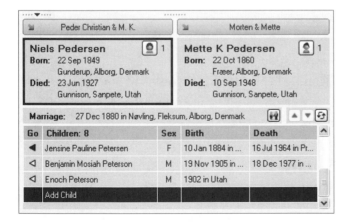

To add a child using the Add button

Click the **Add** button beneath the main toolbar and choose **Add Child**.

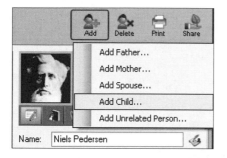

Adding a Father or Mother to a Family

To add a father or mother from the Person menu

Go to the People workspace. Choose **Person>Add Person>Add Father/ Mother**. (If the child already exists in the tree, choose **Person>Attach/Detach Person>Attach Father/Mother** to link the parent to a family.)

To add a father or mother in the pedigree view

Go to the Family tab on the People workspace. In the pedigree view, click **Add Father** or **Add Mother**.

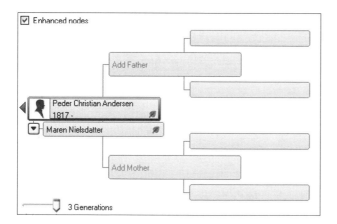

To add a father or mother in the family group view

Go to the Family tab on the People workspace. In the family group view, click **Add Parents**.

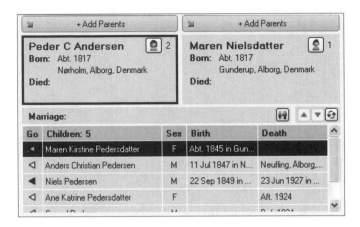

To add a father or mother using the Add button

Click the **Add** button beneath the main toolbar and choose **Add Father** or **Add Mother**.

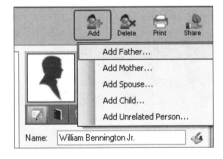

Chapter Four

Importing and Exporting

When you first start your family tree, you spend most of your time entering the names and events you've been gathering. But the longer you're at it, the more you'll focus on collaborating, whether it's exporting your tree for a family member or merging multiple trees together.

Because there are so many types of genealogy software (and so many versions!), variables in how data is input and converted, and even compatability issues with different computer systems, it's impossible for me to describe every importing and exporting situation you may encounter. Instead this chapter informs you of what Family Tree Maker is capable of and gives you guidelines, tips, and cautions to help you successfully share your family tree.

Importing Family Tree Maker Files

When you import or open a file created in Family Tree Maker 2008, 2009, or 2010, Family Tree Maker converts the tree to a new file format. You won't notice any

Genealogy File Extensions

Sometimes a family member or researcher will send you a family tree file in a format you don't recognize. You can identify the file type by looking at the file extension:

.FTM—Family Tree Maker (2008, 2009, 2010, 2011).

.FTMB—Family Tree Maker backup (2008, 2009, 2010, 2011).

.FTW—Family Tree Maker (2005, 2006, version 16).

.FBK or **.FBC**—Family Tree Maker backup (2005, 2006, version 16).

.FTMM—Family Tree Maker for Mac 2010.

.FTMD—Family Tree Maker for Mac 2010 backup.

.GED—The file extension for a GEDCOM, the universal format used for transferring data between genealogy software programs.

.PAF—FamilySearch™ Personal Ancestral File 5.

.PJC—The Master Genealogist™ 7.

.LEG or **.FDB**—Legacy™ Family Tree 7.

.RMG—RootsMagic™ 4.

changes on the user side and none of your information will be lost; however, this new file can be opened only in Family Tree Maker 2011.

You can also import or open files created in version 2005, 2006, and version 16. If your Place fields include slash marks (/), data before the slash will be imported to Description fields; data after the slash will be imported into Place fields. If you need to you can swap Description and Place fields using the Resolve All Place Names tool or Manage Facts feature (see "Editing Facts as a Group" on page 227).

If you are using Family Tree Maker 4.0 (or earlier) or you have a .FBC file, you cannot import or open the file in Family Tree Maker 2011. You will need to use the Family Tree Maker 2005 Starter Edition to convert the file to a compatible format. To download the Starter Edition, go to the KnowledgeBase at <www.familytreemaker.com>; then enter "3673" in the search field and click **Search**.

Importing GEDCOMs

Most genealogy software programs let you export a file as a GEDCOM so it can be opened in other programs. The downside to this format is that it can't include images, audio and video items, or saved charts and reports. Family Tree Maker can import GEDCOMs, version 5.5 or later. If the file was created before version 5.5, you cannot import or open the file in Family Tree Maker 2011. You will need to use the Family Tree Maker 2005 Starter Edition to convert the GEDCOM to a format that can be read by Family Tree Maker 2011. To download the Starter Edition, go to the KnowledgeBase at <www.familytreemaker.com>; then enter "3673" in the search field and click **Search**.

Importing Other Files

You can import FamilySearch™ Personal Ancestral Files (PAFs), Legacy™ Family Tree files, and The Master Genealogist™ files directly into Family Tree Maker; these file types do not need to be converted to GEDCOMs.

Family Tree Maker automatically imports new trees into the Family Tree Maker folder in your My Documents folder. If the file you are importing includes media items, you need to save the new tree in the same folder where it was located previously; otherwise the links to your media items will be lost. When you are importing a tree, you can select the location where the new tree will be saved by clicking the **File Location** button on the Getting Started window (fig. 4-1).

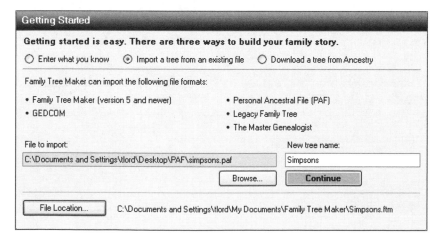

Figure 4-1

The Getting Started window on the Plan workspace.

Importing Large Trees

If you are having problems importing a tree (or you know the file you're importing is extremely large), you may want to try a low memory import. Instead of copying the tree to the computer's memory, Family Tree Maker copies the file directly to the computer's hard drive. Although this method takes more time—often several hours—it makes it possible to import large trees.

Note: This option is rarely needed.

1. Choose **File>Import As New Tree**.

2. Navigate to the file you want to import and click **Open**.

3. Place your cursor in the **New tree name** field; then press **CTRL+SHIFT+I**. A message alerts you that the low memory import will be used on the next file you import.

4. Click **OK**; then click **Continue** to import the tree.

Viewing and Resolving Import Errors

When you import a tree, Family Tree Maker keeps track of information that doesn't import correctly, such as incompatible date formats. You can view a list of import errors on the To-Do list on the Plan workspace (fig. 4-2).

Figure 4-2

Import errors on the To-Do list.

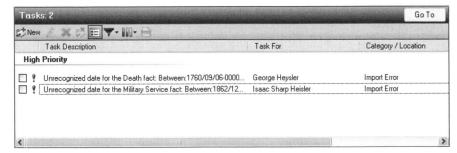

To fix an error, simply right-click the individual's name in the To-Do list and choose **Edit Person** from the drop-down list. The Edit Individual window opens (fig. 4-3). Make the appropriate changes and click **OK**.

Figure 4-3

Editing an individual in the To-Do list.

Another trick I like to use is the Find and Replace tool. Once I received a file from a friend who had used UN instead of Unknown in her Date fields. Because Family Tree Maker couldn't interpret this abbreviation, the dates were all marked as errors—hundreds of them. I used Find and Replace to search for all instances of UN in Facts and change them to Unknown, saving myself from a lot of manual data entry. Before you start making changes, see if Family Tree Maker tools like Find and Replace or the Global Spell Checker can make the necessary changes for you.

Merging Files

At some point you may find that you need to merge two trees together: maybe you originally created multiple trees and now you want to combine them, or you might have received a tree from a family member. Family Tree Maker lets you merge the two files together so you don't have to manually enter the new information. You can choose which individuals will be merged into your tree (and how), and even determine how differences between individuals should be handled.

Let's be honest though. The thought of introducing loads of new information into your own tree can be disconcerting, and there's always the potential to make a mess of your data. But if you back up your tree before you begin, you should feel confident knowing that you can always return to where you started.

Through lots of trial and error, reverting to backups, and suggestions from other users, I've come up with a workflow (see fig. 4-4 on the opposite page) and tips that I hope will make your merging go smoothly and maybe prevent you from having to do repair work later on.

> **TIP**
>
> Although merging files is not difficult, it can be time-consuming, especially if the files you are merging contain a large number of potentially matching people. Make sure you plan an adequate amount of time to go through each individual to specify how Family Tree Maker should handle differences in facts. You might also consider breaking the merging file into several smaller trees that you can merge individually.

1. Open your tree and choose **File>Merge**.

2. If you haven't backed up your tree already, click **Yes** to back up the file.

3. Navigate to the file you want to merge into your tree and click **Open**.

   Note: You can merge these types of genealogy files: Family Tree Maker (.ftm and .ftw), Personal Ancestry File (.paf), The Master Genealogist (.pjc), Legacy (.leg and .fdb), Generations (.uds), and GEDCOMs.

Merging Files

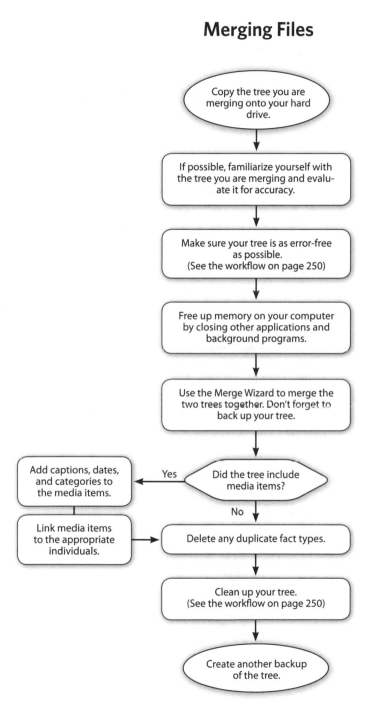

Figure 4-4

A workflow to help you merge files together.

When the Merge Wizard opens, you'll see the name of the host file (your original tree) and the name of the import file (the tree you want to merge).

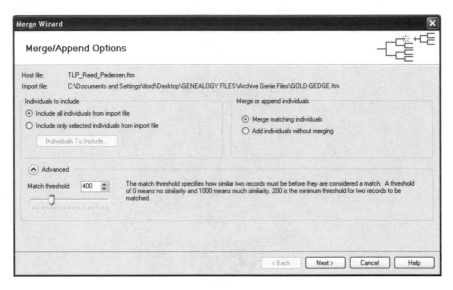

4. First select the individuals in the import file that you want to merge into your tree. Select **Include all individuals** to merge all individuals in the file into your tree; select **Include only selected individuals** to choose specific individuals or groups of individuals. (For help on selecting a group of individuals, see page 46.)

5. After you've selected the appropriate individuals, you can decide how to add them to your tree. Select **Add individuals without merging** to add the individuals as a separate tree without merging anyone together (basically you'll have a tree within a tree.) Select **Merge matching individuals** to have Family Tree Maker match people when merging trees together.

6. If you want, you can choose how similar individuals must be before they are considered a "match." Click the **Advanced** arrow then drag the **Match threshold** slider to the desired number. The higher the match number the more closely individuals need to match in able to be merged together—

a zero means that the individuals do not match at all; a 1,000 means the individuals are extremely similar.

Note: If you don't choose a match threshold, Family Tree Maker uses 400— the default.

Match Threshold: An Example

I have a small family tree on Ancestry that I use to store odds and ends. Recently I decided it was time to merge it with my main Family Tree Maker database to make sure I had all my family history in one spot. In the process I wanted to experiment with match threshold numbers to see just what they did. Because both trees had the same people, I figured that the highest match possible would work the best. What I discovered was that at a match threshold of 1,000, people I believed to be "perfect" matches didn't merge together. Things as simple as a comma in a different location in a Place field kept identical individuals from matching up. After some evaluation I found that the best option is a threshold number between 400 and 500. That way you'll create fewer new individuals and more individuals will be flagged as potential matches.

To give you an idea of how match threshold numbers work, here's what happened in my small tree of 162 people:

Threshold Number	400	700	900
Flagged individuals	116	94	77
Merged individuals	27	27	11
New individuals	19	41	74

Don't be afraid to experiment when choosing a threshold match number. If you don't like the results a certain threshold gives you, you can click the **Back** button on the Merge Wizard and choose a different number.

7. Click **Next**.

   Family Tree Maker analyzes your file, comparing people based on the match theshold you've chosen. A list of individuals appears so you can see how they will be added to your tree; each person will be categorized in one of three ways:

   - **Flagged.** Indicates that Family Tree Maker has found similarities between two individuals but needs you to resolve conflicting details. You cannot complete the merge until all flagged individuals have been marked as "resolved."
   - **Merged.** Indicates that the individuals meet the match threshold, do not have conflicting details, and will be merged together.
   - **New.** Indicates the new individuals who will be added to your tree.

8. Select an individual in the list. Notice that the window now reflects this individual's information.

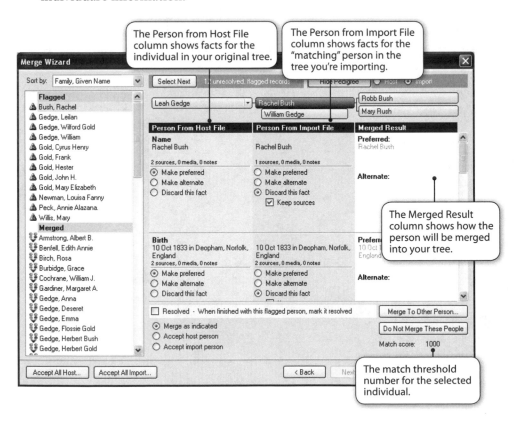

The Person from Host File column shows facts for the individual in your original tree.

The Person from Import File column shows facts for the "matching" person in the tree you're importing.

The Merged Result column shows how the person will be merged into your tree.

The match threshold number for the selected individual.

> **TIP**
>
> It can be hard to determine who an individual is simply by a looking at a name. If you click **View Pedigree**, you can display a mini pedigree tree for the selected individual. Seeing how the individual is related to others in your tree can help clarify whether you're looking at matching individuals. Click **Host** to view the pedigree for the individual in your original tree; click **Import** to view the pedigree for the individual in the merging tree.

9. If you don't want to go through each individual, you can make global changes that apply to every flagged individual in the merge. Use this chart to determine how the flagged individuals will be merged; then skip to step 13.

To do this	Do this
Keep *all* facts in your original tree as "preferred" facts	Click **Accept All Host**. Then choose one of these options: • Select **Save import differences** to add facts from the merging tree as alternate facts. (In the Person from Import File column, the "Make alternate" option will be selected for each fact.) • Select **Discard import differences** to exclude all conflicting facts in the merging tree. (In the Person from Import File column, the "Discard this fact" option will be selected for each fact.)
Accept *all* facts in the merging tree as "preferred" facts	Click **Accept All Import**. Then choose one of these options: • Select **Save host differences** to keep the facts already in your tree but mark them as alternate facts. (In the Person from Import File column, the "Make preferred" option will be selected for each fact.) • Select **Discard host differences** to delete all facts in your original tree.

10. Although you only need to resolve flagged individuals, I like to go through every individual involved in the merge to make sure the information is being added in the way I want it. Use this chart to determine how facts for each individual are merged:

To do this	Do this
Choose which individual's facts will be kept during the merge	Select **Accept host person** to keep the facts associated with the individual from your original tree; or, click **Accept import person** to keep the facts associated with the individual from the imported tree.
	If you want to keep the other individual's fact as an alternate, select **Save differences as alternate facts**. If you want to discard facts from the other individual that don't match, select **Discard differences**.
Choose how specific facts for an individual will be merged into your tree	In the Person from Import File column, choose how you want specific facts for the individual in the merging tree to be added to your tree:
	• Select **Make preferred** to merge the information as the "preferred" fact for the individual.
	• Select **Make alternate** to merge the information as an alternate fact for the individual.
	• Select **Discard this fact** to *not* merge the information into your tree. You may choose to discard some facts for a person, although it is usually a good idea to include all facts in case they turn out to be relevant.
	Select the **Keep sources** checkbox to merge the source information for the discarded fact.
	Note: Don't forget to use the scroll bar on the right side of the window; there may be additional facts for the individual that cannot be viewed on just one screen.

11. When you have resolved an individual's conflicting facts, select the **Resolved** checkbox. The individual will be moved from the "flagged" list to the "resolved" list.

12. Click **Select Next** at the top of the window to move to the next individual. (You can also choose any individual by clicking his or her name in the panel on the left side of the window.)

   Note: If you do not want to merge an individual with the person he or she is matched with, you can click the **Do Not Merge These People** button. Also, if you think the individual matches a person not suggested by Family Tree Maker, you can click the **Merge to Other Person** button and choose the person you want the individual to be merged with.

13. When you've made all the selections you want for the merging files, click **Merge**.

Exporting Trees

If you want to share your family tree with someone, you can export all or part of a file as a Family Tree Maker file or as a GEDCOM—the standard file format used to transfer data between different genealogy software.

Exporting a Tree as a GEDCOM

The easiest way to share a family tree with someone is to export it as a GED-COM because this file type can be opened by almost any genealogy software program, Mac or PC. However, while Family Tree Maker lets you add digital images, sound, and videos to your tree, these items cannot be included in GEDCOMs. (Saved charts and reports, books, and to-do tasks are not included either.)

> **TIP**
> Some genealogy programs let you import a Family Tree Maker file without first converting it to a GEDCOM. Before you export a tree as a GEDCOM (and lose all your media items and to-do items), check the software's website to see what formats the software can import.

1. Choose **File**>**Export**. The Export window opens.

2. Select the individuals you want to include in the exported file. For help, see "Selecting Individuals to Include in an Exported File" on page 73.

3. Choose one of these options from the **Output format** drop-down list:

   - **GEDCOM 5.5.** This is the standard format that can be opened by most genealogy programs.

   - **GEDCOM for FTM 16.** This GEDCOM allows a Family Tree Maker file to be more easily imported into Family Tree Maker version 16.

4. Choose how you want content included in the exported file:

Select this checkbox	To do this
Include private facts	Include facts you have designated as private.
Include private notes	Include notes you have designated as private.

5. Click **OK**. The Export To window opens. Navigate to the location where you want to save the exported file; then click **Save**. A message tells you when your file has been exported successfully.

Exporting a Tree as a Family Tree Maker File

Family Tree Maker lets you export your tree in formats that can be opened in various versions of Family Tree Maker. These files will include media items.

1. Choose **File**>**Export**. The Export window opens.

2. Select the individuals you want to include in the exported file. For help, see the next task, "Selecting Individuals to Include in an Exported File."

3. Choose one of these options from the **Output format** drop-down list:

   - **Family Tree Maker.** This format can be opened only in Family Tree Maker 2011.

   - **Family Tree Maker 2010.** This format can be opened in Family Tree Maker 2010 and 2011.

- **Family Tree Maker 2008/2009.** This format can be opened only in Family Tree Maker 2008 or 2009. (If you want to open this file in 2011, you will need to import and convert it.)

4. Choose how you want content included in the exported file:

Select this checkbox	To do this
Include private facts	Include facts you have designated as private.
Include private notes	Include notes you have designated as private.
Include media files	Include all media files that are linked to the tree.
Include tasks	Include tasks you've added to your To-Do lists.
Include charts, reports, and books	Include saved charts, reports, and books you've created.
	Note: This option is available only if you are exporting a file in the Family Tree Maker 2011 format.
Include only items linked to selected individuals	Include only tasks, notes, and media items that are linked to the individuals you're exporting.

5. Click **OK**. The Export To window opens. Navigate to the location where you want to save the exported file; then click **Save**. A message tells you when your file has been exported successfully.

Selecting Individuals to Include in an Exported File

When sharing a Family Tree Maker tree, you may want to export a file that includes only certain individuals or branches of your tree. I am creating a website about my mother's ancestry and I want to add a downloadable GED-COM. Because my Family Tree Maker database contains the maternal and paternal sides of my family, I'm going to export a GEDCOM that contains only my maternal ancestors. That way family members accessing the website will see only people they are directly related to. When exporting a tree, you can pick which individuals are included in the exported file, by clicking **Selected**

How Does Family Tree Maker Calculate Living Individuals?

We all have concerns about sharing our family history and inadvertently revealing details about family members who are still alive. When you export a tree (or upload a tree to Ancestry.com), Family Tree Maker lets you "privatize" living individuals. That way, only names of living individuals (not names or facts) will be included. Family Tree Maker considers individuals to be "living" if:

He or she has no death date or place (or burial date or place).
AND
He or she was born less than 120 years ago.

If an individual has no recorded birth, marriage, or death facts, Family Tree Maker looks at the person's parents and spouse(s) and considers the individual "living" if:

The individual's spouse is living.
OR
The individual's parents are living.

If you know someone is deceased but you don't have a death date, you can enter "Deceased" or "Dead" into the Death Date field.

individuals on the Export window. For help on choosing specific individuals, see "Selecting a Group of Individuals" on page 46.

When you export a tree, you have the option to privatize living individuals. (To learn how Family Tree Maker calculates living individuals, see the sidebar on this page.) If you use this option, here's how a living individual's information is exported:

- Given names are replaced with the word "Living."

- Relationships are exported.

- Facts about the individual are not exported.

- Shared facts are not exported even if the other individual is deceased.

Creating a Family Tree Maker for Mac File

If you have a Family Tree Maker 2010 or 2011 for Windows file, you can convert it so it can be opened in Family Tree Maker for Mac 2010.

Downloading and Installing the Migration Utility

You will need to have access to the FTM File Migration Utility on a PC in order to convert your files. To download the utility, go to the KnowledgeBase at <www.familytreemaker.com>; then enter "5313" in the search field and click **Search**.

1. After downloading the utility to your PC, double-click the **FTMFileMigrationSetup.exe** icon. The automated installer will start.

2. Follow the instructions that appear on the screen. Once installation is complete, the conversion tool will launch automatically.

Converting a File

1. If necessary, open the conversion tool by choosing **Start>Programs> FTM File Migration Utility>FTM File Migration Utility**. The migration wizard opens.

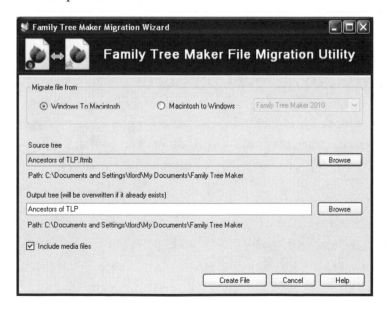

2. Select **Windows to Macintosh**. (You can also convert a Family Tree Maker for Mac file to a Windows file by selecting **Macintosh to Windows**.)

3. Click the **Browse** button to locate the Family Tree Maker file you want to convert. You can choose between a .ftm file ("regular" tree file) or a .ftmb file (a backup).

4. Enter a name for the tree in the **Output tree** field and also select a location for the new tree.

5. If you want to include media items linked to the tree, make sure the **Include media files** checkbox is selected.

   Note: If you are converting a .ftm file, the utility will search for the tree's Media folder. If the tool locates the folder, your media items will be included in the new tree. If you've moved the Media folder from the Family Tree Maker folder, the utility may not be able to locate it. To ensure that your new tree contains your media items, you might want to convert a .ftmb backup file instead of a .ftm file (backup files already include your media items).

6. Click **Create File**. A message tells you when the conversion is complete. Click **Close**.

   Note: Because of formatting changes, Family Tree Maker 2011 files that are converted into Mac files will not include saved charts, reports, and books.

Moving a Tree to a New Computer

When you purchase a new computer system, it's always a little nerve-racking trying to make sure that all your files from your old computer make it onto the new one—especially when they involve years of work on your family tree. This task will help you get your Family Tree Maker software and files up and running in no time.

Making a Backup of the File

The first step in moving your tree is to create a backup of your tree (which includes your media files) on the old computer.

1. Choose **File>Backup** to create a backup file of the Family Tree Maker tree(s) that you want to transfer to the new computer. The Backup window opens.

2. If you want a new name to distinguish this backup file from your original tree, enter a new name for the tree in the **Backup file name** field. For example, a name like "PedersenTree_NEW.ftmb".

    Note: If you change the file's name, make sure you leave the .ftmb extension at the end of the name; otherwise Family Tree Maker might not recognize the file.

3. Insert a CD or DVD in the disk drive or connect a flash drive to the old computer.

4. In "Backup location" select **Removeable Media** and choose your CD-ROM drive, DVD drive, or USB drive from the drop-down list.

5. Select the **Include linked media files** checkbox. If you don't, photos, videos, and audio items you've linked to your tree won't be included in the backup file.

6. Click **OK**. A series of messages shows the progress of the backup.

Copying the Backup to the New Computer

Because Family Tree Maker doesn't let you open trees from CDs, DVDs, or flash drives, you must copy the backup of your tree to your computer's hard drive.

1. Insert the CD or DVD in the disk drive of the new computer or connect your flash drive to the new computer.

2. On the new computer, browse to the drive where your backup file is stored (CD, DVD, or flash drive).

3. Once you have found the backup (.ftmb) file, right-click it and select **Copy**.

4. Find the folder on your hard drive where you want to store the tree (usually this is the Family Tree Maker folder in your My Documents folder); Right-click inside the folder and select **Paste**. The backup file is now copied to the hard drive.

Opening the Tree on the New Computer

1. Disable any anti-virus software you may be using.

2. Install your most current version of Family Tree Maker on the new computer.

3. Open Family Tree Maker; then choose **File>Restore**. The Choose File to Restore window opens.

4. Navigate to the backup (.ftmb) file you just copied to the hard drive and click **Open**. The Name for Restored File window opens.

5. Choose a location for the new tree (if necessary), enter a name, and click **Save**. Your tree opens in Family Tree Maker. Notice that your media items are saved in the same folder where you just saved your new tree.

    Note: Don't forget to reenable your anti-virus software.

Maintaining a Tree on Two Computers

Many of us have a desktop computer at home and a laptop we take with us to the libary or on research trips. While having two computers makes it more convenient to do family history, it also means that you have to maintain two databases and constantly update them so they contain the same information.

The process you'll use to transfer information back and forth between your computers depends on whether you have made changes to a tree on only one computer or whether you've been working actively on both computers.

Making Changes on One Computer

You may have your main Family Tree Maker database on your home computer and use a laptop to enter information when you visit family members, go on vacation, or visit a library. You can keep your two trees up-to-date by copying the tree on the laptop and replacing or overwriting the tree on your desktop—you won't need to merge your files together. The workflow on the opposite page (fig. 4-5) explains how this process works.

Making Changes on One Computer

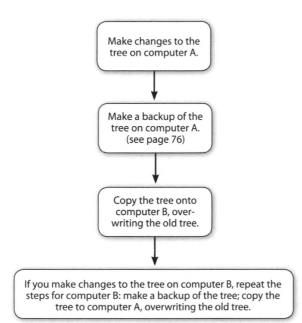

Make changes to the tree on computer A.

Make a backup of the tree on computer A. (see page 76)

Copy the tree onto computer B, over-writing the old tree.

If you make changes to the tree on computer B, repeat the steps for computer B: make a backup of the tree; copy the tree to computer A, overwriting the old tree.

Figure 4-5

A workflow to help you transfer files from one computer to another.

Making Changes on Two Computers

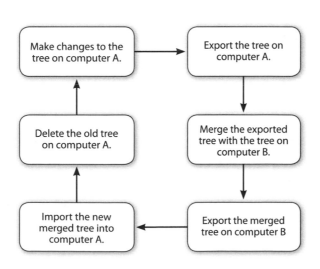

Make changes to the tree on computer A.

Export the tree on computer A.

Delete the old tree on computer A.

Merge the exported tree with the tree on computer B.

Import the new merged tree into computer A.

Export the merged tree on computer B.

Figure 4-6

A workflow to help you merge files from two computers.

Making Changes on Two Computers

You may keep your tree on two computers and make changes simultaneously; for example you may make changes on one computer while your spouse is making changes to the same tree on another computer.

If you have two trees, both with changes, you will need to export the file on one computer and merge it with the database on the other computer. Figure 4-6 on the previous page shows how this process works.

Unfortunately, every time you merge trees together, you run the risk of introducing errors and creating duplicate individuals. Instead of exporting my entire tree every time I update my databases, I use the History list (fig. 4-7) to keep track of the changes I've made and then export only the individuals who have been added or changed since the last time I merged trees.

Figure 4-7

The History list shows the date on which the last individual was edited.

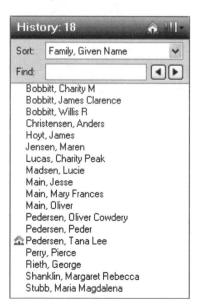

I take a screen capture of the History list and then select these individuals to include in my exported file. (I have tried to create a custom report to recreate this history list but have been unsuccessful so far. It is definitely on my wish list.) If you don't have access to a screen capture program, you can also press **ALT+Print Screen** to capture an image of the Family Tree Maker window and then paste it into a text document.

Chapter Five
Showing Off Your Family

For many family historians, hunting down courthouse records is a breeze and climbing through brambles to read a tombstone is routine. But ask some of these same people to create a family tree chart and they balk. Many of us are hesitant to try new things or worry that we don't have the necessary design skills and creativity. The best way to overcome this is to dive in and experiment. Start simple by adding a background or changing the font. Before you know it you'll be adding family photos, trying out color combinations, and even creating posters.

Using Family Tree Maker you can create a number of useful (and beautiful) charts. Whether you're designing a 10-generation wall poster to display at a family gathering (I will get to this some day!) or making an easy-to-follow pedigree to include in a family history book, Family Tree Maker has the robust tools to help you.

Be aware that some charts are available in book and poster format; others can only be created as posters. This chapter illustrates each type of chart you can create and also gives specific details on what customization options are available for each chart.

Pedigree Charts

The pedigree chart (sometimes called an ancestor tree) is a familiar sight even to non-genealogists. This type of chart is concise and easy to understand (and a great addition to any family history book). It shows the direct ancestors of one individual—parents, grandparents, great-grandparents, and so on.

Figure 5-1

A standard pedigree chart showing an individual and three generations of ancestors.

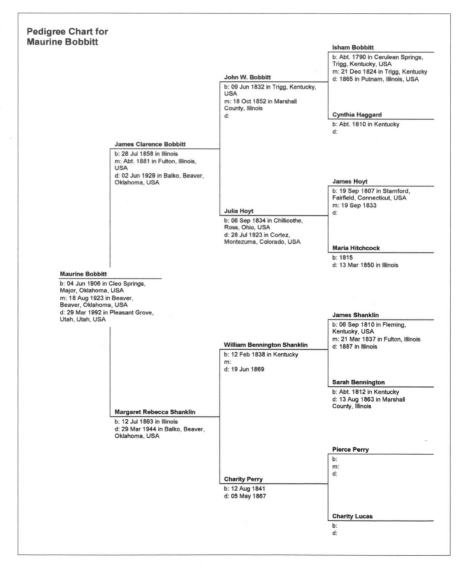

Pedigree Chart for
Maurine Bobbitt

Maurine Bobbitt
b: 04 Jun 1906 in Cleo Springs, Major, Oklahoma, USA
m: 18 Aug 1923 in Beaver, Beaver, Oklahoma, USA
d: 29 Mar 1992 in Pleasant Grove, Utah, Utah, USA

James Clarence Bobbitt
b: 28 Jul 1858 in Illinois
m: Abt. 1881 in Fulton, Illinois, USA
d: 02 Jun 1929 in Balko, Beaver, Oklahoma, USA

Margaret Rebecca Shanklin
b: 12 Jul 1863 in Illinois
d: 29 Mar 1944 in Balko, Beaver, Oklahoma, USA

John W. Bobbitt
b: 09 Jun 1832 in Trigg, Kentucky, USA
m: 18 Oct 1852 in Marshall County, Illinois
d:

Julia Hoyt
b: 06 Sep 1834 in Chillicothe, Ross, Ohio, USA
d: 28 Jul 1923 in Cortez, Montezuma, Colorado, USA

William Bennington Shanklin
b: 12 Feb 1838 in Kentucky
m:
d: 19 Jun 1869

Charity Perry
b: 12 Aug 1841
d: 05 May 1867

Isham Bobbitt
b: Abt. 1790 in Cerulean Springs, Trigg, Kentucky, USA
m: 21 Dec 1824 in Trigg, Kentucky
d: 1865 in Putnam, Illinois, USA

Cynthia Haggard
b: Abt. 1810 in Kentucky
d:

James Hoyt
b: 19 Sep 1807 in Stamford, Fairfield, Connecticut, USA
m: 19 Sep 1833
d:

Maria Hitchcock
b: 1815
d: 13 Mar 1850 in Illinois

James Shanklin
b: 06 Sep 1810 in Fleming, Kentucky, USA
m: 21 Mar 1837 in Fulton, Illinois
d: 1887 in Illinois

Sarah Bennington
b: Abt. 1812 in Kentucky
d: 13 Aug 1863 in Marshall County, Illinois

Pierce Perry
b:
m:
d:

Charity Lucas
b:
d:

Standard Pedigree Charts

In the standard pedigree chart, the primary individual is shown at the left of the tree, with ancestors branching off to the right—paternal ancestors on top and maternal ancestors on the bottom.

The default pedigree chart is shown in figure 5-1 on the opposite page. Figure 5-2 is the same pedigree chart but now it has been enhanced using one of the chart templates included in Family Tree Maker.

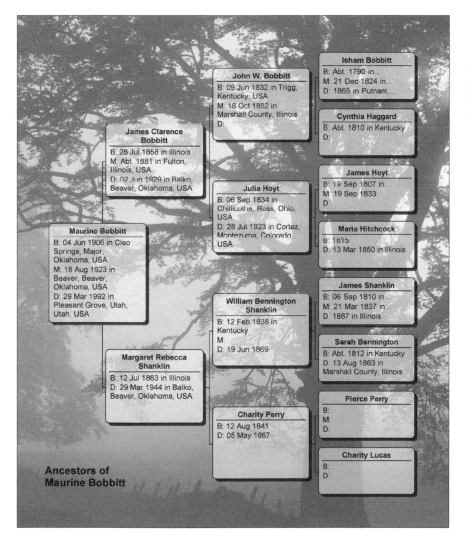

Figure 5-2

A standard pedigree chart customized using the Light Tree template.

Figure 5-3 shows a landscape pedigree chart that includes a page border, thumbnail images, and a textured background.

Figure 5-3

A landscape pedigree chart showing three generations of ancestors.

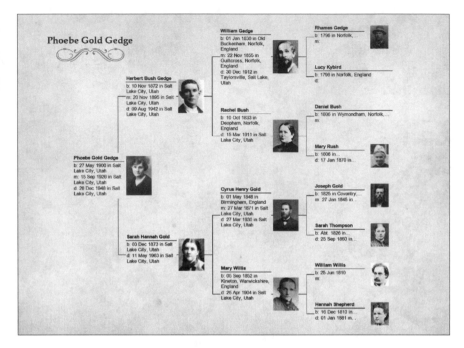

Creating a Standard Pedigree Chart

Go to the Collection tab on the Publish workspace. Under Charts, select **Pedigree Chart**. This chart can be created in book layout or poster layout. Use these options in the editing panel to change the chart:

Include empty branches (Book and Poster layout)

Select this checkbox to display all branches of a tree (even those with no information). This can be useful if you're sharing the chart with other family members and want them to add information for you.

Include duplicate ancestor lines (Book and Poster layout)

If you have people in your tree who have intermarried (for example, cousins who married), select this checkbox to have these individuals appear in every instance where they occur in your tree.

Center tree on page (Poster layout)

Select this checkbox to display the tree in the center of the page.

Include siblings of primary individual (Poster layout)

Select this checkbox to display the brothers and sisters of the chart's primary individual.

Include spouses of primary individual (Poster layout)

Select this checkbox to display the spouse(s) of the primary individual.

Boxes overlap page breaks (Poster layout)

Select this checkbox if you don't want boxes that fall on a page break to be partially printed on both pieces of paper. Family Tree Maker will adjust the chart spacing so that no boxes are split over two pages.

Vertical Pedigree Charts

In the vertical pedigree chart, the primary individual is shown at the bottom of the page, with his or her ancestors branching above the individual   paternal ancestors on the left and maternal ancestors on the right.

The chart in figure 5-4 is the default vertical pedigree chart in Family Tree Maker. In figure 5-5 on the following page, the chart has been customized with a new title, different fonts, additional dates and places, thumbnail photos, and a background color.

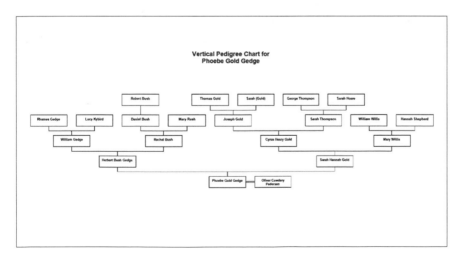

Figure 5-4

A vertical pedigree chart with the default settings.

Figure 5-5

A customized vertical pedigree chart with images and formatted boxes.

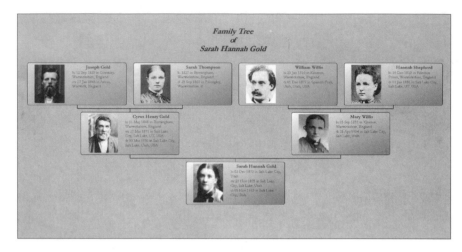

Creating a Vertical Pedigree Chart

Go to the Collection tab on the Publish workspace. Under Charts, select **Vertical Pedigree Chart**. This chart can be created in book layout or poster layout. Use these options in the editing panel to change the chart:

Include spouses of primary individual (Book and Poster layout)

Select this checkbox to display the spouse(s) of the primary individual.

Center tree on page (Poster layout)

Select this checkbox to display the tree in the center of the page.

Include empty branches (Poster layout)

Select this checkbox to display all branches of a tree (even those with no information). This can be useful if you're sharing the chart with other family members and want them to add information for you.

Include siblings of primary individual (Poster layout)

Select this checkbox to display the brothers and sisters of the chart's primary individual.

Boxes overlap page breaks (Poster layout)

Select this checkbox if you don't want boxes that fall on a page break to be partially printed on both pieces of paper. Family Tree Maker will adjust the chart spacing so that no boxes are split over two pages.

Descendant Charts

The descendant chart shows the direct descendants of an individual—children, grandchildren, great-grandchildren, and so on. The primary individual is shown at the top of the chart, with descendants underneath in horizontal rows. Because of the number of individuals contained in this report, it can quickly become unwieldy and stretch over multiple pages. If you're planning on including this chart in a book you might consider creating a descendant report instead (see page 144 for more information).

The chart in figure 5-6 shows a portion of a default descendant chart. Even though the chart includes only two generations of descendants, the full chart covers four pages. The descendant chart on the following page (fig. 5-7) has been customized with a background, embellishments, and a family photograph. In addition the last generation of descendants are arranged vertically to save room.

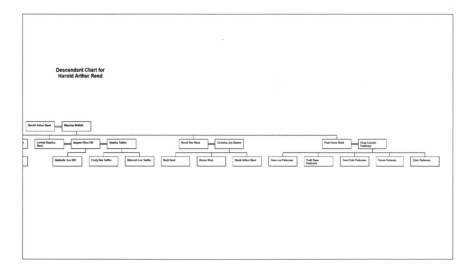

Figure 5-6

A portion of a two-generation chart with the default settings.

Figure 5-7

A customized
descendant
chart.

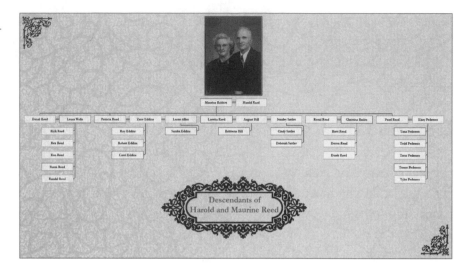

Creating a Descendant Chart

Go to the Collection tab on the Publish workspace. Under Charts, select
Descendant Chart. This chart can be created in book layout or poster layout.
Use these options in the editing panel to change the chart:

Include spouses of primary individual (Book and Poster layout)

Select this checkbox to display the spouse(s) of the primary individual.

Center tree on page (Poster layout)

Select this checkbox to display the tree in the center of the page.

Last descendant generation vertically (Poster layout)

Select this checkbox to list the last generation vertically under their parents
(see fig. 5-7 for an example).

Include siblings of primary individual (Poster layout)

Select this checkbox to display the brothers and sisters of the chart's primary
individual.

Boxes overlap page breaks (Poster layout)

Select this checkbox if you don't want boxes that fall on a page break to be
partially printed on both pieces of paper. Family Tree Maker will adjust the
chart spacing so that no boxes are split over two pages.

Hourglass Charts

An hourglass chart shows both the ancestors and descendants of a specific individual. The individual appears in the middle of the chart, with ancestors and descendants branching off in a shape similar to an hourglass. Because of its shape and the number of individuals included, most hourglass charts look best as posters.

Standard Hourglass Charts

In the standard hourglass chart, the primary individual appears in the middle of the chart, with ancestors branching above and descendants extending below the person.

The chart in figure 5-8 shows a default hourglass chart; it is laid out as a poster and uses landscape orientation. In figure 5-9 (on the following page), the chart is laid out as a poster and has been enhanced using a custom template. Notice the white spaces running vertically and horizontally across the pages. These show the margins of a standard 8½" by 11" sheet of paper. If you want to print the tree at home, you can use these guides to tape the pages together.

You can also create standard hourglass charts that are useful for including in family history books. When you use the book layout, the chart is condensed into a series of individual family trees that appear on separate pages. The chart in figure 5-10 shows one page of a multi-page book-layout chart. Notice the numbered box to the right of the chart. When you are viewing the chart

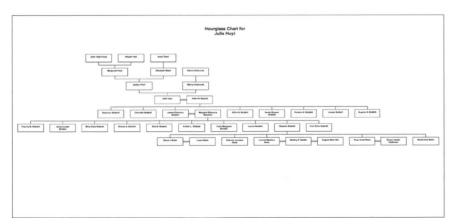

Figure 5-8

A default hourglass chart—three generations of ancestors and descendants.

in Family Tree Maker, you can click one of these boxes to access that page of the chart. And when your chart is printed out, the numbered boxes help you navigate to related individuals found on other pages in the chart.

Figure 5-9

An hourglass chart laid out as a poster.

Figure 5-10

The first page of a hourglass chart laid out for a book.

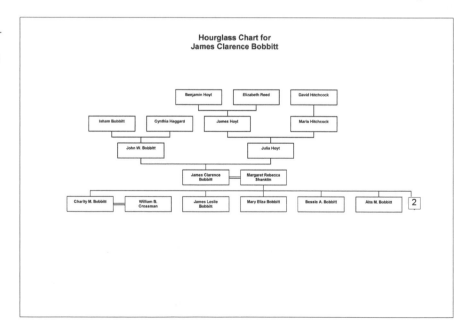

Creating an Hourglass Chart

Go to the Collection tab on the Publish workspace. Under Charts, select **Hourglass Chart**. This chart can be created in book layout or poster layout. Use these options in the editing panel to change the chart:

Include spouses of primary individual (Book and Poster layout)

Select this checkbox to display the spouse(s) of the primary individual.

Center tree on page (Poster layout)

Select this checkbox to display the tree in the center of the page.

Include empty branches (Poster layout)

Select this checkbox to display all branches of a tree (even those with no information). This can be useful if you're sharing the chart with other family members and want them to add information for you.

Last descendant generation vertically (Poster layout)

Select this checkbox to list the last generation vertically under their parents (see fig. 5-7 on page 88 for an example).

Include siblings of primary individual (Poster layout)

Select this checkbox to display the brothers and sisters of the chart's primary individual.

Boxes overlap page breaks (Poster layout)

Select this checkbox if you don't want boxes that fall on a page break to be partially printed on both pieces of paper. Family Tree Maker will adjust the chart spacing so that no boxes are split over two pages.

Horizontal Hourglass Charts

In the horizontal hourglass chart, the primary individual appears in the middle of the chart with ancestors branching to the right and descendants extending to the left of the person. The chart in figure 5-11 shows a default horizontal hourglass chart. The customized chart in figure 5-12 uses a map as the background image, thumbnail images have been added, and siblings and spouses have been removed.

Figure 5-11

A default horizontal hourglass chart.

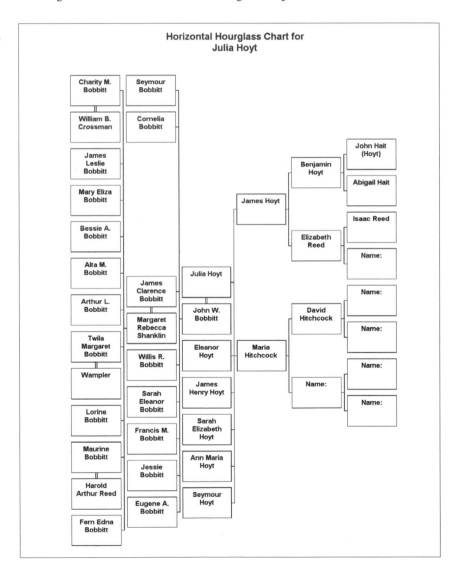

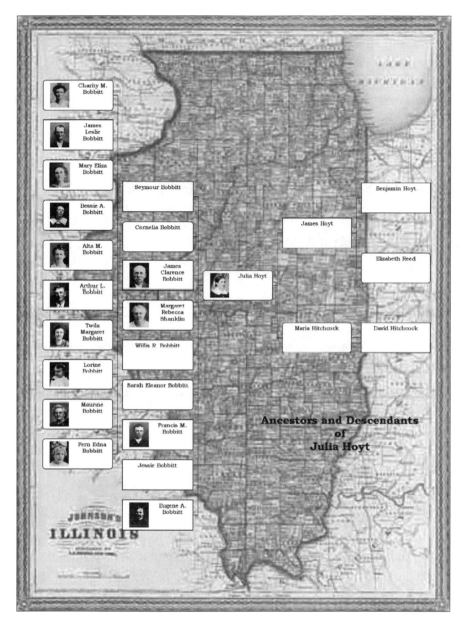

Figure 5-12

A customized
horizontal
hourglass
chart.

Creating a Horizontal Hourglass Chart

Go to the Collection tab on the Publish workspace. Under Charts, select **Horizontal Hourglass Chart**. This chart can be created in poster layout only. Use these options in the editing panel to change the chart:

Center tree on page

Select this checkbox to display the tree in the center of the page.

Include empty branches

Select this checkbox to display all branches of a tree (even those with no information).

Include siblings of primary individual

Select this checkbox to display the brothers and sisters of the chart's primary individual.

Include spouses of primary individual

Select this checkbox to display the spouse(s) of the primary individual.

Boxes overlap page breaks

Select this checkbox if you don't want boxes that fall on a page break to be partially printed on both pieces of paper. Family Tree Maker will adjust the chart spacing so that no boxes are split over two pages.

Bow Tie Charts

The bow tie chart is a great way to display both maternal and paternal lines. The primary individual appears in the middle with paternal ancestors branching off to the left and maternal ancestors branching to the right. Because of its shape and the number of individuals included, this chart is available only in poster layout.

The chart in figure 5-13 on the opposite page shows the default settings. In figure 5-14, the chart has been customized with a background image and birth and death facts.

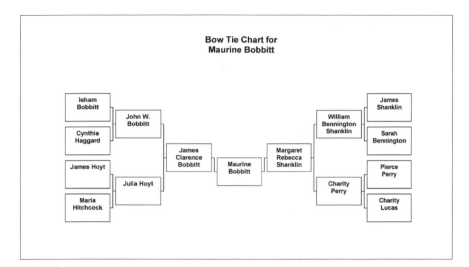

Figure 5-13

A default bow
tie chart.

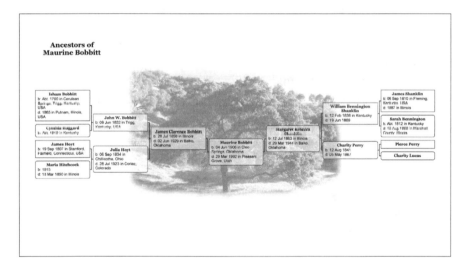

Figure 5-14

A customized
bow tie chart.

Creating a Bow Tie Chart

Go to the Collection tab on the Publish workspace. Under Charts, select **Bow Tie Chart**. This chart can be created in poster layout only. Use these options in the editing panel to change the chart:

Center tree on page

Select this checkbox to display the tree in the center of the page.

Include empty branches

Select this checkbox to display all branches of a tree (even those with no information). This can be useful if you're sharing the chart with other family members and want them to add information for you.

Include siblings of primary individual

Select this checkbox to display the brothers and sisters of the chart's primary individual.

Boxes overlap page breaks

Select this checkbox if you don't want boxes that fall on a page break to be partially printed on both pieces of paper. Family Tree Maker will adjust the chart spacing so that no boxes are split over two pages.

Fan Charts

A fan chart displays an individual's ancestors in a circular shape, one generation per level. The primary individual is at the center or bottom of the chart. You can choose between a full circle, semi-circle, quarter-circle, and more. Because of its shape and the number of individuals included, this chart is available only in poster layout.

The key to creating an attractive fan chart is figuring out which shape works best for the number of generations you've selected and the facts you've included. Too few generations can make a chart look sparse, and including too many facts and individuals can make the chart unreadable. If you're creating a chart with more than six generations, the fan chart looks best if you stick with the 360° or 180° chart.

Figure 5-15 gives examples of a four-generation fan chart displayed in each of the five shapes available in Family Tree Maker.

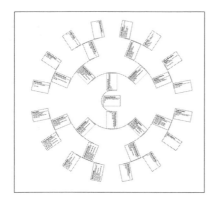 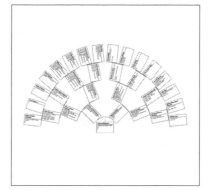

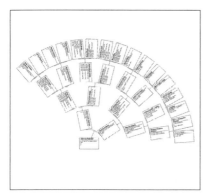 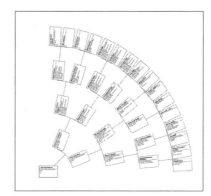

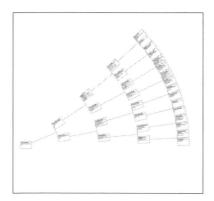

Figure 5-15

Above left, a 360° chart; *above right*, a 180° chart; *middle left*, a 135° chart; *middle right*, a 90° chart; *below*, a 45° chart.

Creating a Fan Chart

Go to the Collection tab on the Publish workspace. Under Charts, select **Fan Chart**. This chart can be created in poster layout only. Use these options in the editing panel to change the chart:

Center tree on page

Select this checkbox to display the tree in the center of the page.

Include empty branches

Select this checkbox to display all branches of a tree (even those with no information). This can be useful if you're sharing the chart with other family members and want them to add information for you.

Root node at fan origin

Select this checkbox if you want the primary individual displayed horizontally. Leave the checkbox blank if you want the primary individual displayed in-line with the rest of the fan.

Fan shape

Click the icon that corresponds to the shape you want for the chart.

Family Tree Charts

In the family tree chart, the primary individual appears at the bottom of the chart, with ancestors branching above him or her in a shape similar to a tree. Because of its shape and the number of individuals included, this chart is available only in poster layout.

The chart in figure 5-16 on the opposite page shows the default tree chart. In figure 5-17, the chart has been customized with thumbnails, a historical photo background, and new box borders and fonts.

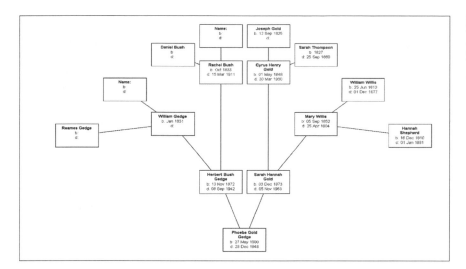

Figure 5-16

A default family tree chart.

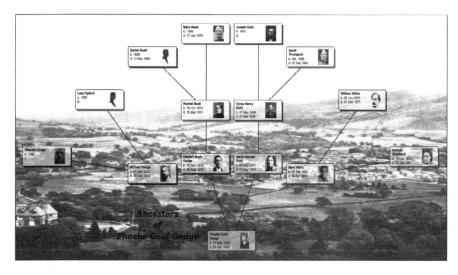

Figure 5-17

A customized family tree chart.

Creating a Family Tree Chart

Go to the Collection tab on the Publish workspace. Under Charts, select **Family Tree Chart**. This chart can be created in poster layout only. Use these options in the editing panel to change the chart:

Center tree on page

Select this checkbox to display the tree in the center of the page.

Include empty branches

Select this checkbox to display all branches of a tree (even those with no information). This can be useful if you're sharing the chart with other family members and want them to add information for you.

Boxes overlap page breaks

Select this checkbox if you don't want boxes that fall on a page break to be partially printed on both pieces of paper. Family Tree Maker will adjust the chart spacing so that no boxes are split over two pages.

Finding an Individual on a Chart

You can quickly find a specific individual on a chart using the Person Locator option located at the bottom of a chart's editing panel. To find an individual, choose his or her name from the **Person Locator** drop-down list. The chart will immediately re-center and the specific individual will be highlighted. If an individual appears in the chart more than once (for example, in families where cousins marry), you can view each occurrence using the **Instances** drop-down list. You can also click the **Select Root Person of Chart** button to display the chart's primary individual.

Although the Person Locator option works on all charts, it's especially useful on the extended family chart because the chart can display hundreds and even thousands of individuals.

Extended Family Charts

The extended family chart can display every individual you've entered in your tree or just the people you select. The chart is arranged so that each generation appears on a separate horizontal row: children, parents, and grandparents, etc. Because of its shape and the number of individuals included, this chart is available only in poster layout.

The chart in figure 5-18 shows a portion of a default extended family chart. In figure 5-19 the chart has been customized with new box borders and fonts and a template background image.

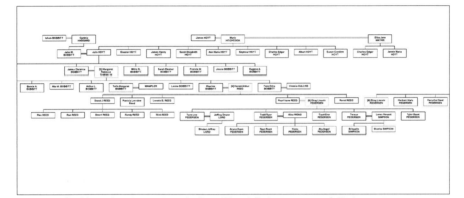

Figure 5-18

A section of a default extended family chart.

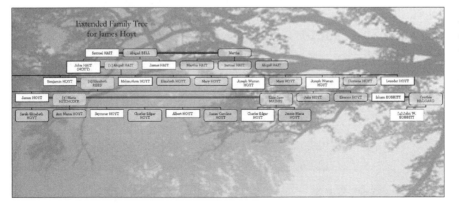

Figure 5-19

A section of a customized extended family chart.

Creating an Extended Family Chart

Go to the Collection tab on the Publish workspace. Under Charts, select **Extended Family Chart**. This chart can be created in poster layout only. Use these options in the editing panel to change the chart:

Center tree on page

Select this checkbox to display the tree in the center of the page.

Include all individuals

Select this checkbox to display every person in your tree. Families or individuals who are not attached to the main tree will be displayed in separate trees at the bottom of the chart.

Boxes overlap page breaks

Select this checkbox if you don't want boxes that fall on a page break to be partially printed on both pieces of paper. Family Tree Maker will adjust the chart spacing so that no boxes are split over two pages.

Relationship Charts

The relationship chart is a graphical representation of one person's relationship to another—including the relationship of each person in between. The common relative is shown at the top of the chart, with direct-line ancestors and descendants shown vertically beneath the individual.

Figure 5-20 on the opposite page shows the relationship chart customized with different fonts, thumbnail images, a tiled background, and a defined footer.

Creating a Relationship Chart

Go to the Collection tab on the Publish workspace. Under Charts, select **Relationship Chart**. Use these options in the editing panel to change the chart:

Relation from

To select the first person whose relationship you are calculating, click the index card icon. Find the individual you want and click **OK**.

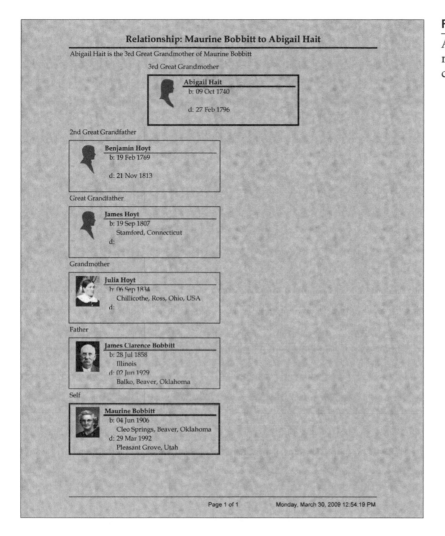

Figure 5-20

A customized relationship chart.

Relation to

To select the second person whose relationship you are calculating, use the mini pedigree tree below the main toolbar; click the person's name in the tree or the index card icon to select an individual.

Display relationship label for each node

Select this checkbox if you want each person in the tree to be labeled, showing how he or she is related to the primary individual.

Show thumbnail

Select this checkbox to include thumbnail images of the individuals on the chart.

Include civil/canon information

Select this checkbox to include canon and civil numbers in the report. (For more information on civil and canon numbers, see the sidebar on page 166.)

Customizing a Chart

What family historian doesn't want to brag a little about their latest find or display their hard work for all to see? Family Tree Maker lets you showcase your family with a variety of ancestor and descendant charts, and with a little effort (and practice) you can make charts that add color and personality to your history.

Because each Family Tree Maker chart is a little different and you can use a wide variety of formatting options, I recommend spending some time experimenting with the software using the basic guidelines explained here. It may take a little practice before you get the results you want.

The chart shown in figure 5-21 (on the opposite page) shows some ways in which you can customize a chart. It can be as simple as choosing a new font or adding a background or as complicated as changing colors for different ancestral lines or changing the layout and spacing.

> **TIP**
> Don't forget to save a customized chart by either saving the actual chart or saving the design as a template. Trust me, charts can be hard to recreate even if you're holding a printed copy right in front of you.

Figure 5-21

Customizing
options for
charts.

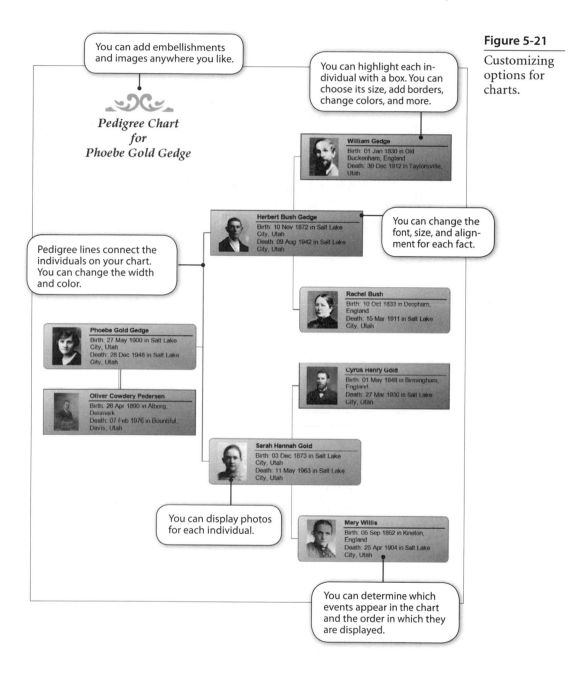

You can add embellishments
and images anywhere you like.

You can highlight each individual with a box. You can
choose its size, add borders,
change colors, and more.

*Pedigree Chart
for
Phoebe Gold Gedge*

William Gedge
Birth: 01 Jan 1830 in Old
Buckenham, England
Death: 30 Dec 1912 in Taylorsville,
Utah

Herbert Bush Gedge
Birth: 10 Nov 1872 in Salt Lake
City, Utah
Death: 09 Aug 1942 in Salt Lake
City, Utah

You can change the
font, size, and align-
ment for each fact.

Pedigree lines connect the
individuals on your chart.
You can change the width
and color.

Rachel Bush
Birth: 10 Oct 1833 in Deopham,
England
Death: 15 Mar 1911 in Salt Lake
City, Utah

Phoebe Gold Gedge
Birth: 27 May 1900 in Salt Lake
City, Utah
Death: 28 Dec 1948 in Salt Lake
City, Utah

Cyrus Henry Gold
Birth: 01 May 1848 in Birmingham,
England
Death: 27 Mar 1930 in Salt Lake
City, Utah

Oliver Cowdery Pedersen
Birth: 26 Apr 1890 in Alborg,
Denmark
Death: 07 Feb 1976 in Bountiful,
Davis, Utah

Sarah Hannah Gold
Birth: 03 Dec 1873 in Salt Lake
City, Utah
Death: 11 May 1963 in Salt Lake
City, Utah

You can display photos
for each individual.

Mary Willis
Birth: 05 Sep 1852 in Kineton,
England
Death: 25 Apr 1904 in Salt Lake
City, Utah

You can determine which
events appear in the chart
and the order in which they
are displayed.

Choosing Facts to Include in a Chart

You can add, delete, and rearrange the order of facts in a chart. As you add facts, keep in mind that the more facts you use the larger your chart will be.

1. Access the chart you want to change. In the editing toolbar, click the **Items to include** button. In the Include facts section you can see the default facts included in the chart.

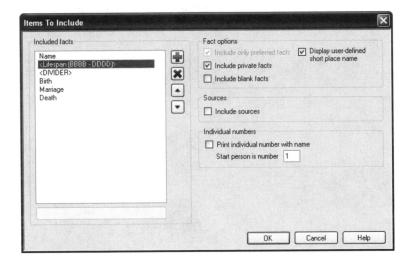

2. Use this chart to add, delete, and organize the chart's facts:

To do this	Do this
Add a fact	Click the **Add fact** (+) button. Select a fact in the list; then click **OK**.
Delete a fact	Select a fact in the list; then click the **Remove fact** (X) button.
Change the display order	Select a fact in the list. Then click the **Move fact up** and **Move fact down** arrows to change the order of the fact.
Add a line or blank space between names or facts	Click the **Add fact** (+) button. Select <DIVIDER> or <BLANKLINE> and click **OK**.

> **TIP**
>
> You can select multiple facts by clicking each fact while holding down the **CTRL** key.

Note: You may have multiple facts for the same event. By default Family Tree Maker charts display only those facts you've marked as preferred. However, you can change this by individual fact type. For example, if you want to include alternate facts for the Birth fact, select "Birth" in the facts list and click the **Options** button. Then deselect the **Include only preferred facts** checkbox.

3. By default Family Tree Maker charts display facts you've marked as private. You may want to deselect the **Include private facts** checkbox if you want to exclude these facts. For example, if you are preparing a chart that will be distributed outside your immediate family, you may want to exclude information about adoptions, illegitimate births, causes of death, and criminal records.

4. Select the **Include blank facts** checkbox to include a fact label even if an individual's fact contains no information. You may want to use this option if you are sharing the chart with family members and want them to help you fill in the blanks.

5. If you have entered shortened place names for locations, select **Display user-defined short place name** to use these locations in the report.

Formatting Name Facts

You can determine how names appear in a chart. For example, you may want to split names onto two lines or have the surname appear before the given name.

1. Access the chart you want to change. In the editing toolbar, click the **Items to include** button. In the Items to Include window, select the name fact and click **Name Options**. The Options window opens.

2. Use the **Format** drop-down list to choose how you want names to appear on the chart (for example, you can display surnames first or use initials instead of names).

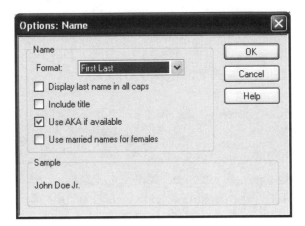

Note: Double backslashes indicate where a line break will appear in the name. For example, if you choose "First \\ Last" the given name and surname will be placed on separate lines. This option can be useful if you want to condense box sizes and save space.

3. Change these options as necessary:

   • **Display last name in all caps.** Select this checkbox to display surnames in capital letters.

   • **Include title.** Select this checkbox to include titles entered in the Title fact (for example, Captain Benjamin Hoyt).

   • **Use AKA if available.** Select this checkbox to include alternate names in quotes (for example, Mary Eliza "Mollie" Bobbitt).

   • **Use married names for females.** Select this checkbox to use a woman's married name in addition to her maiden name.

   To get an idea of how the name will appear on the chart, look at the Sample at the bottom of the window.

4. When you're finished making changes, click **OK**.

Formatting Facts

For each fact you've included in a chart, you can determine which of its fields are displayed (Date, Place, Description) and also how each fact is labelled. Figure 5-22 shows the default fact format (Date and Place fields are included and the fact label is a lowercase abbreviation) and a customized format (Place fields have been excluded and the fact label is the fact's full name capitalized).

Harold Arthur Reed
b: 02 Aug 1895 in Haddam, Washington, Kansas
m: 18 Aug 1923 in Beaver County, Oklahoma
d: 21 Dec 1971 in Boise, Ada, Idaho

Harold Arthur Reed
Birth: 02 Aug 1895
Marriage: 18 Aug 1923
Death: 21 Dec 1971

Figure 5-22

Fact labels in a pedigree chart.

1. Access the chart you want to change. In the editing toolbar, click the **Items to include** button. In the Items to Include window, select a fact and click **Options**. The Options window opens.

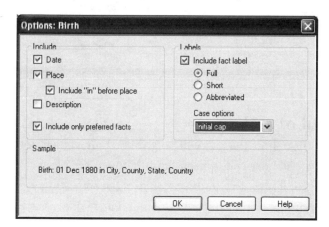

2. Select the fields (Date, Place, Description) you want to include for the fact.

3. By default, the chart will include only preferred facts. If you want to include all facts for a specific fact type, deselect the **Include only preferred facts** checkbox. For example, you may want the chart to display all Birth facts for individuals but display only one Residence fact.

4. Select a label for this fact: **Full** displays the entire fact name; **Short** displays the shortened fact name (generally the first 6 characters of the full name); **Abbreviated** displays the abbreviated fact name (generally the first 3 characters of the full name). You can also deselect the **Include fact label** checkbox to if you don't want to use a label.

    Note: You can view the default labels for a fact on the Manage Facts window.

5. In **Case options** choose the capitalization for the fact label: **All caps** uses uppercase letters for the entire label; **Initial cap** starts each word in the label with an uppercase letter; **Lowercase** uses lowercase letters for the entire label.

> **TIP**
>
> If you change the label for one fact, you'll most likely want to make the same change to all facts included in the chart. That way you won't have one label abbreviated and capitalized and another with the full fact name in lowercase letters.

6. Click **OK**.

Changing the Layout of a Chart

The layout of a chart determines how the tree will be arranged on a page. Will there be lots of white space? Will boxes be squished tightly together? When you're adjusting the layout you'll want to create a balance between getting the right number of people on the chart while still making it attractive—and more importantly, readable. You may also be able to determine how many pages a tree stretches across by changing the layout.

Changing the Horizontal Spacing

Access the chart you want to change. Use the Overlap drop-down in the editing panel to change the horizontal spacing of a chart. (This can be useful when you want to include more generations on a single page.) Figure 5-23 shows the various options you can choose from: **No Overlap** displays boxes in equally spaced columns; **Columns Overlap** displays the chart in columns that overlap slightly; **Only Root Overlaps** displays the chart with only the parents' column overlapping the primary individual's column; **Fish Tail** overlaps all columns except for the last generation.

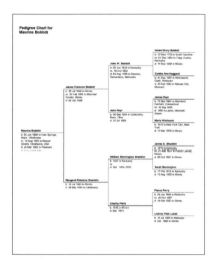

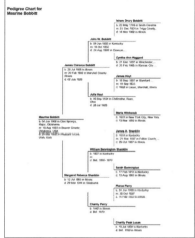

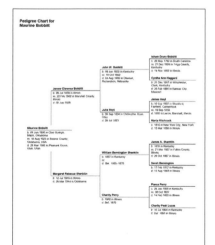

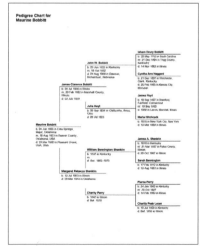

Figure 5-23

Chart overlap options. *Above left*, No Overlap; *above right*, Columns Overlap; *below left*, Only Root Overlaps; *below right*, Fish Tail.

Changing the Vertical Spacing

Access the chart you want to change. Use the Spacing drop-down to change the vertical spacing of a chart. Figure 5-24 shows the various options you can choose from: **Perfect** displays rows with even spacing; **Collapsed** displays rows closer together; **Squished** displays rows with minimal space between them; **Custom** uses the settings selected in the Advanced Layout mode. (For more information about the Advanced Layout mode, see "Changing the Layout of a Wall Chart" on page 130.)

Figure 5-24

Chart spacing options. *Above left,* Perfect; *above right,* Collapsed; *below left,* Squished; *below right,* Custom.

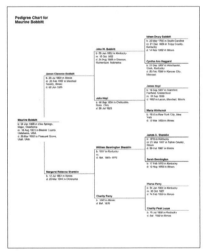
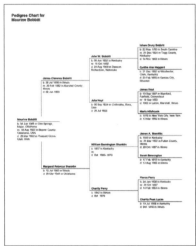
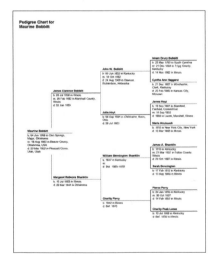
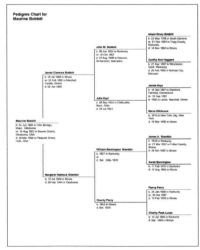

Moving Boxes Manually

If you're using the poster layout, you can change the shape of a tree chart by dragging boxes individually or in groups. Figure 5-25 shows two versions of the same pedigree chart. The chart on the left shows the default layout. In the chart on the right, I have moved the boxes further apart to emphasize the paternal and maternal branches of my tree.

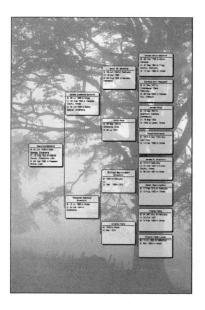 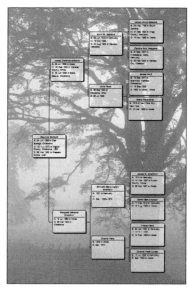

Figure 5-25

Moving boxes on a chart. *Left*, the default layout in a pedigree chart; *right*, boxes have been moved to emphasize the paternal and maternal branches.

To move boxes, access the chart you want to change. Click on a box to select it and drag it in position; you can use the CTRL key to select multiple items and drag them at the same time. You can also make more precise adjustments using the arrow keys.

A few warnings if you want to use this feature: if you are printing your chart professionally, I recommend you print out a copy of the chart at home first. Occasionally the chart looks different in the program than it does printed. Also, make sure the chart is exactly how you want it before you start moving boxes. If you choose a new spacing option, change the page orientation, or add generations to the chart, the boxes you have moved will revert to their original position and you will have to start over.

Tips for Saving Space on Charts

Most of us want to display the most amount of information in the smallest amount of space possible. When you're creating a chart in Family Tree Maker, some small adjustments can make a big difference in overall chart size. The figure on the opposite page shows how I took a vertical pedigree chart that spanned ten pages and resized it to four pages—without discarding any information. Here's a list of some of the space-saving options you might want to try:

- **Experiment with layout options.** Choosing "Collapsed" or "Squished" spacing condenses the space individuals use on a page. Likewise, you'll fit more generations of people on a page if you let the columns overlap.

- **Limit box sizes.** You may want to limit the width and height of boxes. Although this gives you room for more individuals, you'll have less room for facts. You also have the option to make all boxes the same size within a chart. This option can waste valuable space; turn this option off and boxes will be sized based on the amount of information they contain.

- **Use shortened place names.** You can enter shortened place names for each location in your tree (for example, you can use a city and state instead of a city, county, state, and country). Using these shortened names in charts leads to less text wrapping and changes the width of the boxes.

- **Change the paper's orientation.** Most charts can display additional generations if you use landscape mode instead of portrait mode.

- **Change fonts.** Select a more condensed font style or smaller font size.

- **Exclude siblings.** If the chart's primary individual has many brothers and sisters, you might want to leave them out.

- **Be selective with facts.** Decreasing the number of events included in a chart can affect the overall size of the chart significantly. Also, experiment with the formatting options available for each fact. You can use abbreviated labels (such as b., m., and d., for birth, marriage, and death) and also exclude descriptive terms.

- **Use the Advanced Layout option.** If you're creating a wall chart or poster, you can used the Advanced Layout option to change the vertical and horizontal spacing of a chart (for instructions, see "Changing the Layout of a Wall Chart" on page 130).

The first figure shows a vertical pedigree chart that uses default Family Tree Maker settings and displays six generations of ancestors. The chart stretches over ten sheets of paper and measures 44.54" by 12.11". As you can see, almost two pages are completely blank—not a great use of space.

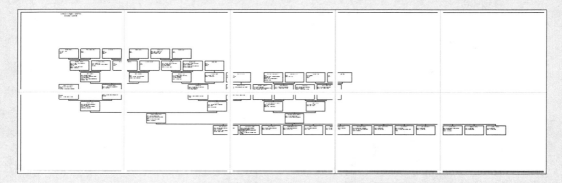

The second figures shows the same six-generation vertical pedigree chart with these adjustments:

- **Boxes.** The minimum box width has been changed and the option to make all boxes the same size has been turned off.
- **Place names.** Facts are using user-defined shortened place names.
- **Facts.** Blank facts have been excluded and labels have been changed to abbreviations.
- **Fonts.** The font style was not changed but the size was reduced from 8 to 7.

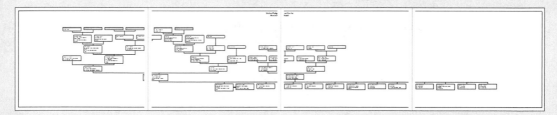

The final result is a chart that stretches over only four sheets of paper and measures 22.5" by 6.57"—almost half its original size. And if I had chosen to exclude the primary individual's siblings, the chart would be reduced to three pages.

Formatting Boxes

You can enhance the appearance of your chart and call attention to individuals by adding boxes. Figure 5-26 shows a bow tie chart using the default boxes and the same bow tie chart with customized boxes.

Figure 5-26

Box formatting. *Above*, default boxes in a bow tie chart; *below*, boxes for males have a double border and are semi-transparent; boxes for females have rounded corners and are semi-transparent.

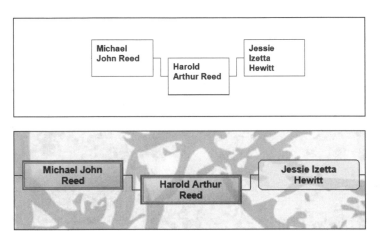

1. Access the chart you want to change. In the editing toolbar, click the **Box and line styles** button. The options window opens.

   On the left side of the window you can see the different groups of individuals for whom you can format boxes: all females, all males, individuals who don't have specified genders, and marked groups 1, 2, and 3. (For more information on marked groups, see "Selecting a Group of People in a Chart" on page 128.)

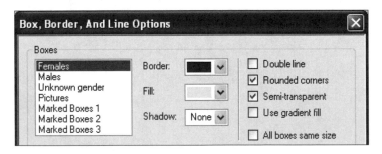

2. Select the group you want to work with (for example, select "Males").

3. To add borders to boxes, choose a color from the **Border** drop-down list. You can also select **Double line** to make the border two lines and/or select **Rounded corners** to round the corners of the border.

4. To add backgrounds to boxes, do one or more of these options:

   • Choose a color for the background from the **Fill** drop-down list.

   • Choose a color for a drop shadow from the **Shadow** drop-down list.

   • Select **Semi-transparent** to make the chart's background image partially visible through the box. This option works even if you are using a fill color.

   • Select **Use gradient fill** to make a box's fill color change from light (at the top, left corner) to dark (at the bottom, right corner).

5. If you want all boxes on the chart to be the same size (regardless of how much information is included for each individual) select the **All boxes same size** checkbox. You might want to use this option if you want a uniform look to your chart. If you don't select this option, the size of each box will be determined by the amount of text in the box. This can be useful when you want to conserve space.

6. Do one of these options:

   • If you're creating a book chart, you can set a maximum width and height for boxes (in inches). If the facts you have included don't fit in the box, the information will be truncated (fig. 5-27).

Harold Arthur Reed
b: 02 Aug 1895 in...

   Figure 5-27

   Truncated text in a book chart box.

   • If you're creating a wall chart, you can set the width and height for boxes (in inches). You can adjust these sizes later by clicking the **Advanced** button on the chart's editing panel.

Changing Pedigree Lines

You can determine how pedigree lines connect people in a chart and also choose the color and thickness of these lines.

To change the alignment

Access the chart you want to change. Use the Align nodes drop-down to change the alignment of the pedigree lines. Figure 5-28 shows the various options you can choose from: **Top** connects individuals at the lines beneath their names (the traditional style); **Center** connects individuals at the center of each person's information; **Bezier** connects individuals with curved lines; **Straight** connects individuals with diagonal lines.

Figure 5-28

Alignment options for pedigree lines. *Above left,* Top; *above right,* Center; *below left,* Bezier; *below right,* Straight.

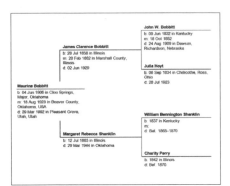
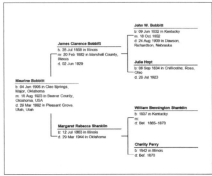
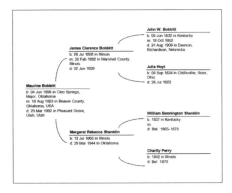
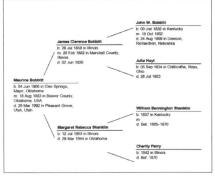

To change the color or thickness

Access the chart you want to change. In the editing toolbar, click the **Box and line styles** button. In "Pedigree lines" choose the color and thickness of the lines.

Changing Fonts

You can change the appearance of text in charts to make it more formal, more fun, or maybe just more readable. For wall charts you'll want to choose a style and size that can be read from a distance. For books you'll want to choose a font that is easy to read; some standard options are Times New Roman and Palatino using a 10 or 12 point size. Figure 5-29 shows some of the text elements for which you can change the font.

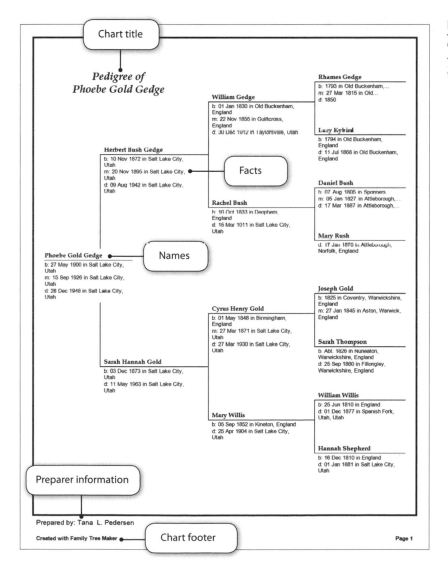

Figure 5-29

Chart elements you can change the font for.

1. Access the chart you want to change. In the editing toolbar, click the **Fonts** button.

   On the left side of the window you can see the different text elements for which you can change the font. The items listed above the divider line are the facts that are currently displayed in the chart. You can change the font for each fact type if you want. Beneath the divider you'll see the rest of the chart elements you can change, such as the title and footer.

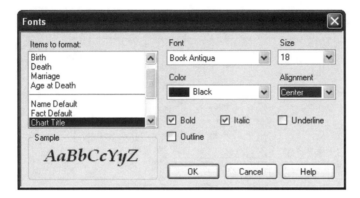

2. In the **Items to format** list select the text element, such as chart title, you would like to change.

   Note: Select "Fact Default" if you want to choose the font for all new facts you add to the chart. For example, if you decide to include the marriage fact, it will use this default font and style.

3. Choose a font from the **Font** drop-down list. You can also change the size, style, color, and alignment. The Sample box shows how your text will appear in the chart.

4. Click **OK** to save your changes.

Using Decorative Photos or Embellishments

In addition to adding backgrounds and portraits to charts, you can personalize your tree and make it more appealing by adding family photographs, borders, and embellishments (fig. 5-30). You can add images from your computer, pictures in the Media Collection, or use the borders and images included in Family Tree Maker.

Figure 5-30

Embellishments and photos added to a chart.

Adding an Image to a Chart

Access the chart you want to change. In the editing toolbar, click the **Insert Image** button. To use an image you've added to your tree, choose **Insert from Media Collection**; then select an image and click **OK**. To use an item on your computer's hard drive, choose **Insert from File**; then select an image and click **Open**.

> Note: You'll find a variety of decorative images in the Embellishments folder located in the Family Tree Maker folder.

Adjusting an Image

After you've added an image to a chart, Family Tree Maker has tools to help you add borders, resize and align images, and even combine images into layered objects.

To add a border

You can add a border to an image you've inserted into a chart. However, you cannot change the border's width or color. To add a border to an image, right-click the image and choose **Border** (fig. 5-31). Then choose **None**, **Single**, or **Double**.

Figure 5-31

Adding a border to an image.

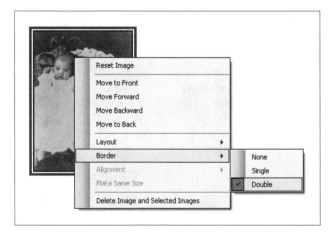

To move an image

Move the pointer over an image until the pointer changes shape. Drag the image to the location you want. You can also make more precise adjustments using the arrow keys on the keyboard. As you drag an image, notice that it becomes semi-transparent, which makes it easier to position (fig. 5-32). You can use the CTRL key to select multiple images and move them at the same time.

Figure 5-32

When you move an image it becomes semi-transparent.

To resize an image

When you insert an image, it is placed in a frame. To resize an image move the cursor over the handle in the bottom-right corner of the frame (fig. 5-33); then drag the image to the size you want. Family Tree Maker will size the image proportionally.

Figure 5-33

The handle in the bottom-right corner of the image lets you resize it.

To fit an image to its frame

As you drag an image, you might notice that the frame no longer fits the image. This can be a problem if you try to align the image with another object. Because alignment is based on the frame (rather than the image) the two images will not line up as expected.

To fit an image to its frame, right-click the image and choose **Layout**. Figure 5-34 shows the various options you can choose from: **Center** resizes the image to fit the width or height of the frame (whichever is smaller); **Stretch** resizes the image to fit the entire frame, which may cause some

Figure 5-34

Image frame options. *Above left,* Center; *above right,* Stretch; *middle left,* Zoom; *middle right,* Tile; *below,* Top.

distortion; **Zoom** resizes the image to fit the width or height of the frame (whichever is larger); **Tile** fills the frame with a series of the image; and **Top** resizes the image to fit the width of the frame, which may cut off the bottom of the image.

To align images

You can align a selected group of images. I use this when I want to line up photographs of a husband and wife or even images for a specific generation (fig. 5-35). Images are positioned based on the first image you select. Click the image you want other images to line up with. Then hold the **CTRL** key and click the other images you want. Right-click and choose **Alignment**. Then choose **Top**, **Bottom**, **Left**, **Right**, or **Center**.

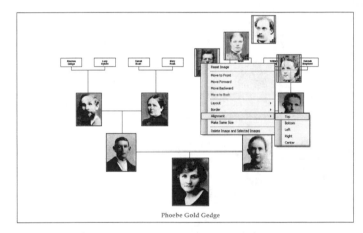

Figure 5-35

Aligning a group of images.

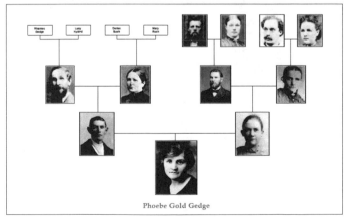

To make all images the same size

You can make selected images the same size with the click of a mouse (fig. 5-36). Images are sized based on the first image you select. Click the image you want other images to be the size of. Then hold the **CTRL** key and click the other images. Right-click and choose **Make Same Size**.

Figure 5-36

Making all images the same size on a chart.

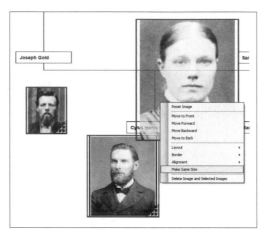

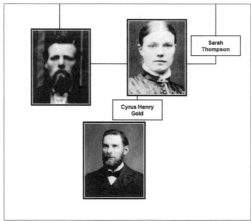

To layer images

You can layer images together to make your own unique embellishment. Figure 5-37 shows how I combined a family photo, an image of a picture frame, and a border into one simple image. You can order images in layers by changing their sort order. To do this, right-click the image you want to change the order of and choose one of these options from the drop-down list: **Move to Front** moves the image in front of the chart and all other images; **Move Forward** moves the image up one layer; **Move Backward** moves the image down one layer; **Move to Back** moves the image behind the chart and all other images.

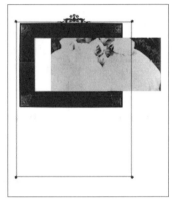

Figure 5-37
Working with images in layers.

To return an image to its original settings

If you've made so many changes to your image that it's unrecognizable, you can return an image to its original settings by right-clicking the image and choosing **Reset Image**.

Selecting a Group of People in a Chart

If you want to apply formatting (such as box lines and colors) to specific individuals or groups, you first need to select and mark them as a group.

1. Access the chart you want to work with. In this example I'll use the bow tie chart and make four separate groups (one for each of the four branches of my tree). That way I can make each branch a different color. Here's an example of what the chart will look like when it's finished:

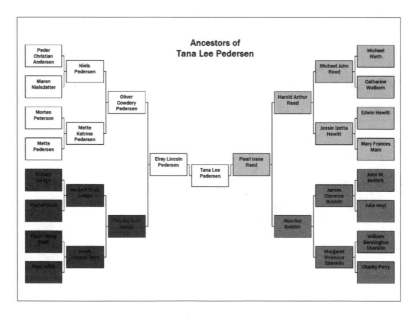

2. First I'll right-click my maternal grandfather in the chart and choose "Select Person and All Ancestors." The individuals who are selected currently are highlighted with blue frames.

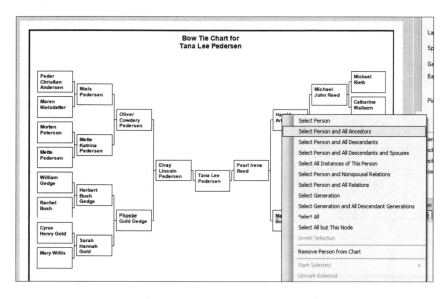

3. Right-click the group again and choose **Mark Selected>Marking 1**. The highlighted individuals are now included in the "Marked Boxes 1" group.

4. Now I'll repeat steps 2 and 3 for my maternal grandmother (designated as Marking 2) and paternal grandmother (designated as Marking 3).

Note: If you accidentally select an individual you don't want to include in a group, you can right-click the individual on the chart and choose Unmark Selected from the drop-down list.

> ### TIP
> You can also select or deselect specific individuals by pressing the **CTRL** key and clicking on an individual. For me, this is an efficient way to create a group, and I always know exactly who is being excluded and included.

Creating a Wall Chart

Smaller charts are great when you want to share information about a specific individual or display only a few generations. But to really showcase your family tree, you'll want to create a wall chart. Headed to a reunion? Create a descendant chart you can hang on the wall (or lay across a table) to show everyone how they're related. Need some perspective while researching? Hang a wall chart above your desk and you'll always be able to see family connections.

Changing the Layout of a Wall Chart

When you're creating a wall chart, you can use the Advanced Layout for posters to adjust the spacing, overlap, and position of elements on a chart. You can change the layout to make it taller, wider, or just to fit the chart onto the desired number of pages.

1. Access the chart you want to change. Choose **Poster** from the Layout drop-down list. Then click the **Advanced** button. The Advanced Layout window opens.

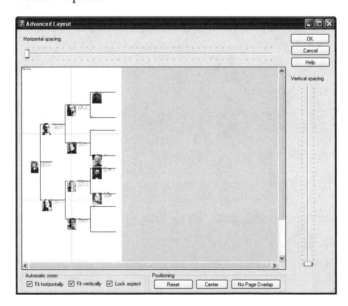

Notice the light gray lines running vertically and horizontally across the tree. These lines represent the margins of a standard 8½" by 11" sheet of paper.

In this example, the chart is spread over six vertical sheets of paper. You can adjust the spacing of the poster to fit on the desired number of pages.

2. Drag the **Horizontal spacing** bar from side to side to control the amount of horizontal space between boxes. Drag the **Vertical spacing** bar up and down to control the amount of vertical space between boxes; if you condense the vertical spacing too much, the text in one box may overlap the text in the box beneath it.

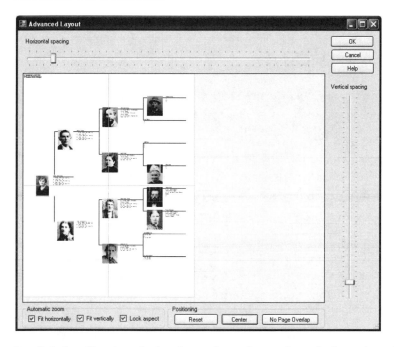

By slightly adjusting the horizontal spacing and vertical spacing, this chart is now condensed to four sheets of paper.

TIP

You can change how the viewer displays the chart. This does *not* affect how the chart prints. Click **Fit horizontally** to scale the chart to fit the window horizontally; click **Fit vertically** to scale the chart to fit the window vertically; and click **Lock aspect** to keep the chart in proportion vertically and horizontally.

3. You can also change the position of the chart using these options:

   - Click **Reset** to move the chart back to its original position.

   - Click **Center** to center the chart on the current number of pages.

   - Click **No Page Overlap** to prevent boxes and photos from printing partially on two different sheets of paper.

4. Click **OK**.

Tips for Making Wall Charts

Because wall charts are generally for display and are often viewed from a distance, there are some unique considerations you don't usually face when making a single-page chart that will go in a book. Here are some tips that can help:

- **Maximize space.** Choose a suitable paper orientation. For example, descendant posters usually look best in portrait mode while extended family trees look best in landscape mode. (See the sidebar on pages 114–15 for more space-saving tips.) Don't forget to leave a margin around the edge if you plan on framing the chart.

- **Choose fonts carefully.** Pick a font that is easy to read. A highly decorative font may be attractive, but if your family can't decipher it, style doesn't matter. Also, adjust the font size so that names and important details can be read from several feet way. You might want to make names a size larger than other facts so they really stand out.

- **Emphasize family ties.** Use thick pedigree lines so family relationships can be identified from far away.

- **Use backgrounds and colors sparingly.** Use subtle backgrounds that won't distract people from the real purpose of the chart—your family history. Also, be aware that the more color you use, usually the more expensive the chart is to print.

- **Preview your chart before printing.** Sometimes charts look different on-screen than when they're printed. Check your chart for errors or formatting problems. You might even want to print a few test pages. You don't want to spend money getting your wall chart printed commercially only to find out that the colors clash and the font is unreadable.

Printing a Wall Chart

When I was growing up, we had a large family tree chart that my grandparents had made. Part of it was handwritten, part of it was typed, and because it was always folded, there were little tears at all the corners—and of course, no photos. Technology has made it much simpler to show off your family history and the results are usually more attractive too. With Family Tree Maker you can print a large chart at home (if you have a large-format printer) or you can create a file to take to your local print shop.

Using a Plotter

If you're fortunate enough to have access to a large format printer, commonly called a plotter, you can print out a wall chart at home.

1. When you're ready to print, click the **Page Setup** button on the chart editing toolbar.

2. Click the **Printer** button; then choose the plotter from the **Name** dropdown list and click **OK**.

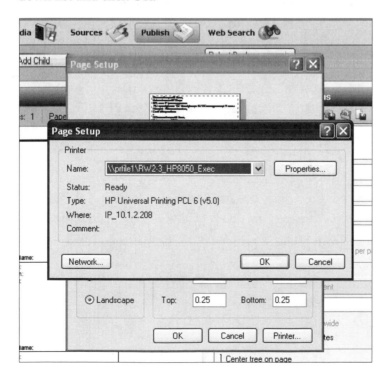

3. On the Page Setup window, choose the size of paper you'll be using from the **Size** drop-down. Then click **OK**.

4. Make sure the chart will fit on the paper size you've chosen. The size of the chart is displayed in the toolbar on top of the chart.

TIP

You can also print a wall chart using a regular printer and tape the pages together. This is a good option if you are using a chart for research purposes and don't plan on keeping it long.

Taking a Chart to a Print Shop

If you don't have a large-format printer, your local copy or print shop will probably be able to print it for you. It's not hard to find a place with reasonable prices and quality products. Most shops accept PDF files and some even let you upload your files to their websites.

1. Access the chart you want to print. Click the **Share** button in the toolbar above the editing panel and choose **Export to One Page PDF.** This option exports the chart as one page (regardless of size).

   Note: Because of PDF restrictions, you can only export charts that are smaller than 200" by 200".

2. Change formatting options as necessary. Because of the size of the chart, you will probably want to keep the image quality as high as possible.

3. Once you've made your selections, click **OK**. A file management window opens.

4. Navigate to the location where you want to save the chart. Then enter a name for the chart and click **Save**.

Chart Ideas

I love creating charts that can be displayed—for my home, my desk at work, and for my family. What's the fun in entering all that information if I can't enjoy it too? Family Tree Maker has quite a few basic templates that can get you started. But with some creativity, and some embellishments and photographs, you can transform your ancestry into an artistic family tree you're proud to show off. This section shows some examples of my favorite charts. You may want to recreate them or maybe you'll be inspired to try your own.

A Photo Family Tree

Photographs inspire me. I'm always looking at old family images trying to see who I resemble most or discover whose nose I have. Because all my family history photos are already organized in Family Tree Maker, it's easy to use them to make a photo family tree (fig. 5-38).

Figure 5-38

A photo family tree.

Chart Options

- Chart: Family Tree Chart.

- Spacing: Perfect. (I then adjusted this by clicking the **Advanced** layout button and adding more vertical spacing.)

- Generations: Three.

- Background: Tree in Mist (in the Backgrounds/Trees folder included with Family Tree Maker). The image is centered and is 0% transparent.

- Items to Include: When you create any chart, you must have at least one fact displayed. I keep the Name fact so I can see where people belong on the chart. In order to make the name as compact as possible (so it can be hidden behind the photos), click the **Name Options** button and choose "First Last" or "F. Last" for the name format.

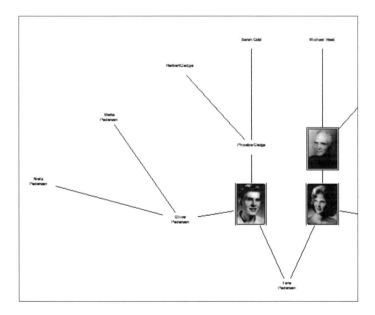

- Box, Border, and Line Options: You can't delete boxes so I made sure the name fact in the box used the smallest font size possible and was centered. Again, this is so the name can be hidden behind the photo.

How-to

After you've chosen all the chart options, you're ready to add and arrange the photos. A word of caution here. Get your chart options set up exactly the way you want before adding photos. If you make any changes to box borders, facts, etc., after adding your photos you will lose your changes; the chart will revert back to its default position and shape. Figure 5-39 shows how the pedigree lines moved after I made changes to the spacing.

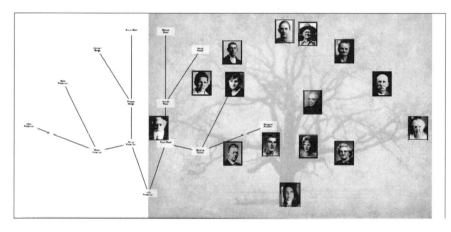

Figure 5-39

A tree that has moved back to its default position.

To add the photos to the chart, simply click the **Insert Image** button in the chart editing toolbar and select the images you want. To make the images all the same size, resize one image to the size you like. Then select all the other images, right-click and choose **Make Same Size**.

The challenge is then to line the photos up properly. Using the pedigree lines and name boxes, I placed the photos approximately where they should be. I then used the alignment options to line up photos on opposing sides of the tree.

TIP

Most family photos have different shapes, sizes, and colors, which can lead to some unappealing charts. Every time I receive an individual's photo, I make a copy of it and create a "portrait" image. I crop the photo to show only the person's face, change the color to black and white, and then resize the image to 2" by 2.5". That way, all my charts look more unified.

Just the Names, Please

Not everyone in my family is as interested in family history as I am. My "name tree" (fig. 5-40) is a simple way to acquaint my family with their ancestors without overwhelming them with lots of dates and locations. This type of chart has the additional benefit of being able to show multiple generations in a small amount of space.

Figure 5-40

A bow tie chart with only names.

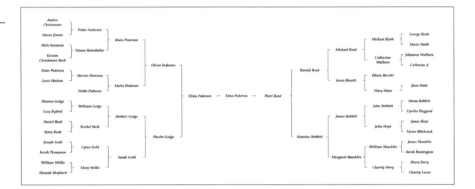

Chart Options

- Chart: Bow Tie.

- Spacing: Collapsed. If the names are squished, you can click the **Advanced** layout button and add more horizontal space.)

- Generations: Five.

- Background: None.

- Items to Include: Name fact only. You can have first and last names displayed on separate lines in the chart, which can make your chart even smaller. To do this, click the **Name Options** button and choose "First Middle\\ Last" or "First\\Last" for the name format.

- Box, Border, and Line Options: Take off the borders around boxes for females and males (the Border and Fill drop-downs should say "None").

- Fonts: Change the font for the Name fact. You can choose any font you want. I decided to use a calligraphy font so it looks more like handwriting. Make sure you select "Center" alignment too.

Embellished Pedigree Chart

When I was creating a pedigree chart for my grandmother, I wanted it to be feminine without being too "cutesy." I settled on a subtle yellow background and then added a portrait and embellishments to finish it off (fig. 5-41).

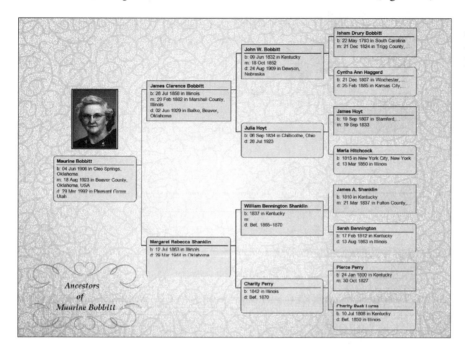

Figure 5-41

An embellished pedigree chart.

Chart Options

- Chart: Pedigree Chart.

- Layout: Book.

- Overlap: No overlap.

- Spacing: Perfect.

- Align nodes: Top.

- Generations: Three.

- Background: Swirls (in the Backgrounds/Patterns folder included with Family Tree Maker). The image is zoomed in on and is at 50% transparency.

- Items to Include: Name, Divider, Birth, Marriage, and Death. I also chose to display user-defined shortened place names to conserve space.

- Box, Border, and Line Options: Boxes for females have rounded corners and are semi-transparent; boxes for males are semi-transparent. You can also choose border and fill colors.

- Fonts: I changed the font used for the title and also chose center alignment.

- Embellishments: I added a design element around the chart title (called Flourish Heading in the Embellishments/Flourishes folder included with Family Tree Maker).

- Photographs: I inserted my grandma's portrait and gave it a double border.

Chapter Six
Analyzing Your Tree

Family Tree Maker includes a number of reports to help you organize and evaluate the information you've entered in your tree. Some reports, such as bibliographies and task lists, can help you keep track of your research. Other reports are full of details about families and allow you to quickly see connections between individuals in your tree. You can share these in-depth reports with interested family members or fellow researchers, use the detailed information to plot out your next steps, or use them to add interest to a family history book.

I also use custom reports quite a bit, whether it's to make an address list for a family reunion or simply doing maintenance on my tree. I have included some of the reports I create most often. Hopefully you will find them useful or they will motivate you to create your own.

Personal Reports

"Personal" reports chronicle the life of an individual or his or her family. These types of reports help you understand where an individual fits in his or her family or ancestral line. They are also useful for including in family history books or for sharing information with other researchers.

Ahnentafels

The Ahnentafel (a German word meaning "ancestor table") is basically a numbered list of individuals. Its format is ancestor-ordered, meaning that it starts with one individual and moves backward in time to that individual's

Figure 6-1

An Ahnentafel.

Ancestors of Emma Gedge

Generation 1

1. **Emma Gedge**, daughter of William Gedge and Rachel Bush was born on 30 Aug 1863 in Utah, USA. She died on 11 Dec 1906 in St George, Washington, Utah, USA. She married **Samuel G. Spencer** on 21 Dec 1883.

Generation 2

2. **William Gedge**, son of George Gedge and Lucy Kybird was born on 01 Jan 1830 in Old Buckenham, Norfolk, England. He died on 30 Dec 1912 in Taylorsville, Salt Lake, Utah, USA. He married **Rachel Bush** on 22 Nov 1855 in Guiltcross, Norfolk, England.

3. **Rachel Bush**, daughter of Robb Bush and Mary Rush was born on 10 Oct 1833 in Deopham, Norfolk, England. She died on 15 Mar 1911 in Salt Lake City, Salt Lake, Utah, USA.

   Rachel Bush and William Gedge had the following children:

   i. Leah Gedge was born about 1859 in Old Buckenham, Norfolk, England. She died on 13 Aug 1862 in Wyoming or Nebraska.

   ii. Mary Gedge was born on 01 Aug 1862 in Nebraska, USA. She died on 30 Aug 1862 in Wyoming, USA. She married.

   iii. Lois Gedge was born on 01 Aug 1862 in Nebraska, USA. She died on 30 Aug 1862 in Wyoming, USA. She married.

   +1. iv. Emma Gedge was born on 30 Aug 1863 in Utah, USA. She died on 11 Dec 1906 in St George, Washington, Utah, USA. She married Samuel G. Spencer on 21 Dec 1883.

   v. Anna Gedge was born on 05 Sep 1865 in Salt Lake City, Salt Lake, Utah, USA. She died on 09 Jun 1945 in Salt Lake City, Salt Lake, Utah, USA. She married William J. Cochrane on 16 Mar 1887 in Logan, Cache, Utah, USA.

   vi. William Reames Gedge was born on 30 Jun 1868 in Salt Lake City, Salt Lake, Utah, USA. He married Margaret A. Gardiner on 12 Nov 1890 in Logan, Cache, Utah, USA.

   vii. Nathan Gedge was born about 1871 in Utah, USA. He died on 11 Jun 1902 in Brighton, Salt Lake, Utah, USA. He married Charlotte Ann Brown Lane on 24 Oct 1894 in Salt Lake City, Salt Lake, Utah, USA.

   viii. Herbert Bush Gedge was born on 10 Nov 1872 in Salt Lake City, Salt Lake, Utah, USA. He died on 09 Aug 1942 in Salt Lake City, Salt Lake, Utah, USA. He married Sarah Hannah Gold on 20 Nov 1895 in Salt Lake City, Salt Lake, Utah, USA, daughter of Cyrus Henry Gold and Mary Willis. She was born on 03 Dec 1873 in Salt Lake City, Salt Lake, Utah, USA. She died on 11 May 1963 in Salt Lake City, Salt Lake, Utah, USA.

Generation 3

4. **George Gedge**. He married **Lucy Kybird**.

5. **Lucy Kybird**.

   Lucy Kybird and George Gedge had the following child:

   +2. i. William Gedge was born on 01 Jan 1830 in Old Buckenham, Norfolk, England. He died on 30 Dec 1912 in Taylorsville, Salt Lake, Utah, USA. He married Rachel Bush on 22 Nov 1855 in Guiltcross, Norfolk, England, daughter of Robb Bush and Mary Rush. She was born on 10 Oct 1833 in Deopham, Norfolk, England. She died on 15 Mar 1911 in Salt Lake City, Salt Lake, Utah, USA.

6. **Robb Bush**. He married **Mary Rush**.

7. **Mary Rush**.

ancestors. This kind of reports is often included in a family history book and is a great way to document your research or share your findings with fellow genealogists.

To read the report, you'll need to understand a bit about its numbering system. The Ahnentafel (see fig. 6-1 on the opposite page) assigns the first (or primary) individual the number 1. His or her father is number 2, and his or her mother is number 3, and so on. Women are always odd numbers, and men are always even numbers (except when they are the primary individual). You can easily determine who the father of an individual is by looking at his or her number—it is twice his or her own number. For example, if a man's number is four, his father's number is eight. The mother of an individual is twice the person's number plus one. So from the previous example, the mother of the individual would be nine.

Creating an Ahnentafel

Go to the Collection tab on the Publish workspace. Under Genealogy Reports, select **Ahnentafel Report**. Use these options in the editing panel to change the report:

List non-vital facts separately

By default the Ahnentafel includes only birth, marriage, and death facts. However, if you've added additional facts, you can determine where they will appear in the report. Select this checkbox to list additional facts after vital facts; leave the checkbox empty to include additional facts in the narrative.

Include parent/child relationship types

Select this checkbox to include parent and child relationships (such as adopted or foster).

Exclude children

Select this checkbox to exclude siblings from the report—only an individual and his or her direct ancestors are included.

Note: If you choose to include sources in an Ahnentafel, they will be printed as endnotes at the end of the report.

Descendant Reports

A descendant report is a narrative genealogy report that includes basic facts and biographical information about an individual. It is descendant-ordered, meaning that it starts with one individual and moves forward in time through that individual's descendants. Family Tree Maker gives you four report options: Register, NGSQ, Henry, and d'Aboville. The main difference between these reports is the numbering system that is used.

Register System

The Register System (fig. 6-2) uses Arabic numerals (1, 2, 3, 4) to indicate primary individuals and Roman numerals (i, ii, iii, iv) to indicate children. A superscript number next to a name (John Bobbitt[1]) indicates which generation the individual belongs to; a plus sign next to a number (+3) indicates that the individual has children/descendants. Be aware that this report's numbering system does not include individuals who have no children.

Figure 6-2

Descendant report using the Register System.

Descendants of James Hoyt

Generation 1

1. **JAMES[1] HOYT** was born on 19 Sep 1807 in Stamford, Fairfield, Connecticut, USA. He died in 1902. He married (1) **MARIA HITCHCOCK** on 19 Sep 1833. She was born in 1815 in New York City, New York, USA. She died on 13 Mar 1850 in Illinois, USA. He married (2) **ELIZA JANE MATHIS** on 28 Jul 1853. She was born in 1830. She died in 1924.

    James Hoyt and Maria Hitchcock had the following children:

    +2. i. **JULIA[2] HOYT** was born on 06 Sep 1834 in Chillicothe, Ross, Ohio, USA. She died on 28 Jul 1923. She married JOHN W. BOBBITT on 18 Oct 1852, son of Isham Drury Bobbitt and Cyntha Ann Haggard. He was born on 09 Jun 1832 in Kentucky, USA. He died on 24 Aug 1909 in Dawson, Richardson, Nebraska, USA.

    ii. **ELEANOR HOYT** was born on 30 Mar 1837 in Chillicothe, Ross, Ohio, USA. She died on 25 Jul 1838. She married.

    iii. **JAMES HENRY HOYT** was born on 01 May 1839 in Lacon, Marshall, Illinois, USA. He died on 01 Oct 1922 in Golden City, Barton, Missouri, USA. He married ESTHER READY.

    Notes for James Henry Hoyt:
    Living in Martinsburg, Missouri, in 1871

    iv. **SARAH ELIZABETH HOYT** was born on 06 Jul 1841 in Marshall County, Illinois, USA. She died on 13 Feb 1929. She married SAMUEL CLIFFORD.

    v. **ANN MARIA HOYT** was born on 20 Jul 1843 in Marshall County, Illinois, USA. She died on 20 Jul 1843 in Marshall County, Illinois, USA. She married.

    vi. **SEYMOUR HOYT** was born on 10 Aug 1844 in Lacon, Marshall, Illinois, USA. He died on 07 May 1940 in Greenfield, Dade, Missouri, USA.

    Notes for Seymour Hoyt:
    In 1871 is living in Greenfield, Dade County, Missouri.

    vii. **CHARLES EDGAR HOYT** was born on 23 Sep 1846 in Marshall County, Illinois, USA. He died on 22 Aug 1847 in Marshall County, Illinois, USA. He married.

NGSQ System

The NGS Quarterly System is the format accepted by the New England Historic Genealogical Society, the oldest genealogical society in the United States. It is sometimes referred to as "modified register" because it is based on the Register numbering system. The only difference between the two is that all individuals are assigned numbers regardless of whether they had children or not (fig. 6-3).

Descendants of James Hoyt

Generation 1

1. JAMES[1] HOYT was born on 19 Sep 1807 in Stamford, Fairfield, Connecticut, USA. He died in 1902. He married (1) MARIA HITCHCOCK on 19 Sep 1833. She was born in 1815 in New York City, New York, USA. She died on 13 Mar 1850 in Illinois, USA. He married (2) ELIZA JANE MATHIS on 28 Jul 1853. She was born in 1830. She died in 1924.

    James Hoyt and Maria Hitchcock had the following children:

    +2. I. JULIA[2] HOYT was born on 06 Sep 1834 in Chillicothe, Ross, Ohio, USA. She died on 28 Jul 1923. She married JOHN W. BOBBITT on 18 Oct 1852, son of Isham Drury Bobbitt and Cyntha Ann Haggard. He was born on 09 Jun 1832 in Kentucky, USA. He died on 24 Aug 1909 in Dawson, Richardson, Nebraska, USA.

    3. ii. ELEANOR HOYT was born on 30 Mar 1837 in Chillicothe, Ross, Ohio, USA. She died on 25 Jul 1838. She married.

    4. iii. JAMES HENRY HOYT was born on 01 May 1839 in Lacon, Marshall, Illinois, USA. He died on 01 Oct 1922 in Golden City, Barton, Missouri, USA. He married ESTHER READY.

        Notes for James Henry Hoyt:
        Living in Martinsburg, Missouri, in 1871

    5. iv. SARAH ELIZABETH HOYT was born on 06 Jul 1841 in Marshall County, Illinois, USA. She died on 13 Feb 1929. She married SAMUEL CLIFFORD.

    6. v.   ANN MARIA HOYT was born on 20 Jul 1843 in Marshall County, Illinois, USA. She died on 20 Jul 1843 in Marshall County, Illinois, USA. She married.

    7. vi. SEYMOUR HOYT was born on 10 Aug 1844 in Lacon, Marshall, Illinois, USA. He died on 07 May 1940 in Greenfield, Dade, Missouri, USA.

        Notes for Seymour Hoyt:
        In 1871 is living in Greenfield, Dade County, Missouri.

    8. vii. CHARLES EDGAR HOYT was born on 23 Sep 1846 in Marshall County, Illinois, USA. He died on 22 Aug 1847 in Marshall County, Illinois, USA. He married.

    9. viii. ALBERT HOYT was born on 10 Feb 1848 in Marshall County, Illinois, USA. He died on 10 Feb 1848 in Marshall County, Illinois, USA. He married.

    10. ix. SUSAN CAROLINE HOYT was born on 22 Apr 1849 in Marshall County, Illinois, USA. She died on 22 Aug 1849 in Marshall County, Illinois, USA. She married.

    James Hoyt and Eliza Jane Mathis had the following children:

    11. i.   CHARLES EDGAR[2] HOYT was born on 21 Oct 1857 in Marshall County, Illinois, USA.

    12. ii. JENNIE MARIA HOYT was born on 28 Jul 1861 in Marshall County, Illinois, USA.

Generation 2

2. JULIA[2] HOYT (James[1]) was born on 06 Sep 1834 in Chillicothe, Ross, Ohio, USA. She died on 28 Jul 1923. She married JOHN W. BOBBITT on 18 Oct 1852, son of Isham Drury Bobbitt and Cyntha Ann Haggard. He was born on 09 Jun 1832 in Kentucky, USA. He died on 24 Aug 1909 in Dawson, Richardson, Nebraska, USA.

    John W. Bobbitt and Julia Hoyt had the following children:

    13. i.   SEYMOUR[3] BOBBITT was born about 1854 in Illinois, USA.

    14. ii. CORNELIA O. BOBBITT was born in Mar 1857 in Illinois, USA. She married HERMON P. SHIER on 02 Feb 1873 in Varna, Marshall, Illinois, USA.

    15. iii. WILLIS R. BOBBITT was born about 1861 in Illinois, USA.

Figure 6-3

Descendant report using the NGSQ System.

Modified Henry System

The Modified Henry System (fig. 6-4) lets you see the relationships between individuals by the number they are assigned. Like the other numbering systems, the primary individual is designated number 1. Children are assigned their parent's number with their birth order after it. For example, if a woman's number is 14, her first child would be 141, her second 142, and so on. If an individual has more than nine children, subsequent children are assigned letters (starting with X, then A, B, C . . .).

Figure 6-4

Descendant report using the Modified Henry System.

Descendants of James Hoyt

Generation 1

1. **JAMES[1] HOYT** was born on 19 Sep 1807 in Stamford, Fairfield, Connecticut, USA. He died in 1902. He married (1) **MARIA HITCHCOCK** on 19 Sep 1833. She was born in 1815 in New York City, New York, USA. She died on 13 Mar 1850 in Illinois, USA. He married (2) **ELIZA JANE MATHIS** on 28 Jul 1853. She was born in 1830. She died in 1924.

James Hoyt and Maria Hitchcock had the following children:

11. JULIA[2] HOYT was born on 06 Sep 1834 in Chillicothe, Ross, Ohio, USA. She died on 28 Jul 1923. She married JOHN W. BOBBITT on 18 Oct 1852, son of Isham Drury Bobbitt and Cyntha Ann Haggard. He was born on 09 Jun 1832 in Kentucky, USA. He died on 24 Aug 1909 in Dawson, Richardson, Nebraska, USA.

12. ELEANOR HOYT was born on 30 Mar 1837 in Chillicothe, Ross, Ohio, USA. She died on 25 Jul 1838. She married.

13. JAMES HENRY HOYT was born on 01 May 1839 in Lacon, Marshall, Illinois, USA. He died on 01 Oct 1922 in Golden City, Barton, Missouri, USA. He married ESTHER READY.

Notes for James Henry Hoyt:
Living in Martinsburg, Missouri, in 1871

14. SARAH ELIZABETH HOYT was born on 06 Jul 1841 in Marshall County, Illinois, USA. She died on 13 Feb 1929. She married SAMUEL CLIFFORD.

15. ANN MARIA HOYT was born on 20 Jul 1843 in Marshall County, Illinois, USA. She died on 20 Jul 1843 in Marshall County, Illinois, USA. She married.

16. SEYMOUR HOYT was born on 10 Aug 1844 in Lacon, Marshall, Illinois, USA. He died on 07 May 1940 in Greenfield, Dade, Missouri, USA.

Notes for Seymour Hoyt:
In 1871 is living in Greenfield, Dade County, Missouri.

17. CHARLES EDGAR HOYT was born on 23 Sep 1846 in Marshall County, Illinois, USA. He died on 22 Aug 1847 in Marshall County, Illinois, USA. He married.

18. ALBERT HOYT was born on 10 Feb 1848 in Marshall County, Illinois, USA. He died on 10 Feb 1848 in Marshall County, Illinois, USA. He married.

19. SUSAN CAROLINE HOYT was born on 22 Apr 1849 in Marshall County, Illinois, USA. She died on 22 Aug 1849 in Marshall County, Illinois, USA. She married.

James Hoyt and Eliza Jane Mathis had the following children:

1X. CHARLES EDGAR[2] HOYT was born on 21 Oct 1857 in Marshall County, Illinois, USA.

1A. JENNIE MARIA HOYT was born on 28 Jul 1861 in Marshall County, Illinois, USA.

Generation 2

11. **JULIA[2] HOYT** (James[1]) was born on 06 Sep 1834 in Chillicothe, Ross, Ohio, USA. She died on 28 Jul 1923. She married JOHN W. BOBBITT on 18 Oct 1852, son of Isham Drury Bobbitt and Cyntha Ann Haggard. He was born on 09 Jun 1832 in Kentucky, USA. He died on 24 Aug 1909 in Dawson, Richardson, Nebraska, USA.

John W. Bobbitt and Julia Hoyt had the following children:

111. SEYMOUR[3] BOBBITT was born about 1854 in Illinois, USA.

d'Aboville System

The d'Aboville System (fig. 6-5) is similar to the Henry System. The same numbering system is used, but periods are included between the numbers. The primary individual is assigned number 1; his or her first child would be 1.1, the second 1.2, and so on. In addition, all individuals are assigned numbers—even families that have more than nine children.

Figure 6-5

Descendant report using the d'Aboville System.

Descendants of James Hoyt

Generation 1

1. **JAMES[1] HOYT** was born on 19 Sep 1807 in Stamford, Fairfield, Connecticut, USA. He died in 1902. He married (1) **MARIA HITCHCOCK** on 19 Sep 1833. She was born in 1815 in New York City, New York, USA. She died on 13 Mar 1850 in Illinois, USA. He married (2) **ELIZA JANE MATHIS** on 28 Jul 1853. She was born in 1830. She died in 1924.

James Hoyt and Maria Hitchcock had the following children:

1.1. **JULIA[2] HOYT** was born on 06 Sep 1834 in Chillicothe, Ross, Ohio, USA. She died on 28 Jul 1923. She married **JOHN W. BOBBITT** on 18 Oct 1852, son of Isham Drury Bobbitt and Cyntha Ann Haggard. He was born on 09 Jun 1832 in Kentucky, USA. He died on 24 Aug 1909 in Dawson, Richardson, Nebraska, USA.

1.2. **ELEANOR HOYT** was born on 30 Mar 1837 in Chillicothe, Ross, Ohio, USA. She died on 25 Jul 1838. She married.

1.3. **JAMES HENRY HOYT** was born on 01 May 1839 in Lacon, Marshall, Illinois, USA. He died on 01 Oct 1922 in Golden City, Barton, Missouri, USA. He married **ESTHER READY**.

Notes for James Henry Hoyt.
Living in Martinsburg, Missouri, in 1871

1.4. **SARAH ELIZABETH HOYT** was born on 06 Jul 1841 in Marshall County, Illinois, USA. She died on 13 Feb 1929. She married **SAMUEL CLIFFORD**.

1.5. **ANN MARIA HOYT** was born on 20 Jul 1843 in Marshall County, Illinois, USA. She died on 20 Jul 1843 in Marshall County, Illinois, USA. She married.

1.6. **SEYMOUR HOYT** was born on 10 Aug 1844 in Lacon, Marshall, Illinois, USA. He died on 07 May 1940 in Greenfield, Dade, Missouri, USA.

Notes for Seymour Hoyt:
In 1871 is living in Greenfield, Dade County, Missouri.

1.7. **CHARLES EDGAR HOYT** was born on 23 Sep 1846 in Marshall County, Illinois, USA. He died on 22 Aug 1847 in Marshall County, Illinois, USA. He married.

1.8. **ALBERT HOYT** was born on 10 Feb 1848 in Marshall County, Illinois, USA. He died on 10 Feb 1848 in Marshall County, Illinois, USA. He married.

1.9. **SUSAN CAROLINE HOYT** was born on 22 Apr 1849 in Marshall County, Illinois, USA. She died on 22 Aug 1849 in Marshall County, Illinois, USA. She married.

James Hoyt and Eliza Jane Mathis had the following children:

1.10. **CHARLES EDGAR[2] HOYT** was born on 21 Oct 1857 in Marshall County, Illinois, USA.

1.11. **JENNIE MARIA HOYT** was born on 28 Jul 1861 in Marshall County, Illinois, USA.

Generation 2

1.1. **JULIA[2] HOYT** (James[1]) was born on 06 Sep 1834 in Chillicothe, Ross, Ohio, USA. She died on 28 Jul 1923. She married **JOHN W. BOBBITT** on 18 Oct 1852, son of Isham Drury Bobbitt and Cyntha Ann Haggard. He was born on 09 Jun 1832 in Kentucky, USA. He died on 24 Aug 1909 in Dawson, Richardson, Nebraska, USA.

John W. Bobbitt and Julia Hoyt had the following children:

1.1.1. **SEYMOUR[3] BOBBITT** was born about 1854 in Illinois, USA.

1.1.2. **CORNELIA O. BOBBITT** was born in Mar 1857 in Illinois, USA. She married **HERMON P. SHIER** on 02 Feb 1873 in Varna, Marshall, Illinois, USA.

1.1.3. **WILLIS R. BOBBITT** was born about 1861 in Illinois, USA.

1.1.4. **SARAH ELEANOR BOBBITT** was born about 1863 in Illinois, USA.

1.1.5. **FRANCIS MARION BOBBITT** was born in 1868 in Illinois, USA. He died on 03 Jun 1906 in Topeka, Shawnee, Kansas, USA. He married **JULIA L. COMSTOCK** on 23 Mar 1890 in North Platte, Lincoln, Nebraska, USA.

Creating a Descendant Report

Go to the Collection tab on the Publish workspace. Under Genealogy Reports, select **Descendant Report**. Use these options in the editing panel to change the report:

Generations

Select the number of generations of descendants you want to display.

Generation indicators

Select how generations are identified. A generation indicator is a superscript number or letter next to a name (John Bobbitt[1]) that identifies which generation the individual belongs to. You can choose from:

- **Simple.** Numbering is based on the primary individual of the report. Ancestors are not numbered.

- **Oldest paternal ancestor.** Numbering is based on the oldest male ancestor in the same blood line as the primary person. For example, if the primary individual in the report has a grandfather included in your tree, the grandfather would be assigned 1, the father would be assigned 2, and the primary individual would be assigned 3.

- **Primary individual.** Numbering is based on the primary individual in the report and he or she will be assigned number 1 regardless of previous generations. If the primary individual has ancestors in the tree, they will be identified by letters, (A, B, C, D . . .).

Number system

Select a numbering system: Register, NGSQ, Modified Henry, or d'Aboville.

List non-vital facts separately

Select this checkbox to include only birth, marriage, and death facts in the narrative.

Include parent/child relationship types

Select this checkbox to include parent and child relationships (such as adopted or foster).

Outline Descendant Report

The Outline Descendant Report displays an individual's descendants—his or her children, grandchildren, great-grandchildren, and so on—in a simple outline form (fig. 6-6). Each individual's information is shown on a separate line, with following generations indented underneath. You can include generation numbers next to each name to make the report easier to understand. If the primary person is 1, his or her children will be 2, grandchildren 3, and so on. Spouses are indicated with a plus sign (+).

Outline Descendant Report for Abigail Hait

..... 1 Abigail Hait b: 09 Oct 1740 in Stamford, Fairfield, Connecticut, USA, d: 27 Feb 1796 in Stamford, Fairfield, Connecticut, USA
..... + John Hoyt b: 24 Nov 1740 in Stamford, Fairfield, Connecticut, USA, m: 31 Dec 1761, d: 01 Mar 1825
.... 2 Samuel Hoyt b: 08 Nov 1762 in Stamford, Fairfield, Connecticut, USA, d: 22 Sep 1838 in Stamford, Fairfield, Connecticut, USA
.... 2 William Hoyt b: 01 Aug 1764 in Stamford, Fairfield, Connecticut, USA, d: 25 Aug 1828
.... 2 John Hoyt b: 02 Dec 1765 in Stamford, Fairfield, Connecticut, USA, d: 15 Dec 1812 in Burlington, Chittenden, Vermont, USA
.... 2 Abigail Hoyt b: 31 Oct 1767 in Stamford, Fairfield, Connecticut, USA, d: 26 Aug 1840 in Norwalk, Fairfield, Connecticut, USA
.... 2 Benjamin Hoyt b: 19 Feb 1769 in Stamford, Fairfield, Connecticut, USA, d: 21 Nov 1813
.... + Elizabeth Reed b: 15 Nov 1774, m: 23 Dec 1792, d: 11 Jun 1818
.... 3 Sarah Hoyt b: 23 Feb 1794 in Tarrytown, Westchester, New York, USA
.... 3 Seymour Hoyt b: 22 Mar 1796 in Stamford, Fairfield, Connecticut, USA, d: 29 Oct 1866 in Stamford, Fairfield, Connecticut, USA
.... 3 Benjamin Hoyt b: 28 Jul 1798 in Stamford, Fairfield, Connecticut, USA, d: 13 Feb 1801 in Stamford, Fairfield, Connecticut, USA
.... 3 Elizabeth Hoyt b: 05 Aug 1800 in Stamford, Fairfield, Connecticut, USA, d: Aft. 1871
.... 3 Benjamin Hoyt b: 26 Nov 1802 in Stamford, Fairfield, Connecticut, USA
.... 3 Emeline Hoyt b: 02 Jun 1805 in Stamford, Fairfield, Connecticut, USA, d: 09 Jan 1854
.... 3 James Hoyt b: 19 Sep 1807 in Stamford, Fairfield, Connecticut, USA, d: 1902
.... + Maria Hitchcock b: 1815 in New York City, New York, USA, m: 19 Sep 1833, d: 13 Mar 1850 in Illinois, USA
.... 4 Julia Hoyt b: 06 Sep 1834 in Chillicothe, Ross, Ohio, USA, d: 28 Jul 1923
.... + John W. Bobbitt b: 09 Jun 1832 in Kentucky, USA, m: 18 Oct 1852, d: 24 Aug 1909 in Dawson, Richardson, Nebraska, USA
.... 5 Seymour Bobbitt b: Abt. 1854 in Illinois, USA
.... 5 Cornelia O. Bobbitt b: Mar 1857 in Illinois, USA
.... + Hermon P. Shier m: 02 Feb 1873 in Varna, Marshall, Illinois, USA
.... 5 Willis R. Bobbitt b: Abt. 1861 in Illinois, USA
.... 5 Sarah Eleanor Bobbitt b: Abt. 1863 in Illinois, USA
.... 5 Francis Marion Bobbitt b: 1868 in Illinois, USA, d: 03 Jun 1906 in Topeka, Shawnee, Kansas, USA
.... + Julia L. Comstock m: 23 Mar 1890 in North Platte, Lincoln, Nebraska, USA
.... 5 Jessie Julia Bobbitt b: 03 Mar 1872 in Illinois, USA, d: 15 Nov 1951 in Los Angeles, Los Angeles, California, USA
.... + Robert E. Loudon b: Abt. 1867 in Indiana, USA
.... 5 Eugene Allen Bobbitt b: 1877 in Illinois, USA
.... + Ella (Bobbitt) b: 1879 in Missouri, USA
.... 5 Unknown Female Bobbitt b: 02 Mar 1872 in Varna, Marshall, Illinois, USA
.... 5 James Clarence Bobbitt b: 28 Jul 1858 in Illinois, USA, d: 02 Jun 1929
.... + Margaret Rebecca Shanklin b: 12 Jul 1863 in Illinois, USA, m: 20 Feb 1882 in Marshall County, Illinois, USA, d: 29 Mar 1944
.... 6 Charity Bobbitt b: 10 Mar 1883 in Nebraska, USA, d: May 1982
.... + William Burdette Crossman b: 1882 in Michigan

Figure 6-6

An Outline Descendant Report.

Creating an Outline Descendant Report

Go to the Collection tab on the Publish workspace. Under Relationship Reports, select **Outline Descendant Report**. Use these options in the editing panel to change the report:

Generations

Select the number of generations of descendants to include from the dropdown list.

Starting no. and Include generation number

You can display numbers in the report to help readers easily identify which generation each individual belongs to. This can be particularly useful in long reports. To display generation numbers, select the **Include generation number** checkbox. Then in **Starting no.** select a number for the primary individual (by default, this is 1, or the first generation). You may want to change this number if this report is just one in a series and the primary individual is assigned a different generation number on other reports.

Indentation

By default, each line is indented with "leaders," a series of dots. To use a different leader character, enter it in the **Character** field. You can also choose the number of leader characters to use before each entry (the default is 6 characters). To fit as many generations as possible on a page, choose fewer characters; to make it obvious which generation each individual belongs to, increase the number of characters.

Spaces between individuals

If you find that the report is too condensed, you can add blank lines between each individual to make the report more readable.

Include spouses

Select this checkbox to include spouses for all descendants (the spouse will be listed beneath the individual).

Include (B-D)

Select this checkbox to include an individual's life span in parentheses after his or her name.

Family Group Sheet

A family group sheet (fig. 6-7) is one of the most easily recognized reports used in genealogy. It contains information about a single family unit (parents and children) including names; birth, death, and marriage events; notes; and sources. Be aware that individuals who have more than one spouse can have multiple family groups sheets, one for each family unit.

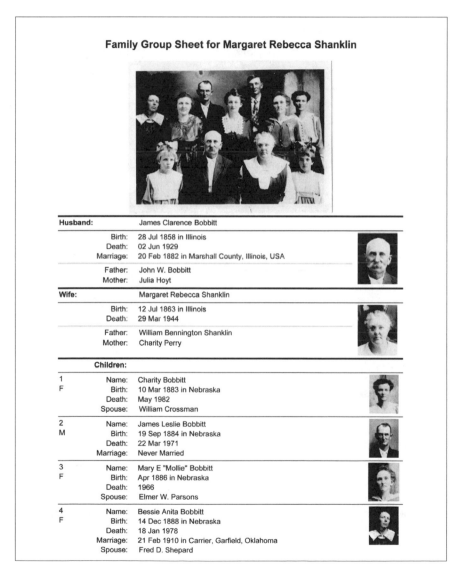

Figure 6-7

A family group sheet with a family picture and thumbnail images.

> **TIP**
>
> Children are listed on the family group sheet in the sort order you've specified on the family group view. If you want children listed in birth order, go to the family group view on the People workspace and click the **Sort children by birth order** button before you create the report.

Creating a Family Group Sheet

Go to the Collection tab on the Publish workspace. Under Relationship Reports, select **Family Group Sheet**. Use these options in the editing panel to change the report:

Spouse(s)

If the primary individual has more than one spouse, choose the spouse you want in the report from the drop-down list.

Extra children

If you want to print blank spaces for additional children, choose the number of spaces from the drop-down list.

Pictures

If you have assigned portraits to individuals, you can click **Include thumbnails** to add these images to the report. Click **Use silhouettes** to display an icon for those individuals who don't have portraits assigned to them.

Family picture

If you have linked photos to the parents' relationship, you can choose one of these from the drop-down list. The photograph appears at the top of the report.

Include other spouses

Select this checkbox to include the names of all the individual's spouses.

Include LDS section

Select this checkbox to include LDS-specific facts, such as baptisms and sealings.

Individual Report

The Individual Report (fig. 6-8) lists every fact and source you have recorded for a specific individual and includes names of parents, spouses, and children.

Figure 6-8

An Individual Report with sources.

Individual Report for Margaret Rebecca Shanklin

Individual Summary:	Margaret Rebecca Shanklin
Sex:	Female [1, 2, 3, 4, 5]
Father:	William Bennington Shanklin
Mother:	Charity Perry

Individual Facts:

Birth:	12 Jul 1863 in Illinois, USA [1, 4, 6]
1870 U.S. Census:	1870 in Bell Plain, Marshall, Illinois, USA [4]
1900 U.S. Census:	1900 in Stone, Woods, Oklahoma, USA [1]
1910 U.S. Census:	1910 in Kokomo, Beaver, Oklahoma, USA [2]
1920 U.S. Census:	1920 in Kokomo, Beaver, Oklahoma, USA [3]
1930 U.S. Census:	1930 in Kokomo, Beaver, Oklahoma [5]
Death:	29 Mar 1944 [6]
Burial:	Balko, Beaver, Oklahoma, USA [6]

Shared Facts: **James Clarence Bobbitt**

Marriage:	20 Feb 1882 in Marshall County, Illinois, USA [7]
Children:	Charity Bobbitt
	James Leslie Bobbitt
	Mary E "Mollie" Bobbitt
	Bessie Anita Bobbitt
	Alta Maud Bobbitt
	Arthur Leroy Bobbitt
	Twila Bobbitt
	Maurine Bobbitt
	Fern Edna Bobbitt
	Lorine Bobbitt
	Veda M. Bobbitt
	Clyde S. Bobbitt

Sources:

1 Ancestry.com, 1900 United States Federal Census (Provo, UT, USA, The Generations Network, Inc., 2004), www.ancestry.com, Database online. Stone, Woods, Oklahoma, ED , roll , page. Record for James C Bobbitt.
2 Ancestry.com, 1910 United States Federal Census (Provo, UT, USA, The Generations Network, Inc., 2006), www.ancestry.com, Database online. Kokomo, Beaver, Oklahoma, ED , roll T624_1242, part , page. Record for James C Bobbitt.
3 Ancestry.com, 1920 United States Federal Census (Provo, UT, USA, The Generations Network, Inc., 2005), www.ancestry.com, Database online. Kokomo, Beaver, Oklahoma, ED , roll , page , image 1062. Record for James L Bunfill.
4 Ancestry.com, 1870 United States Federal Census (Provo, UT, USA, The Generations Network, Inc., 2003), www.ancestry.com, Database online. Year: 1870; Census Place: Bell Plain, Marshall, Illinois; Roll: M593_; Page: ; Image:. Record for Maggie Shanklin.
5 Ancestry.com, 1930 United States Federal Census (Provo, UT, USA, The Generations Network, Inc., 2002), www.ancestry.com, Database online. Year: 1930; Census Place: Kokomo, Beaver, Oklahoma; Roll: 1892; Page: 5B; Enumeration District: 18; Image: 568.0.
6 Pleasant Hill Cemetery (Balko, Beaver, Oklahoma), Margaret R. and James C.
7 License to Marry. Feb 20, Jas C Bobbitt of Salem, Neb., to Margaret Rebecca Shanklin of Belle Plain.., *Henry Republican*, Henry, Illinois, online transcription.

Creating an Individual Report

Go to the Collection tab on the Publish workspace. Under Person Reports, select **Individual Report**. Use these options in the editing panel to change the report:

Use chronological order for facts

Select this checkbox if you want the individual's facts to be listed by date. Otherwise, the report lists a preferred fact first and then additional facts in the order in which you entered them.

TIP

By default, every fact you've entered for a person will appear in their individual report. To delete a fact from the report, click the **Items to Include** button on the editing toolbar. Click the fact in the "Included facts" list and click the **Delete Fact** (**X**) button.

Show individual thumbnail

If you have assigned portraits to individuals, select this checkbox to include the photos in the report.

Timeline Report

A Timeline Report (fig. 6-9) is a great way to illustrate how an individual fits into historical times. You can view all the events you've entered for an individual; each entry shows the date and location of the event and the person's age at the time. You can also choose to include important events in an individual's immediate family (such as the birth of family members) and historical events.

Timeline Report for John W. Bobbitt

	Yr/Age	Event	Date/Place
	1832	Birth	09 Jun 1832 Kentucky, USA
	1834 2	Birth (Spouse) Julia Hoyt	06 Sep 1834 Chillicothe, Ross, Ohio, USA
	1850 17	1850 U.S. Census	1850 Tazewell County, Illinois, USA
	1852 20	Marriage Julia Hoyt	18 Oct 1852
	1854 21	Birth (Son) Seymour Bobbitt	Abt. 1854 Illinois, USA
	1857 24	Birth (Daughter) Cornelia O. Bobbitt	Mar 1857 Illinois, USA
	1858 26	Birth (Son) James Clarence Bobbitt	28 Jul 1858 Illinois, USA
	1860 27	1860 U.S. Census	1860 Roberts, Marshall, Illinois, USA
	1861 28	Birth (Son) Willis R. Bobbitt	Abt. 1861 Illinois, USA
	1862 30	Death (Father) Isham Drury Bobbitt	14 Nov 1862
	1863 30	Birth (Daughter) Sarah Eleanor Bobbitt	Abt. 1863 Illinois, USA
	1868 35	Birth (Son) Francis Marion Bobbitt	1868 Illinois, USA
	1870 37	1870 U.S. Census	1870 Roberts, Marshall, Illinois, USA
	1872 39	Birth (Daughter) Unknown Female Bobbitt	02 Mar 1872 Varna, Marshall, Illinois, USA
	1872 39	Birth (Daughter) Jessie Julia Bobbitt	03 Mar 1872 Illinois, USA
	1873 40	Marriage (Daughter) Cornelia O. Bobbitt	02 Feb 1873 Varna, Marshall, Illinois, USA
	1877 44	Political Office Assessor	1877 Bell Plain, Marshall, Illinois, USA

Figure 6-9

A Timeline Report.

Creating a Timeline Report

Go to the Collection tab on the Publish workspace. Under Person Reports, select **Timeline Report**. Use these options in the editing panel to change the report:

Include event type icons

Select this checkbox to display icons that identify each type of event.

Include family events

Select this checkbox to include life events for parents, siblings, spouses, and children.

Include historical events

Select this checkbox to include historical events that occurred during the individual's lifetime.

> Note: Family Tree Maker comes with a set of default historical events that you can edit, delete, and add to. For more information, see "Customizing Historical Timelines" on page 229.

Include private facts

Select this checkbox to include events you have marked as private.

Research Reports

Family Tree Maker has a number of reports that can help you track your
progress, see potential errors in your data, and help your organize your
research.

Documented Facts Report

As you look over your tree it's important to be able to understand where the
information about your family came from. A great way to do this is by creating a Documented Facts Report for an individual (fig. 6-10). For each person
you include in the report, you'll see all the events for which you have entered
sources (facts without sources will not be included).

Figure 6-10

A Documented
Facts Report.

Creating a Documented Facts Report

Go to the Collection tab on the Publish workspace. Under Source Reports,
select **Documented Facts**.

Source Usage Report

The Source Usage Report (fig. 6-11) includes each source you have created and lists the individuals and facts associated with that source. This report helps you determine which recorded facts are supported by sources. It can be useful in keeping track of the sources you've researched and lets you compare notes with other researchers. You can choose whether to include individuals and facts for sources or only individuals.

Note: If you have not assigned a source to any facts, the report will include the fact and the message, "Not associated with any facts."

Figure 6-11

A Source Usage Report that shows each citation associated with a source.

Source Usage Report

Source Title: 1850 United States Federal Census
Repository: www.ancestry.com
Citation: Ancestry.com, 1850 United States Federal Census (Provo, UT, USA, The Generations Network, Inc., 2005), www.ancestry.com, Database online. Year: 1850; Census Place: District 1, Fleming, Kentucky; Roll: M432_199; Page: 346A; Image:. Record for Sarah Shanklin. [Source citation includes media item(s)]
    Bennington, Sarah

Source Title: 1860 United States Federal Census
Repository: www.ancestry.com
Citation: Ancestry.com, 1860 United States Federal Census (Provo, UT, USA, The Generations Network, Inc., 2004), www.ancestry.com, Database online. Year: 1860; Census Place: Bell Plain, Marshall, Illinois; Roll: ; Page: ; Image:. Record for Sarah Shanklin. [Source citation includes media item(s)]
    Bennington, Sarah

Source Title: A Genealogical History of the Hoyt, Haight, and Hight Families
Repository: Family History Library
Citation: A Genealogical History of the Hoyt, Haight, and Hight Families (Chicago, Illinois, The S.J. Clarke Publishing Company, 1886), Family History Library, 35 North West Temple Street
Salt Lake City, Utah 84150-3440, pg 477. [Source citation includes media item(s)]
    Hoyt, James
Citation: A Genealogical History of the Hoyt, Haight, and Hight Families (Chicago, Illinois, The S.J. Clarke Publishing Company, 1886), Family History Library, 35 North West Temple Street
Salt Lake City, Utah 84150-3440, pg 478. [Source citation includes media item(s)]
    Hoyt, James
Citation: A Genealogical History of the Hoyt, Haight, and Hight Families (Chicago, Illinois, The S.J. Clarke Publishing Company, 1886), Family History Library, 35 North West Temple Street
Salt Lake City, Utah 84150-3440, pg 566. [Source citation includes media item(s)]
    Hoyt, James

Source Title: Connecticut Town Birth Records, pre-1870 (Barbour Collection)
Repository: www.ancestry.com
Citation: Ancestry.com, Connecticut Town Birth Records, pre-1870 (Barbour Collection) (Provo, UT, USA, Ancestry.com Operations Inc, 2006), www.ancestry.com, Database online. Record for James Hoyt. [Source citation includes media item(s)]
    Hoyt, James

Source Title: Ellsworth, Spencer, Records of Olden Time: Fifty Years on the Prairies
Citation: Spencer Ellsworth, *Records of Olden Time: Fifty Years on the Prairies: Embracing Sketches of the Discovery, Exploration and Settlement of the Country the Organization of the Counties of Putnam and Marshall, Incidents and Reminiscences Connected*

Creating a Source Usage Report

Go to the Collection tab on the Publish workspace. Under Source Reports, select **Source Usage Report**. Use these options in the editing panel to change the report:

Show facts

Select this checkbox to include specific facts associated with each source citation.

Show notes

Select this checkbox to include notes you've entered for each source citation.

Show citations

Select this checkbox to include each citation you've entered for a source. Each individual associated with a citation will be listed underneath it. However, you will not be able to see how the citation was used unless you select the **Show facts** checkbox.

Bibliographies

A bibliography lists all the sources you have cited and is a great addition to a book to help readers locate and evaluate the resources you've used in your research. You can create a simple bibliography that lists only the titles of sources or you can create an annotated bibliography (fig. 6-12) that includes repositories, reference notes, and more.

Figure 6-12

An annotated bibliography.

Source Bibliography

Loretta Young, Heritage Glimpses (, 1983).

Merideth, Lois (Barney). *Unknown Nebraska Newspaper*, 1885. Online archives. Original paper in possession of author

Missouri. State Board of Health. Death certificates.

Nebraska State Gazetteer & Business Directory - Adams County Nebraska 1890 (Omaha, Nebraska, Wolf & Co., 1890).
Found in Ancestry.com database called Adams County, Nebraska Directory, 1890

Nebraska. Lincoln. Marriage certificates. Tana Pedersen Personal Holdings.

New England Historic Society, Utah City Directories 1934 (Ancestry.com), www.ancestry.com.

Northwest Arkansas Times. Arkansas. Fayetteville, Arkansas.

Oklahoma. Beaver. Marriage certificates.

Oklahoma. Beaver. Marriage certificates. Tana Pedersen Personal Holdings.

Oklahoma. Marriage certificates.

Online Resource.

Orange County California Genealogical Society. *For King or Country: Revolutionary War Era Ancestors with 200 Years of Descendants*. Vol 1-2 volumes. : Orange County California Genealogical Society, 1976.

Pattonsburg-Moss Cemetery (Pattonsburg, Marshall, Illinois). Grave markers.

Pedersen, Oliver Cowdery. Diary. Denmark, 1924-26.

Creating a Bibliography

Go to the Collection tab on the Publish workspace. Under Source Reports, select **Source Bibliography**. Use this option in the editing panel to change the report:

Annotated bibliography

Select this checkbox to include summary information, such as repository and reference notes, for each source.

Task List

You may want to use the task list (fig. 6-13) to track your research tasks. For example, you may want to keep a list of questions you need to answer, resources you need to search, or a list of documents you want to find. The task list lets you see categories you've assigned to tasks, creation and due dates, and tasks that have already been completed; you can even sort the list by task priority.

Task List

☐	Write to Berks County Historical Society for Reed/Rieth church records	Priority: High Owner: General Task Categories: Reed Date Created: 3/24/2010 Date Due: 3/26/2010
☐	Write to Peoria County for Milton Hewitt's death record.	Priority: High Owner: General Task Categories: Hewitt Date Created: 2/17/2010 Date Due: 4/30/2010
☐	Look for marriage record for Joseph Thompson and "Jane" between 1840 and 1845 in Warwickshire, England	Priority: Medium Owner: General Task Categories: Records Date Created: 3/24/2010 Date Due: 6/30/2010
☐	Look up name of Brighton church book (GEDGE family) in Family History Library for source citation.	Priority: Medium Owner: General Task Categories: Gedge Date Created: 2/17/2010 Date Due: 4/30/2010
☐	Send Aunt Chris an email about the family photos.	Priority: Low Owner: General Task Categories: Communication Date Created: 2/17/2010 Date Due: 6/30/2010
☒	Find out when Phoebe Gedge went to the U of U and see if you can get a diploma.	Priority: Medium Owner: General Task Categories: Gedge Date Created: 2/17/2010 Date Due: 8/31/2010

Figure 6-13

A task list that includes completed tasks.

Creating a Task List

Go to the Collection tab on the Publish workspace. Under Person Reports, select **Task List**. Use this option in the editing panel to change the report:

Include completed tasks

Select this checkbox to include tasks that have been marked as completed. (Completed tasks that have been deleted will not be included.)

Research Note Report

The Research Note Report (fig. 6-14) lists an individual's name, life span, and the research notes associated with him or her.

Figure 6-14

A Research
Note Report.

Research Note Report

Elizabeth Gentry
Birth - Death: 14 Aug 1731 - 28 Jul 1820
Research Note: Had ten children, six of whom were sons.

Bartlett Haggard
Birth - Death: 04 Feb 1764 - 18 May 1846
Research Note: Bartlett and David were twins and married sisters.

Martha Haggard
Birth - Death: 1795 - 1871
Research Note: Married names of Routt and Newton.

Edwin Hewitt
Birth - Death: 1833 - ?
Research Note: Edwin is living with the Main family in Pennsylvania in 1850. Was he living with them at the time of the 1840 census? When did he move to Pennsylvania and why?

Maria Hitchcock
Birth - Death: 1815 - 13 Mar 1850
Research Note: County histories show that Maria married James in New York City abt. 1837. Need to see if New York City kept marriage records that early. Census records also indicate that she was born in New York state.

George Thompson
Birth - Death: Abt. 1833 - ?
Research Note: Thomas Ward is the person who registered the death. Son in law?

Joseph Thompson
Birth - Death: Abt. 1821 - ?
Research Note: Wife's name is possibly Jane. They are both listed as witnesses on Sarah Thompson and Joseph Gold's marriage certificate.

Catharine Walborn
Birth - Death: 13 Dec 1826 - 09 Mar 1903
Research Note: According to 1900 census, Catharine was the mother of 7 children, four of whom were dead before 1900. Amanda, Michael, and George all lived past 1900. Find out when Maria died and who the other three children are.

Creating a Research Note Report

Go to the Collection tab on the Publish workspace. Under Person Reports, select **Research Note Report**. Use this option in the editing panel to change the report:

Show private research notes

Select this checkbox if you want to include research notes you have marked as "private."

Statistical Reports

Family Tree Maker has several reports that can show you statistical information about your database; for example, you can see who is married, see the number of people with the same surname, or view parental relationships. Although you can determine which individuals are included in these reports, you cannot choose which facts are included.

Marriage Report

The Marriage Report (fig. 6-15) shows information about each marriage in your tree. Family Tree Maker automatically includes those individuals with marriage data. You'll see the names of husbands and wives, their marriage dates, and their relationship status.

Figure 6-15

A Marriage Report.

Marriage Report

Husband:	Wife:	Marriage Date:	Relation:
Andersen, Peder Christian	Nielsdatter, Maren		Spouse - Ongoing
Andersen, Peder Christian	Peterson, M. K.		Spouse - Ongoing
Bennington, William Jr.	Smith, Margaret	16 Apr 1793	Spouse - Ongoing
Bobbitt, Isham Drury	Haggard, Cyntha Ann	21 Dec 1824	Spouse - Ongoing
Bobbitt, James Clarence	Shanklin, Margaret Rebecca	20 Feb 1882	Spouse - Ongoing
Bobbitt, John W.	Hoyt, Julia	18 Oct 1852	Spouse - Ongoing
Bush, Robb	Rush, Mary		Spouse - Ongoing
Dawson, Martin	Carter, Elizabeth		Spouse - Ongoing
Gedge, George	Kybird, Lucy		Spouse - Ongoing
Gedge, Herbert Bush	Gold, Sarah Hannah	20 Nov 1895	Spouse - Ongoing
Gedge, Reames	Kybird, Lucy		Spouse - Ongoing
Gedge, William	Bush, Rachel	22 Nov 1855	Spouse - Ongoing
Gold, Cyrus Henry	Newman, Louisa Fanny	08 Aug 1904	Spouse - Ongoing
Gold, Cyrus Henry	Willis, Mary	27 Mar 1871	Spouse - Ongoing

Creating a Marriage Report

Go to the Collection tab on the Publish workspace. Under Relationship Reports, select **Marriage Report**. Use this option in the editing panel to change the report:

Sort by wife

By default the report is sorted the husband's last name; select this checkbox to sort the report by the wife's last (maiden) name.

Parentage Report

The Parentage Report (fig. 6-16) lists each individual, the individual's parents, and the relationship between the individual and parents (e.g., natural, adopted, foster).

Figure 6-16

A Parentage Report.

Parentage Report		
Name	**Parents**	**Relationship**
Andersen, Peder Christian		
Bell, Abigail		
Bell, Permelia		
Bennington, Sarah	Bennington, William Jr.	Natural
	Smith, Margaret	Natural
Bennington, William Jr.		
Bobbitt, Isham Drury		
Bobbitt, James Clarence	Bobbitt, John W.	Natural
	Hoyt, Julia	Natural
Bobbitt, John W.	Bobbitt, Isham Drury	Natural
	Haggard, Cyntha Ann	Natural
Bobbitt, Maurine	Bobbitt, James Clarence	Natural
	Shanklin, Margaret Rebecca	Natural
Bush, Rachel	Bush, Robb	Natural
	Rush, Mary	Natural
Bush, Robb		
Carter, Elizabeth		
Dawson, Martin		
Dawson, Nancy	Dawson, Martin	Natural
	Carter, Elizabeth	Natural
Gedge, George		
Gedge, Herbert Bush	Gedge, William	Natural
	Bush, Rachel	Natural
Gedge, Phoebe Gold	Gedge, Herbert Bush	Natural
	Gold, Sarah Hannah	Natural
Gedge, Reames		
Gedge, William	Gedge, Reames	Natural
	Kybird, Lucy	Natural
Gedge, William	Gedge, George	Natural
	Kybird, Lucy	Natural
Gentry, Elizabeth		
Gold, Cyrus Henry	Gold, Joseph	Natural
	Thompson, Sarah	Natural

Creating a Parentage Report

Go to the Collection tab on the Publish workspace. Under Relationship Reports, select **Parentage Report**.

Kinship Report

The Kinship Report (fig. 6-17) helps you determine how a specific person in your tree is related to other individuals. While the kinship reports in most software programs show only one relationship per individual, Family Tree Maker shows you all known relationships. For example, if you have third cousins who marry, the report will show both relationships.

Figure 6-17

A Kinship Report sorted by relationship and showing civil and canon numbers.

Kinship Report for Maria Hitchcock

Name:	Birth Date:	Relationship:	Civil:	Canon:
(Bobbitt), Clara	Feb 1851	Wife of grandson		
(Bobbitt), Ella	1879	Wife of grandson		
(Bobbitt), Ella M.	Jun 1853	Wife of grandson		
Comstock, Julia L.		Wife of grandson		
Shanklin, Margaret Rebecca	12 Jul 1863	Wife of grandson		
(Bobbitt), F. Berwyn	18 Aug 1910	Wife of great grandson		
Goodman, Myrtle	19 Jul 1900	Wife of great grandson		
Allen, Lester Phillip	24 Apr 1924	Husband of 2nd great granddaughter		
Eddins, Zane Leroy	10 Dec 1925	Husband of 2nd great granddaughter		
Hill, August Allen	03 Aug 1920	Husband of 2nd great granddaughter		
Pedersen, Elray Lincoln	12 Feb 1938	Husband of 2nd great granddaughter		
Sattler, Stanley	05 Dec 1914	Husband of 2nd great granddaughter		
Baslee, Christina Joy		Wife of 2nd great grandson		
Wells, Leora		Wife of 2nd great grandson		
Bobbitt, John W.	09 Jun 1832	Son-in-law		
Clifford, Samuel		Son-in-law		
Crossman, William Burdette	1882	Husband of great granddaughter		
Cullins, James Clonnie	20 Aug 1900	Husband of great granddaughter		
Ford, Alonzo W.	1886	Husband of great granddaughter		
Parsons, Unknown		Husband of great granddaughter		
Reed, Harold Arthur	02 Aug 1895	Husband of great granddaughter		
Shepard, Fred D.	23 Oct 1886	Husband of great granddaughter		
Wampler, Claud Daniel	01 Dec 1892	Husband of great granddaughter		
Guy, Tester		Husband		
Hoyt, James	19 Sep 1807	Husband		
Hitchcock, Maria	1815	Self		
Loudon, Robert E.	Abt. 1867	Husband of granddaughter		
Shier, Hermon P.		Husband of granddaughter		
Ready, Esther		Daughter-in-law		
Hitchcock, David		Father	I	1
Hoyt, Albert	10 Feb 1848	Son	I	1
Hoyt, Charles Edgar	23 Sep 1846	Son	I	1

Civil and Canon Numbers

Canon and civil numbers indicate the degree of relationship between individuals. Canon (commonly used in the United States) measures the number of steps back to a common ancestor and is indicated by an Arabic numeral (1, 2, 3). For example, you and your first cousin have the same grandparents. There is one step from you to your parent and another step from your parent to your grandparent. Therefore the number of steps back to your common ancestor (grandparent) is 2.

Civil measures the total number of steps from one family member to another and is indicated by Roman numerals (I, II, III). For example, your civil relationship to your sibling would be II—one step to your parent and another step back down to your sibling.

Creating a Kinship Report

Go to the Collection tab on the Publish workspace. Under Relationship Reports, select **Kinship Report**. Use these options in the editing panel to change the report:

Show unrelated individuals
Select this checkbox to include people who are not directly related to the primary individual.

Show Civil and Canon
Select this checkbox to show civil and canon numbers.

Show AKA as a separate entry
Select this checkbox to include "Also Known As" names for individuals.

Show all relationships
Select this checkbox to show all the ways in which individuals are related (for example, two people may be married and also be third cousins).

> Note: If you choose to show all relationships, the report may take a long time to generate—from several minutes to more than an hour.

Sort individuals by kinship
Select this checkbox to sort individuals by their relationship to the primary individual (for example, all first cousins will be grouped together).

Surname Report

A Surname Report (fig. 6-18) lists the surnames in your tree, including the total number of individuals with that surname, the number of males and females with that surname, and the earliest and most recent year a surname appears in your tree.

Surname Report

Surname	Count	Male	Female	Earliest	Most recent
Hoyt	34	18	16	1740	1861
Gold	31	16	15	1825	1908
Bobbitt	27	12	15	1793	1909
Haggard	25	14	11	1678	1813
Gedge	23	11	12	1830	1914
Reed	15	7	8	1774	1901
Pedersen	12	7	4	1821	1973
Peterson	10	6	4	1888	1905
Shanklin	7	3	4	1810	1866
Thompson	7	4	3	1796	1835
Bonnington	5	1	3	1802	1812
Hewitt	4	2	2	1833	1865
Rieth	4	2	2	1822	1861
Dawson	3	1	2	1764	1764
Gentry	3	1	2	1731	1731
Hait	3	2	1	1709	1743
Berry	3	1	2		

Figure 6-18

A Surname Report sorted by name count.

Creating a Surname Report

Go to the Collection tab on the Publish workspace. Under Person Reports, select **Surname Report**. Use these options in the editing panel to change the report:

Sort by surname count

Select this checkbox to sort surnames based on the number of individuals with that surname.

Limit counts to included individuals

Select this checkbox to include surnames of only those individuals you've selected; otherwise all surnames entered in your tree will be included.

Place Usage Report

The Place Usage Report (fig. 6-19) lists locations you've entered and each person associated with that location. You can also choose to include the specific events, such as birth or marriage, that occurred in that location.

Figure 6-19

A Place Usage Report.

Place Usage Report

Albemarle County, Virginia, USA
  Haggard, David
    Birth: 1763
  Haggard, Nathaniel
    Birth: 21 Nov 1723

Álborg, Nordjylland, Denmark
  Pedersen, Mette
    Res: May 1924
  Pedersen, Mette Katrina
    Emigr: 05 Oct 1899
  Pedersen, Niels
    Emigr: 20 Apr 1899
  Pedersen, Oliver Cowdery
    Birth: 26 Apr 1891
    Emigr: 05 Oct 1899

Aston Manor, Warwick, England
  Gold, Joseph
    Occu: 1861 Bricklayer

Aston, Warwick, England
  Gold, Joseph
    Marr: 27 Jan 1845
    Marr: 30 Jun 1861
    Marr: 20 Jun 1861
  Thompson, Sarah
    Marr: 27 Jan 1845

Balko, Beaver, Oklahoma, USA
  Bobbitt, James Clarence
    Burial: Pleasant Hill Cemetery
  Hewitt, Jessie Izetta
    Burial: Pleasant Hill Cemetery
  Shanklin, Margaret Rebecca
    Burial: Pleasant Hill Cemetery

Beaver County, Oklahoma, USA
  Bobbitt, Maurine
    Marr: 18 Aug 1923

Creating a Place Usage Report

Go to the Collection tab on the Publish workspace. Under Place Reports, select **Place Usage Report**. Use this option in the editing panel to change the report:

Show facts

Select this checkbox to include specific facts associated with a location.

Data Errors Report

Regardless of how careful I am entering data in my tree, errors seem to creep in. For example, I'll find an individual whose birth date is after their death date or he or she is listed as being born before his or her parents. Because of this, I like to run the Data Errors Report (fig. 6-20) at least once a month to identify any potential problems and keep my tree as error-free as possible.

Data Errors Report

Name	Birth Date	Potential Error
Anna Gedge	05 Sep 1865	The burial date occurred before his/her death.
Nathan Gedge	Abt. 1871	The birth date occurs after the death date. The birth date occurred after his/her mother was 60. The birth date occurred after his/her mother died. The birth date occurred after his/her father was 80. The birth date occurred more than one year after his/her father died.
Kate E. Kline	07 Nov 1857	The birth date occurs after the death date. Death date occurred before individual's birth date.
Mette Katrina Pedersen	22 Oct 1860	The individual has the same last name as her husband, Niels Pedersen. This individual's children sort order may be incorrect.
Mary Shanklin	1866	The birth date occurred more than one year after his/her father died.

Figure 6-20

A Data Errors Report.

Creating a Data Errors Report

Go to the Collection tab on the Publish workspace. Under Person Reports, select **Data Errors Report**. To choose which errors are included in the report, click the **Errors to include** button on the editing toolbar. You can include all errors or select the errors you're interested in. The more errors you include, the longer it will take to run the report.

Include All

Click this button to include all error types in the report.

Exclude All

Click this button to deselect all error types. You can then select specific error types you want to include in the report.

LDS Ordinances Report

The LDS Ordinances Report (fig. 6-21) is useful for members of The Church of Jesus Christ of Latter-day Saints (LDS church) and displays LDS-specific ordinances such as baptisms and sealings.

Figure 6-21

An LDS Ordinances Report.

LDS Ordinances

Gedge, Herbert Bush
Birth:	10 Nov 1872 in Brighton, Salt Lake, Utah
Marriage:	20 Nov 1895 in Salt Lake City, Salt Lake, Utah
Death:	08 Sep 1942 in Salt Lake, Salt Lake City, Utah
Baptism (LDS):	10 Nov 1880
Endowment (LDS):	20 Nov 1895

Gedge, Phoebe Gold
Birth:	27 May 1900 in Salt Lake City, Salt Lake, Utah
Marriage:	15 Sep 1926 in Salt Lake City, Utah
Death:	28 Dec 1948 in Salt Lake City, Salt Lake, Utah
Endowment (LDS):	15 Sep 1926 in Salt Lake City, UT, USA

Gold, Sarah Hannah
Birth:	03 Dec 1873 in Salt Lake City, Utah
Marriage:	20 Nov 1895 in Salt Lake City, Salt Lake, Utah
Death:	05 Nov 1963 in Salt Lake City, Utah
Baptism (LDS):	03 Jan 1882

Creating an LDS Ordinances Report

Go to the Collection tab on the Publish workspace. Under Person Reports, select **LDS Ordinances**.

Media Reports

Media reports can help you share documents and images with other family members. You can also use them to display photographs in a family history book.

Media Item Report

The Media Item Report lets you quickly view a media item's caption, date of origin, description, and individuals associated with it (fig. 6-22).

Figure 6-22

A Media Item Report.

Creating a Media Item Report

Go to the Collection tab on the Publish workspace. Under Media Reports, select **Media Item**. Use this option in the editing panel to change the report:

Media item

Displays the name of the currently selected media item. Click the **Find Media** button next to the name to choose a different media item.

Photo Album

The photo album (fig. 6-23) shows a basic summary of an individual's life
events, such as birth and death dates, and also includes all photos associated
with the person.

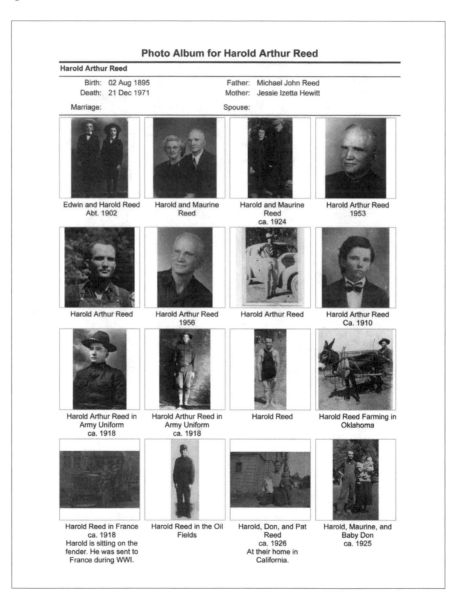

Creating a Photo Album

Go to the Collection tab on the Publish workspace. Under Media Reports, select **Photo Album**. Use these options in the editing panel to change the report:

Type

Choose a photo album type from the drop-down list. You can choose between photos linked to an individual, photos linked to a relationship, or both.

Photos per row

Choose the number of images you want on each row (up to six).

Show person/relationship photos only

Select this checkbox to include only photos that are linked to the selected individual or relationship. Images linked to sources, citations, or facts will not be included.

Include media date

Select this checkbox to include dates you've entered for an item.

Include media description

Select this checkbox to include information you've entered in the Description field for a media item.

Media Usage Report

The Media Usage Report (fig. 6-24) shows a thumbnail of each media item in your tree and lists its caption and location on your computer. It can also show the sources, facts, and individuals each media item is linked to. If you have many media items this report can become quite large. In my tree I have around 1,000 items and the report is 100 pages. Because of this you might want to limit the report to a specific group of people.

Figure 6-24

A Media Usage Report showing items linked to source citations.

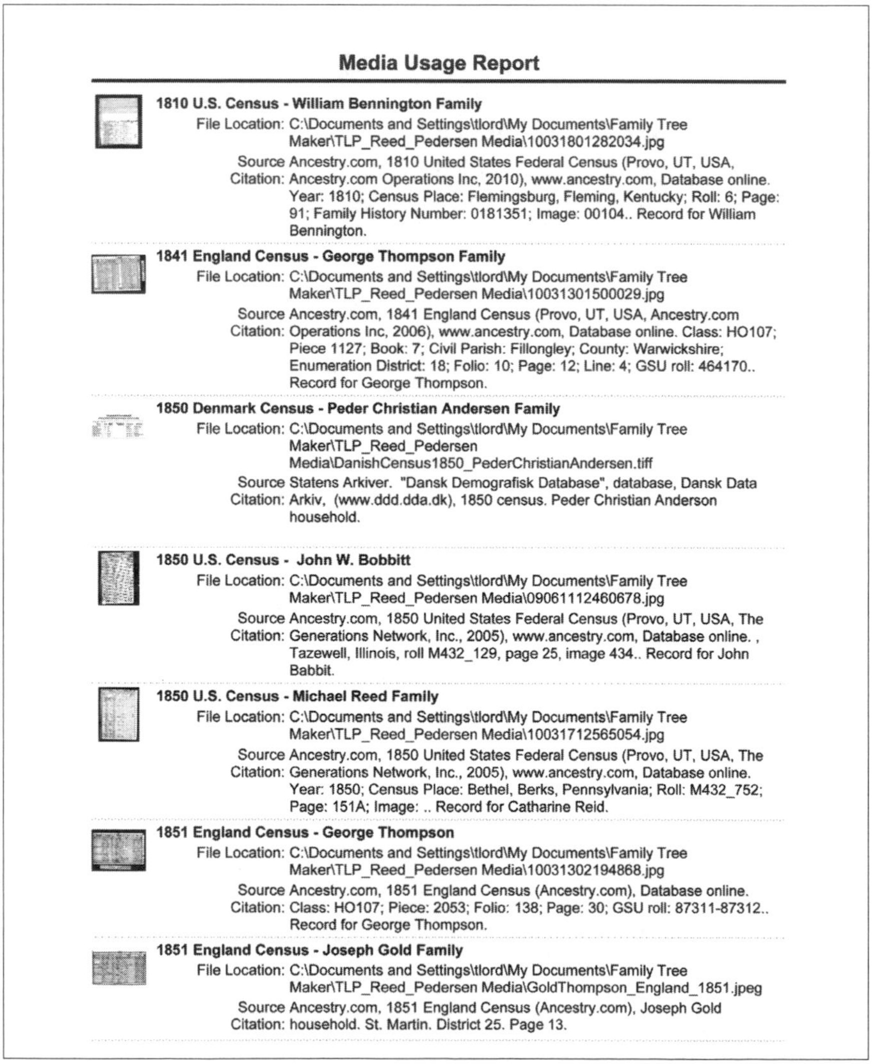

Media Usage Report

1810 U.S. Census - William Bennington Family
File Location: C:\Documents and Settings\tlord\My Documents\Family Tree Maker\TLP_Reed_Pedersen Media\10031801282034.jpg
Source Ancestry.com, 1810 United States Federal Census (Provo, UT, USA, Citation: Ancestry.com Operations Inc, 2010), www.ancestry.com, Database online. Year: 1810; Census Place: Flemingsburg, Fleming, Kentucky; Roll: 6; Page: 91; Family History Number: 0181351; Image: 00104.. Record for William Bennington.

1841 England Census - George Thompson Family
File Location: C:\Documents and Settings\tlord\My Documents\Family Tree Maker\TLP_Reed_Pedersen Media\10031301500029.jpg
Source Ancestry.com, 1841 England Census (Provo, UT, USA, Ancestry.com Citation: Operations Inc, 2006), www.ancestry.com, Database online. Class: HO107; Piece 1127; Book: 7; Civil Parish: Fillongley; County: Warwickshire; Enumeration District: 18; Folio: 10; Page: 12; Line: 4; GSU roll: 464170.. Record for George Thompson.

1850 Denmark Census - Peder Christian Andersen Family
File Location: C:\Documents and Settings\tlord\My Documents\Family Tree Maker\TLP_Reed_Pedersen Media\DanishCensus1850_PederChristianAndersen.tiff
Source Statens Arkiver. "Dansk Demografisk Database", database, Dansk Data Citation: Arkiv, (www.ddd.dda.dk), 1850 census. Peder Christian Anderson household.

1850 U.S. Census - John W. Bobbitt
File Location: C:\Documents and Settings\tlord\My Documents\Family Tree Maker\TLP_Reed_Pedersen Media\09061112460678.jpg
Source Ancestry.com, 1850 United States Federal Census (Provo, UT, USA, The Citation: Generations Network, Inc., 2005), www.ancestry.com, Database online. , Tazewell, Illinois, roll M432_129, page 25, image 434.. Record for John Babbit.

1850 U.S. Census - Michael Reed Family
File Location: C:\Documents and Settings\tlord\My Documents\Family Tree Maker\TLP_Reed_Pedersen Media\10031712565054.jpg
Source Ancestry.com, 1850 United States Federal Census (Provo, UT, USA, The Citation: Generations Network, Inc., 2005), www.ancestry.com, Database online. Year: 1850; Census Place: Bethel, Berks, Pennsylvania; Roll: M432_752; Page: 151A; Image: .. Record for Catharine Reid.

1851 England Census - George Thompson
File Location: C:\Documents and Settings\tlord\My Documents\Family Tree Maker\TLP_Reed_Pedersen Media\10031302194868.jpg
Source Ancestry.com, 1851 England Census (Ancestry.com), Database online. Citation: Class: HO107; Piece: 2053; Folio: 138; Page: 30; GSU roll: 87311-87312.. Record for George Thompson.

1851 England Census - Joseph Gold Family
File Location: C:\Documents and Settings\tlord\My Documents\Family Tree Maker\TLP_Reed_Pedersen Media\GoldThompson_England_1851.jpeg
Source Ancestry.com, 1851 England Census (Ancestry.com), Joseph Gold Citation: household. St. Martin. District 25. Page 13.

Creating a Media Usage Report

Go to the Collection tab on the Publish workspace. Under Media Reports, select **Media Usage Report**.

Show source media

Select this checkbox to include media items linked to sources.

Show citation media

Select this checkbox to include media items attached to source citations.

Show relationship media

Relationship media items are those linked to a couple in the Edit Relationship window. Select this checkbox to include these items in the report. I like to use this option to view marriage certificates and wedding photos.

Show fact media

Select this checkbox to include media items linked to specific facts (for example, in my tree I link tombstone photos to Burial facts).

Show person media

Select this checkbox to include media linked to specific individuals. Most of your media items will fall into this category.

Show unlinked media

Select this checkbox to include media items that are not linked to people, facts, sources, or source citations.

Custom Reports

I think one of the most under-utilized features in Family Tree Maker is its powerful reporting capability. You can use reports to mine your data and open up new research possibilities; you can use them to locate where you're missing or duplicating information; you can even create reports to alert family members of medical dangers lurking in their health history.

And while Family Tree Maker comes with an array of default reports, it also includes the ability to create reports with your own criteria. Don't see a report that you want? Create it yourself. In this section, I'll explain the basic options available in the custom report and also give you examples of some of my most used custom reports.

Custom Report Options

Before you create a custom report, it's good to have a general idea of the information you want to include in the report. Are you interested in finding all individuals with multiple spouses? Do you want to know which couple had the most children? Are you grouping individuals and facts together by location? The data your want to see in your report will determine the options you use, whether you're searching for useful research facts or simply want interesting ways to look at your family tree.

1. Open the **Custom Report** (located on the Publish workspace under Person Reports) and click the **Reset** button to clear any previous settings.

    When you first open the custom report, it includes birth, marriage, and death information and notes.

2. To change the facts that appear in the report, click the **Items to include** button in the reports toolbar.

3. In the "Included facts" list, you can click the **Add fact** (+) button to include additional facts in the report or select a fact and click the **Delete fact** (-) button to discard the fact.

    Note: To determine how facts look in the report, see "Formatting Name Facts" on page 107 and "Formatting Facts" on page 109.

4. If you want, you can select a primary and secondary sort for the report. For example, if you're creating a birthday report, you'll want to sort the list by the Birth fact (Date field) and then by Name. Each sort option can be sorted in ascending order (from A to Z or oldest to newest) or descending order (from Z to A or newest to oldest).

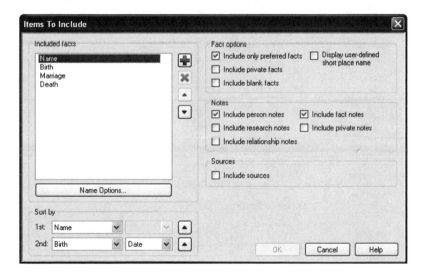

5. After you've selected your options, click **OK**. You can also determine which individuals appear in the report. For instructions see "Selecting a Group of Individuals" on page 46.

Address Report

Every year when my Reed family holds its annual reunion, someone has to gather the addresses of every family member in order to send out instructions, assignments, and directions to the location. I discovered that an easy way to gather this information is by putting each family's address (or e-mail address) in Family Tree Maker and then creating an address report that organizes them all (fig. 6-25).

This type of report can also be useful when creating mailing lists for family newsletters or making a list of relatives you want to send Christmas cards or wedding invitations to. You can include addresses, e-mail addresses, and even phone numbers.

Figure 6-25

An Address Report.

Addresses

Alvin Peterson	
	2927 Clifford Street Dublin, CA 94568
Bud Seitz	
	4338 Caldwell Road Rochester, NY 14620
Donal Reed	
	50 East 1800 South Bountiful, Utah 84010
Eleanor Hoyt	
	16301 Meadowhouse Ave San Bernardino, CA 92407
Elizabeth Hoyt	
	4475 W 59th Pl Los Angeles, CA 90012
Florence Loudon	
	19013 Grovewood Dr Corona, CA 92881
George Reed	
	3581 Canis Heights Drive Los Angeles, CA 90017
Isaac Reed	
	562 Cimmaron Road Riverside, CA 92501
John Routt	
	379 James Martin Circle Westerville, OH 43081
Kate Kline	
	3117 Single Street Waltham, MA 02154

Before You Begin

Enter contact information for all relevant individuals in the Address fact (Place field). You may also want to add the Phone Number and Email facts.

Creating an Address Report

1. Open the **Custom Report** (located on the Publish workspace under Person Reports) and click the **Reset** button to clear any previous settings.

2. Click the **Items to include** button in the reports toolbar. Delete the unnecessary facts (Birth, Marriage, and Death) by selecting the fact in the **Included facts** list and clicking the **Delete fact** (**X**) button.

3. Add the Address fact to the report. (You might want to add the "Phone Number" and "Email" facts, also.)

> **TIP**
>
> Because these addresses are for living individuals, I have marked the Address, Phone Number, and Email facts as private. In order to display these facts in the report, I have to click the **Include private facts** checkbox.

4. To change name formats, select the Name fact and click the **Name Options** button. From the Format list, select "First Last" to exclude middle names. Then click **OK**.

5. To change addresses formats, select the Address fact and click the **Address Options** button. You won't need dates or a fact label so deselect these checkboxes. Then click **OK**.

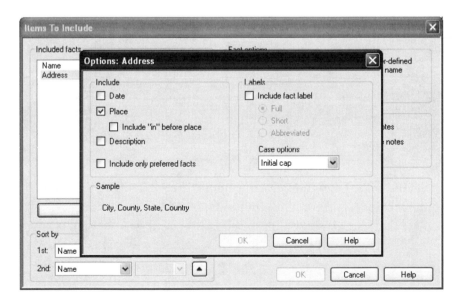

Now you can choose who you want to include in the report. The quickest option is to include everyone in your tree by choosing "All individuals." However, you can filter the list if you want. In this example, I want to select only individuals for whom I've entered addresses.

6. In **Individuals to include**, click **Selected individuals**. The Filter Individuals window opens. No individuals should be included in the report at this point; if there are, click **Exclude All** to clear the report.

7. Click **Filter In**. The Filter Individuals by Criteria window opens.

8. Click **All facts**.

9. Select "Address" and "Place" from the **Search where** drop-down lists. Then select "Is not blank" from the next drop-down list and click **OK**. The Filter Individuals window now shows all the individuals for whom I have entered an address.

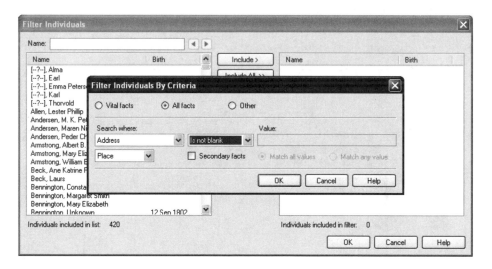

10. Click **OK** on the Filter Individuals window. The Address Report opens.

All-in-One Report

The All-in-One Report (fig. 6-26) is an alphabetical list of every family member you have entered in a tree—even if the only information you've entered for them is a name. The report can be quite long, especially if you have a large number of people in your tree. Depending on the number of facts you include in the report, about ten people will fit on a page. In this example, only names and birth, marriage, and death dates are included in the report. However, you can choose other facts you'd also like to include.

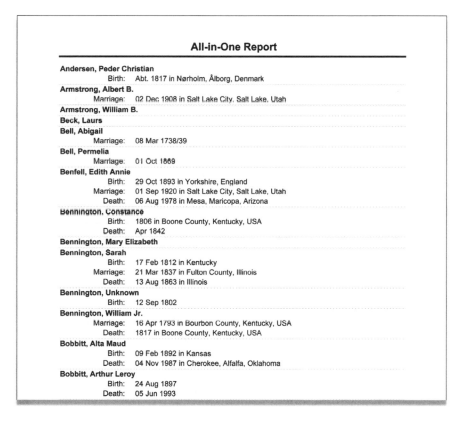

Figure 6-26

An All-in-One Report.

1. Open the **Custom Report** (located on the Publish workspace under Person Reports) and click the **Reset** button to clear any previous settings.

2. In **Individuals to include**, click **All individuals**.

Cemetery Report

One year for a Memorial Day celebration, I decided to visit a nearby cemetery where at least fifteen family members are buried. I wanted to take a photo of each tombstone to include in my tree and also compare dates with the information I already have. In anticipation of the event, I created a custom cemetery report (fig. 6-27) that showed the names (and dates) of every family member buried in that cemetery. I took the report with me so I wouldn't have to rely on my own memory and perhaps miss someone.

Figure 6-27

A Cemetery Report.

Cemetery Report

Salt Lake City Cemetery

Name:	Anna Gedge
Birth:	05 Sep 1865 in Salt Lake City, Salt Lake, Utah
Death:	09 Jun 1945 in Salt Lake City, Salt Lake, Utah
Burial:	12 Jun 1942 in Salt Lake City, Salt Lake, Utah; Salt Lake City Cemetery
Name:	Annie Jane Gold
Birth:	27 Dec 1895 in Utah
Death:	28 Feb 1956 in Salt Lake City, Salt Lake, Utah
Burial:	03 Mar 1956 in Salt Lake City, Salt Lake, Utah; Salt Lake City Cemetery
Name:	Cyrus Henry Gold
Birth:	01 May 1848 in Birmingham, Warwick, England
Death:	27 Mar 1930 in Salt Lake City, Salt Lake, Utah
Burial:	30 Mar 1930 in Salt Lake City, Salt Lake, Utah; Salt Lake City Cemetery
Name:	Cyrus William Gold
Birth:	28 Mar 1876 in Salt Lake City, Salt Lake, Utah
Death:	22 Nov 1956 in Salt Lake City, Salt Lake, Utah
Burial:	26 Nov 1956 in Salt Lake City, Salt Lake, Utah; Salt Lake City Cemetery
Name:	Edith Annie Benfell
Birth:	29 Oct 1893 in Yorkshire, England
Death:	06 Aug 1978 in Mesa, Maricopa, Arizona
Burial:	09 Aug 1978 in Salt Lake City, Salt Lake, Utah; Salt Lake City Cemetery
Name:	Edwin Robert Newman Gold
Birth:	22 Jun 1905
Death:	03 Nov 1986
Burial:	Salt Lake City, Salt Lake, Utah; Salt Lake City Cemetery
Name:	Emma Gedge
Birth:	30 Aug 1863 in Utah
Death:	11 Dec 1906 in St George, Washington, Utah
Burial:	15 Dec 1906 in Salt Lake City, Salt Lake, Utah; Salt Lake City Cemetery
Name:	Hannah Shepherd
Birth:	16 Dec 1810 in Pillerton, Warwick, England
Death:	01 Jan 1881 in Salt Lake City, Salt Lake, Utah
Burial:	Salt Lake City, Salt Lake, Utah; Salt Lake City Cemetery

Before You Begin

Enter burial information for all relevant individuals in the Burial fact and enter the name of the cemetery in the Description field.

Creating a Cemetery Report

1. Open the **Custom Report** (located on the Publish workspace under Person Reports) and click the **Reset** button to clear any previous settings.

2. Click the **Items to include** button in the reports toolbar and add the Burial fact to the report.

    I want the report to be sorted by cemetery name so I'll select "Burial" and "Description" from the first **Sort by** drop-down list.

Now you can choose who you want to include in the report. In this case individuals who have been buried in a designated cemetery.

3. In **Individuals to include**, click **Selected individuals**. The Filter Individuals window opens. No individuals should be included in the report at this point; if there are, click **Exclude All** to clear the report.

4. Click **Filter In**. The Filter Individuals by Criteria window opens.

5. Click **All facts**.

6. Choose "Burial" and "Description" from the **Search where** drop-down list (the field you choose depends on where you've entered the cemetery name).

7. Choose "Contains" from the next drop-down list; in the **Value** field, enter the name of the cemetery. Make sure you enter the cemetery name exactly as you've entered it in the Burial fact. Click **OK**. The Filter Individuals window now shows all the individuals who are buried in a particular cemetery.

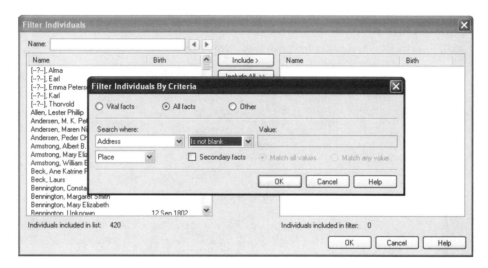

8. Click **OK** on the Filter Individuals window. The Cemetery Report opens.

Family Health Histories

In 2004, the Surgeon General's office launched the Family Health Initiative and encouraged everyone to create a family health history. This type of information can help you know what diseases you are at risk for and perhaps help you prevent illnesses that run in family lines. According to the Surgeon General, the six most useful hereditary diseases to track are (1) heart disease, (2) stroke, (3) diabetes, (4) colon cancer, (5) breast cancer, and (6) ovarian cancer.

One great resource for medical information is death certificates. A few years ago I obtained sixteen death certificates for one branch of my family. Each one listed a cause of death and many included contributing factors.

Family Tree Maker made it easy for me to record all this information and run
a quick report (fig. 6-28). If you have gathered health information about your
family members you might want to give a family health history a try.

Family Health History

Accident; auto
                Mary Elizabeth Gold
Age at death: 51
Accident; crushed by falling house
                Svend Pedersen
Accident; fall resulting in broken hip
                John W. Bobbitt
Age at death: 77
Cancer, colon
                Donal J. Reed
Age at death: 78
Cancer, stomach
                Maurine Bobbitt
Age at death: 86
Cerebral hemorrhage
                Cyrus William Gold
Age at death: 80
                Harold Arthur Reed
Age at death: 76
                Herbert Bush Gedge
Age at death: 70
                Mette Katrina Pedersen
Age at death: 88
                Phoebe Gold Gedge
Age at death: 48
                Seymour Hoyt
Age at death: 96
Consumption
                Nathan Gedge
Age at death: 31
Coronary ???
                Anna Gedge
Age at death: 80
Diptheria
                Herbert Gold Gedge
Age at death: 9
Emphysema
                Benjamin Mosiah Peterson
Age at death: 72
Heart disease, chronic valvular
                Rachel Bush
Age at death: 78
Heart disease, mitral stenosis
                Lorilla Gedge
Age at death: 54
Heart failure
                William Gedge
Age at death: 82
Influenza
                Alvin Peterson
Age at death: 25

Figure 6-28

A family health history sorted by cause of death.

Before You Begin

Enter causes of death for all the relevant individuals in the Cause of Death fact (Description field). You may also want to add the Medical Condition fact.

Creating a Family Health History

1. Open the **Custom Report** (located on the Publish workspace under Person Reports) and click the **Reset** button to clear any previous settings.

2. Click the **Items to include** button in the reports toolbar. Delete the unnecessary facts (Birth, Marriage, and Death) by selecting the fact in the **Included facts** list and clicking the **Delete fact** (**X**) button.

3. Add the Cause of Death fact to the report. (You might want to add the "Medical Condition" and "Age at Death" facts, also.)

   I want the report to be sorted by cause of death so I'll select "Cause of Death" and "Description" from the first **Sort by** drop-down list.

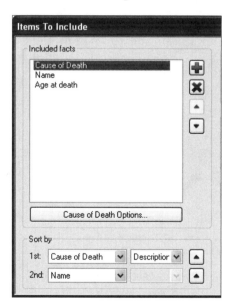

Now you can choose who you want to include in the report. In this case individuals for whom I've entered causes of death and/or medical conditions.

4. In **Individuals to include**, click **Selected individuals**. The Filter Individuals window opens. No individuals should be included in the report at this point; if there are, click **Exclude All** to clear the report.

5. Click **Filter In**. The Filter Individuals by Criteria window opens.

6. Click **All facts**, if necessary.

7. Select "Cause of Death" and "Description" from the **Search where** drop-down lists. Then select "Is not blank" from the next drop-down list and click **OK**. The Filter Individuals window now shows all the individuals who have recorded causes of death. (You may want to repeat this step to include individuals who have recorded medical conditions.)

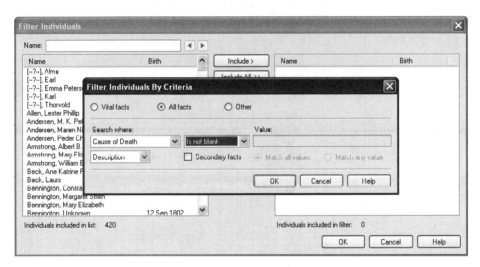

8. Click **OK** again. The health history opens.

Locations Reports

When you're tracking down records or trying to get a clear picture of all the locations where your ancestor lived, it can be helpful to create a report that lists every place you've entered for an individual (fig. 6-29). You might also want to create a report for a specific location.

Locations for Harold Arthur Reed

Beaver County, Oklahoma, USA
Reed, Harold Arthur
Marr: 18 Aug 1923

Benton County, Arkansas
Reed, Harold Arthur
Res: 1924

Boise, Ada, Idaho
Reed, Harold Arthur
Death: 21 Dec 1971

Caldwell, Canyon, Idaho
Reed, Harold Arthur
Burial: Hillcrest Memorial Gardens

Cherbourg, Manche, Basse-Normandie, France
Reed, Harold Arthur
WWI: 1918

Elk City, Washita, Oklahoma
Reed, Harold Arthur
1910: 1910

Haddam, Washington, Kansas
Reed, Harold Arthur
Birth: 02 Aug 1895
1900: 1900

Kansas
Reed, Harold Arthur
Birth: Aug 1895

Kokomo, Beaver, Oklahoma, USA
Reed, Harold Arthur
1920: 1920

Nyssa, Malheur, Oregon
Reed, Harold Arthur
Res: 1938

Santa Clara, Santa Clara, California
Reed, Harold Arthur
1930: 1930

Creating a Locations Report for an Individual

1. Open the **Place Usage Report** (located on the Publish workspace under Place Reports) and click the **Reset** button to clear any previous settings.

2. In **Individuals to include**, click **Selected individuals**. The Filter Individuals window opens. No individuals should be included in the report at this point; if there are, click **Exclude All** to clear the report.

3. Click the name of the person you want to create the report for and click **Include**.

4. Click **OK**. The report will show every location associated with an individual, including facts and dates.

Creating a Report for a Specific Location

1. Go to the Collection tab on the Publish workspace. Under Place Reports, select **Place Usage Report**.

2. Select a location in the **Places** panel.

3. Click the **Share** button beneath the main toolbar. From the drop-down list, choose **Export Place Usage Report for This Place**.

4. Click the export option you want. You can choose from PDF, CSV, RTF, HTML, and Image.

5. After you choose a format type, you may be able to choose options such as page borders and text separators. Once you've made your selections, a file management window opens.

6. Navigate to the location you want. Then enter a name for the report in the field and click **Save**.

Maternal Ancestors Report

You can create a report that includes only your maternal ancestors (your mother and her direct ancestors). This can be helpful when you are focusing on this side of your family tree. (A paternal ancestors report can be found on page 197.)

1. Open the **Custom Report** (located on the Publish workspace under Person Reports) and click the **Reset** button to clear any previous settings.

2. In **Individuals to include**, click **Selected individuals**. The Filter Individuals window opens. No individuals should be included in the report at this point; if there are, click **Exclude All** to clear the report.

3. Click your mother's name in the **Name** list and click **Ancestors**. You can choose the number of ancestral generations to include and whether or not to include all parents and spouses. In this case, I want only direct-line ancestors, so I'll include only preferred spouses and parents.

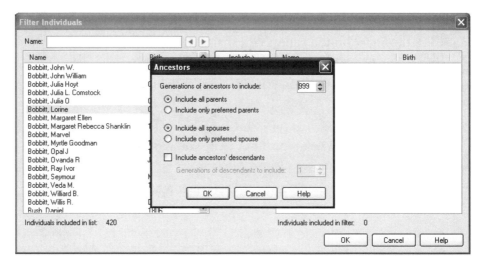

4. Choose your report options and click **OK**.

   The list will include all your maternal ancestors—male and female.

5. Click **OK**. The report opens.

Men-Only Report

If you want to focus on finding information about only your male relatives, it can be helpful to create a report that lists only the men in your family tree.

1. Open the **Custom Report** (located on the Publish workspace under Person Reports) and click the **Reset** button to clear any previous settings.

2. In **Individuals to include**, click **Selected individuals**. The Filter Individuals window opens. No individuals should be included in the report at this point; if there are, click **Exclude All** to clear the report.

3. Click **Filter In**. The Filter Individuals by Criteria window opens.

4. Click **Vital facts**.

5. Select "Sex" from the **Search where** drop-down list. Then select "Equals" from the next drop-down list and select "Male" from the **Value** drop-down list. Click **OK**. The Filter Individuals window now shows all the males in your family tree. You can filter the list further if necessary.

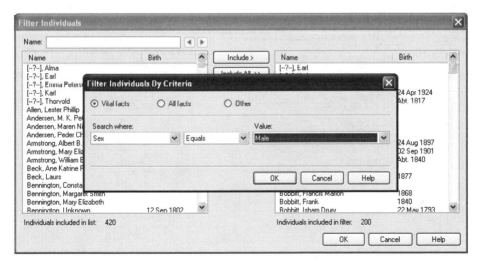

6. Click **OK**. The report opens.

Missing Date Reports

When I first started my family tree it was fairly easy to keep track of which facts I'd found and see gaping holes where I was missing information. But the deeper I went to explore my roots, the more I had a tendency to get side-tracked. The Illinois state censuses just came online? I better go look; right now. And when I found a photo of a tombstone (that no one knew existed) for my grandma's twin on Findagrave.com, you can bet I spent a few days completely ignoring my current research as I hunted through the rest of the website.

If your unexpected finds take you down a different path than the one you were on, you may not realize the blanks you have left in your family tree. Periodically I will run a few custom reports to find out what information I've neglected (fig. 6-30). The missing dates I look for most often are for births, deaths, and marriages.

Figure 6-30

A custom report showing missing birth dates.

Missing Birth Dates

Name	Birth Date	Potential Error
Albert B. Armstrong		The birth date is missing.
Ane Katrine Pedersdatter Beck		The birth date is missing.
Female Bobbitt		The birth date is missing.
Julia L. Comstock Bobbitt		The birth date is missing.
Elizabeth Jessup Bush		The birth date is missing.
Charlotte Ann Brown Lane Gedge		The birth date is missing.
Margaret A. Gardiner Gedge		The birth date is missing.
Rosa Birch Gold		The birth date is missing.
Nancy Dawson Haggard		The birth date is missing.
James Martin Hipkins		The birth date is missing.
Irvin R. Larsen		The birth date is missing.
Leonard T. Lund		The birth date is missing.
George W. Mayes		The birth date is missing.
Harrison Dean Oliver		The birth date is missing.
Svend Pedersen		The birth date is missing.
Olive A. Taylor Perry		The birth date is missing.
Clausen Peterson		The birth date is missing.
Theodor Peterson		The birth date is missing.
Permelia Bell Shanklin		The birth date is missing.
Hermon P. Shier		The birth date is missing.

Creating a Missing Birth Date Report

1. Open the **Data Errors Report** (located on the Publish workspace under Person Reports) and click the **Reset** button to clear any previous settings.

2. Click the **Errors to include** button in the reports toolbar. Then click **Exclude All**.

3. In **Person errors**, select "Birth date missing" and click **OK**.

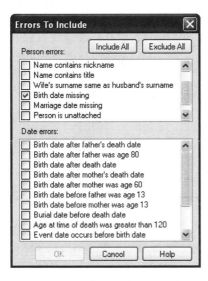

4. In **Individuals to include**, click **All individuals**. The report opens.

Creating a Missing Marriage Date Report

1. Open the **Data Errors Report** (located on the Publish workspace under Person Reports) and click the **Reset** button to clear any previous settings.

2. Click the **Errors to include** button in the reports toolbar and click **Exclude All**.

3. In **Person errors**, select "Marriage date missing" and click **OK**.

4. In **Individuals to include**, click **All individuals**. The report opens.

Creating a Missing Death Date Report

1. Open the **Custom Report** (located on the Publish workspace under Person Reports) and click the **Reset** button to clear any previous settings.

2. Click the **Items to include** button in the reports toolbar. In the **Included facts** list, delete the Birth, Marriage, and Death facts. Then click **OK**.

    Now you can choose who you want to include in the report, in this case individuals who have no death dates.

3. In **Individuals to include**, click **Selected individuals**. The Filter Individuals window opens. No individuals should be included in the report at this point; if there are, click **Exclude All** to clear the report.

4. Click **Filter In**. The Filter Individuals by Criteria window opens.

5. Click **Vital facts**, if necessary.

6. Choose "Death" and "Date" from the **Search where** drop-down lists; then choose "Is blank" from the next drop-down list and click **OK**. The Filter Individuals window shows all the individuals who do not have death dates recorded in your tree.

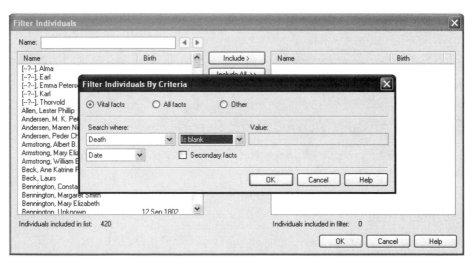

7. Click **OK**. The report opens.

Notes Report

Family Tree Maker comes with a report that lets you view and print all your research notes. If you want you can use the custom report to create a list of your person, relationship, or fact notes (fig. 6-31).

Notes

Abraham John Gold
Person Notes: Gold, Abraham John, an Elder who died while filling a foreign mission, was born Oct. 16, 1882, in Salt Lake City, Utah, the son of Cyrus H. Gold and Mary W. Willis. He was baptized Nov. 4, 1890, by Joseph Keddington and later ordained a Priest. From his earliest youth he took great interest in Church affairs and was universally known as a good boy. After attending the public schools, he entered upon a four years' business course at the L. D. S. University in Salt Lake City. He had completed about three years' study in that institution and was residing in the Cannon Ward, Salt Lake City, when he was called on a mission to the Netherlands. After being set apart for his mission Sept. 2, 1904, he left for his field of labor Sept. 10, 1904, and was, on his arrival in Holland, Oct. 2, 1904, appointed to labor in the Arnhem conference. In February, 1906, his field of labor was changed to Groningen. At that place he was zealously engaged in missionary work, when it fell to his lot to wait on a fellow missionary (Hugh W. Welker), who suffered with black small-pox, and while engaged in this benevolent work, he, himself, was attacked by a malignant form of that dreadful disease. which terminated his life at Groningen, Holland, May 14, 1906. He was buried at the cemetery at Groningen, by the side of Hugh M. Welker, who had died with small-pox two weeks previously. Both graves are inclosed with an iron fence and the ground is owned and taken care of by the Church. A monument is erected on the graves. Elder Gold had required the Dutch language to a high degree of perfection and was a very efficient and energetic missionary.

David Haggard
Relationship Notes: Sureties and witnesses are wedding are David Haggard, Martin Dawson, and Cary M. Carter.

Joseph Gold
Person Notes: From the personal history of Cyrus Henry Gold (Joseph's son). "My father, Joseph Gold, was what was termed a jobbing mason doing all kinds of repair work about buildings and factories. I went with him often. I would carry bricks or mortar or anything he might need in his work."

Leah Gedge
Person Notes: When Leah was barely three years old, her parents left England to travel to the United States. They joined the Homer Duncan Company in Nebraska and headed to Utah. She died enroute somewhere in Wyoming. Her death was followed by the death of her twin sisters who were born on the trail.

Pierce Perry
Person Notes: According to the biography of Pierce's son James, Pierce Perry was 53 when he died and was a life long member of the Baptist church. [Look for Baptist church records in Marshall County, Illinois, and Scott County, Kentucky. They might have birth records for the children.] The biography also states that he was married twice; by first marriage had four sons [this would be with Charity Lucas]; second marriage had ten children, four boys and six girls [this would be with Mary Lucas]. This doesn't make sense because most of the children were born long before he was married to Mary when Charity was still alive. I think the biography assigned the children backwards. At this point, I have connected six girls and two boys to the Pierce Perry/Charity Lucas marriage. This seems to point to the biography being wrong.

Theodor Peterson
Person Notes: In 1924 Oliver Pedersen visited his grandmother in Denmark. He recorded in his journal that he met his cousin Theodor and his wife and two children. He doesn't mention the name of the wife or son (a boy who is 19 at the time of the visit 1924), but he does mention the name of Theodor's daughter, Remore (who is 17 at the time of the visit 1924). I wonder if he named his daughter Remore after this girl or if it is coincidence.

Figure 6-31

A custom report showing relationship and person notes.

1. Open the **Custom Report** (located on the Publish workspace under Person Reports) and click the **Reset** button to clear any previous settings.

2. Click the **Items to include** button in the reports toolbar. Select the person notes, relationship notes, and/or fact notes checkboxes. Then click **OK**.

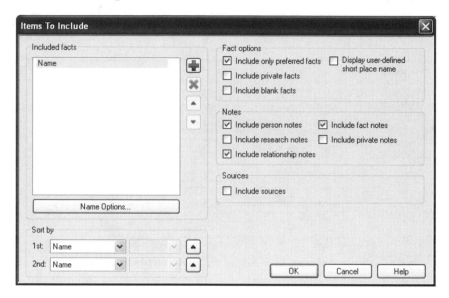

Now you can choose who you want to include in the report. In this case individuals who have notes.

3. In **Individuals to include**, click **Selected individuals**. The Filter Individuals window opens. No individuals should be included in the report at this point; if there are, click **Exclude All** to clear the report.

4. Click **Filter In**. The Filter Individuals by Criteria window opens.

5. Click **Other**.

6. Select "Any People/Fact Notes" from the **Search where** drop-down list. Then select "Exists" from the next drop-down list and click **OK**. The Filter Individuals window now shows all individuals with notes in your database. You can filter the list further if necessary.

7. Click **OK**. The report opens.

Paternal Ancestors Report

You can create a report that includes only your paternal ancestors (your father and his direct ancestors). This can be helpful when you are focusing on this side of your family tree. (A maternal ancestors report can be found on page 190.)

1. Open the **Custom Report** (located on the Publish workspace under Person Reports) and click the **Reset** button to clear any previous settings.

2. In **Individuals to include**, click **Selected individuals**. The Filter Individuals window opens. No individuals should be included in the report at this point; if there are, click **Exclude All** to clear the report.

3. Click your father's name in the **Name** list and click **Ancestors**. You can choose the number of ancestral generations to include and whether or not to include all parents and spouses. In this case, I want only direct-line ancestors, so I'll include only preferred spouses and parents.

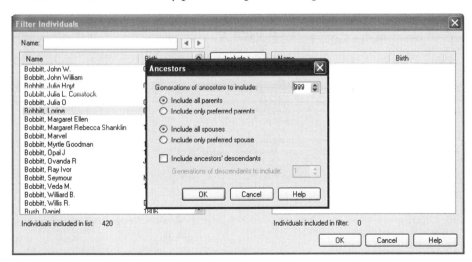

4. Choose your report options and click **OK**.

   The list will include all your paternal ancestors—male and female.

5. Click **OK**. The report opens.

Surname Report of Individuals

Family Tree Maker includes a Surname Report that lets you see the total number of individuals with a specific surname. I like to create my own custom report that lists all the individuals with a specific surname (fig. 6-32). I use it as a checklist to keep track of which individuals I've searched for in a specific index, database, or book. This report can also be useful if you're focusing on one branch of your family.

Figure 6-32

A report listing everyone with the same surname.

Bobbitts

Alta Maud Bobbitt
Birth: 09 Feb 1892 in Kansas, USA
Death: 04 Nov 1987 in Cherokee, Alfalfa, Oklahoma, USA

Arthur Leroy Bobbitt
Birth: 24 Aug 1897
Death: 05 Jun 1993

Bessie Anita Bobbitt
Birth: 14 Dec 1888 in Nebraska, USA
Marriage: 21 Feb 1910 in Carrier, Garfield, Oklahoma, USA
Death: 18 Jan 1978

Celia (Bobbitt)
Birth: 1848 in Pennsylvania, USA

Charity Bobbitt
Birth: 10 Mar 1883 in Nebraska, USA
Death: May 1982

Clara (Bobbitt)
Birth: Feb 1851 in Illinois, USA

Clyde S. Bobbitt
Birth: 02 Sep 1901
Marriage: Never Married
Death: 11 May 1902

Cornelia O. Bobbitt
Birth: Mar 1857 in Illinois, USA
Marriage: 02 Feb 1873 in Varna, Marshall, Illinois, USA

Daisy E Bobbitt
Birth: Sep 1887 in Nebraska, USA

David Bobbitt
Birth: Abt. 1840
Death: Aft. 1885

Edgar A. Bobbitt

1. Open the **Custom Report** (located on the Publish workspace under Person Reports) and click the **Reset** button to clear any previous settings.

2. In **Individuals to include**, click **Selected individuals**. The Filter Individuals window opens. No individuals should be included in the report at this point; if there are, click **Exclude All** to clear the report.

3. Click **Filter In**. The Filter Individuals by Criteria window opens.

4. Click **Vital facts**.

5. Select "Name" from the **Search where** drop-down list. Then select "Contains" from the next drop-down list. In **Value**, enter a surname and click **OK**. The Filter Individuals window now shows all the individuals with the same surname. You can filter the list further if necessary.

6. Click **OK**. The report opens.

Women-Only Report

If you want to focus on finding information about only your female relatives, it can be helpful to create a report that lists only the women in your family tree.

1. Open the **Custom Report** (located on the Publish workspace under Person Reports) and click the **Reset** button to clear any previous settings.

2. In **Individuals to include**, click **Selected individuals**. The Filter Individuals window opens. No individuals should be included in the report at this point; if there are, click **Exclude All** to clear the report.

3. Click **Filter In**. The Filter Individuals by Criteria window opens.

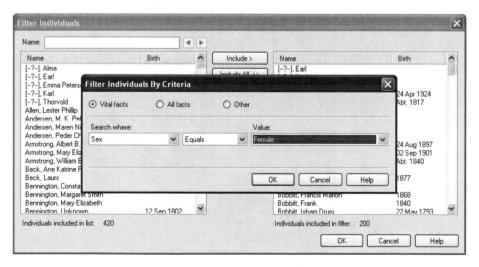

4. Click **Vital facts**.

5. Select "Sex" from the **Search where** drop-down list. Then select "Equals" from the next drop-down list and select "Female" from the **Value** drop-down list. Click **OK**. The Filter Individuals window now shows all the females in your family tree. You can filter the list further if necessary.

6. Click **OK**. The report opens.

Unlinked Media Items Report

I have a tendency to add photos to my tree in large groups, and it's easy to forget to link each of them to a fact or person. Occasionally I will run a report to see which media items in my tree aren't attached to individuals or sources (fig. 6-33). I can then link the media items to the appropriate individuals or delete them.

Figure 6-33

A report showing unlinked media items.

Unlinked Media Items

1870 U.S. Census - Catharine Reed Family
File Location: C:\Documents and Settings\tlord\My Documents\Family Tree Maker\TLP_Reed_Pedersen Media\10031712511484.jpg
[not linked to people, facts, or sources]

Baby Bonnets
File Location: C:\Documents and Settings\tlord\My Documents\Family Tree Maker\TLP_Reed_Pedersen Media\bonnets.jpg
[not linked to people, facts, or sources]

Bobbitt Siblings
File Location: C:\Documents and Settings\tlord\My Documents\Family Tree Maker\TLP_Reed_Pedersen Media\BOBBITTsiblings.bmp
[not linked to people, facts, or sources]

Copenhagen, Denmark in 1890
File Location: C:\Documents and Settings\tlord\My Documents\Family Tree Maker\TLP_Reed_Pedersen Media\Copenhagen_1890.jpg
[not linked to people, facts, or sources]

Cyrus Henry Gold
File Location: C:\Documents and Settings\tlord\My Documents\Family Tree Maker\TLP_Reed_Pedersen Media\cyrus_henry_gold_resized.jpg
[not linked to people, facts, or sources]

Cyrus Henry Gold
File Location: C:\Documents and Settings\tlord\My Documents\Family Tree Maker\TLP_Reed_Pedersen Media\CyrusHenryGOLD_older.jpg
[not linked to people, facts, or sources]

Cyrus Henry Gold Immigration
File Location: C:\Documents and Settings\tlord\My Documents\Family Tree Maker\TLP_Reed_Pedersen Media\cyrusgold_newspaperemigrationpaid.pdf
[not linked to people, facts, or sources]

CyrusBirth.tiff
File Location: C:\Documents and Settings\tlord\My Documents\Family Tree

1. Open the **Media Usage Report** (located on the Publish workspace under Media Reports) and click the **Reset** button to clear any previous settings.

2. Deselect all options except "Show unlinked media." The report opens.

Unrelated Individuals Report

During your family research, you may have added individuals to your tree without linking them to anyone. Because these people don't appear in charts and can be navigated to only in the Index and Index of Individuals, they are easy to forget about. You might want to run an Unrelated Individuals Report periodically to remind yourself of just who is in your tree (fig. 6-34).

Unrelated Individuals

Name	Birth Date	Potential Error
Maurice Desormier dit Cusson		This individual has no parents, no children, and no spouses.
Anna Gedge	Abt. 1865	This individual has no parents, no children, and no spouses.
George Gedge	Abt. 1825	This individual has no parents, no children, and no spouses.
Eva B Shepard	Jan 1890	This individual has no parents, no children, and no spouses.

Figure 6-34

A report showing unrelated individuals.

1. Open the **Data Errors Report** (located on the Publish workspace under Person Reports) and click the **Reset** button to clear any previous settings.

2. Click the **Errors to include** button in the reports toolbar and click **Exclude All**.

3. In **Person errors**, select "Person is unattached" and click **OK**.

4. In **Individuals to include**, click **All individuals**. The report opens.

Exporting Reports

You may want to save a report to a file format compatible with software other than Family Tree Maker; for example, a spreadsheet or word-processing program. These files can be easily shared with others, posted on a website, or have additional facts and data added to them.

Exporting a Report

1. Access the report you want to save.

2. Click the **Share** button above the editing panel. From the drop-down list, choose one of these options: Export to PDF, Export to CSV, Export to RTF, Export to HTML.

3. Change the format options (such as page borders and text separators) as necessary. A file management window opens.

4. Navigate to the location you want. Then enter a name for the report in the field and click **Save**.

Exporting as a PDF

If you want to share a report with a friend or family member, exporting it as a PDF is your best option. Adobe PDF (Portable Document Format) is useful because it keeps the formatting you select—the report will look exactly as you see it on your monitor. You cannot make changes to the PDF within Family Tree Maker, and you need the Adobe Reader in order to view it. When you export a report as a PDF, you can change these options:

- **Page range.** You can choose which pages you want to export.

- **Don't embed these fonts.** All fonts used in the report are automatically embedded in the PDF. If you want, you can enter a font name to prevent it from being embedded. In general, you should embed all fonts so the report's formatting isn't changed.

- **Images quality.** If you want to reduce the size of the PDF, choose medium or low quality images.

- **Compression.** This option will try to reduce the file size of the report without compromising the quality.

Exporting as a Text File

You can export a report as an RTF text file, which can be opened in almost any word-processing application. I like to use this option because RTF keeps the text formatting but allows me to edit the content of the report. I can add missing information, delete redundancies, take out private facts or simply update facts without needing to recreate the entire report. Figure 6-35 shows how I have modified a timeline that was exported as an RTF.

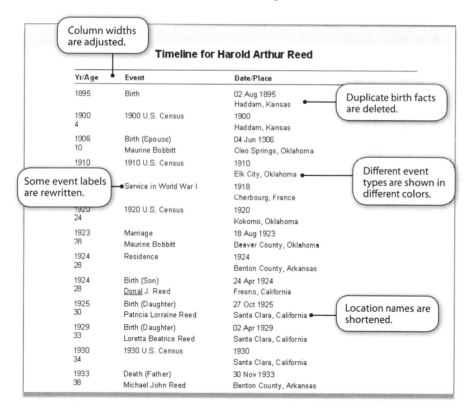

Figure 6-35

A timeline that has been exported to RTF and modified.

Exporting to a Spreadsheet

You can export a report as a CSV (comma-separated values) file, a format that organizes information into fields. CSV files can be imported into a spreadsheet program, which lets you examine your report data in new ways. For example, the Surname Report in Family Tree Maker can only be sorted alphabetically or by surname count. If you export the report to a spreadsheet program, you can also sort the report by date and gender (fig. 6-36).

Figure 6-36

A Surname Report in a spreadsheet program. The report is sorted by gender.

	Surname	Count	Male	Female	Earliest	Most recent
1	Surname	Count	Male	Female	Earliest	Most recent
2	Totals:	408	198	207		
3	Bobbitt	42	17	25	1793	1909
4	Hoyt	34	18	16	1740	1861
5	Gedge	31	16	15	1796	1914
6	Gold	31	16	15	1825	1908
7	Haggard	25	14	11	1678	1813
8	Reed	24	15	9	1774	1938
9	Spencer	15	6	9	1864	1924
10	Perry	10	3	7	1800	1845
11	Pedersen	16	10	5	1821	1973
12	Bush	7	3	4	1806	1839
13	Peterson	10	6	4	1888	1905
14	Shanklin	7	3	4	1810	1866
15	Bennington	5	1	3	1802	1812
16	Dawson	5	2	3	1764	1764
17	Loudon	6	3	3	1867	1915
18	Shepherd	3	0	3	1810	1918
19	Shier	5	2	3		
20	Thompson	7	4	3	1796	1835
21	VanNoy	7	4	3	1873	1928
22	Bell	2	0	2		
23	Eddins	5	3	2	1925	1925
24	Ford	4	2	2	1886	1918
25	Gentry	3	1	2	1731	1731
26	Hewitt	4	2	2	1833	1865
27	Lucas	3	1	2	1807	1808

Although you can export any report as a CSV file, this format is most useful for statistical reports that use columns, such as the Marriage Report, Parentage Report, and Kinship Report. When you export to a CSV file, the report will not include any images or formatting.

Exporting to the Web

You can export a report to HyperText Markup Language (HTML), the standard language used when creating and formatting Web pages. HTML files can be opened in any Internet browser and are a great way to share information on a personal or family website. When you export to HTML, the report will include all the images and formatting you've chosen. You can also change these options:

- **Export mode.** You can format pages in a single file (regardless of the number of pages in the original report, the HTML report will be one continuous page); page-by-page (each page in the report is separate but they are all contained within one HTML file); and different files (each page in the report is saved as a separate HTML file).

- **Page range.** You can choose which pages you want to export.

- **Borders.** You can determine the size and color of the report's border. Choose "Transparent" if you don't want a border.

Chapter Seven
Preserving Your History

For many family historians the ultimate goal—and reward—is to publish a record of their ancestry. And what could be more convenient than using the same software to organize your family history and create a book to tell your ancestral story? Family Tree Maker gives you the power to combine your choice of printouts—from ancestor trees, kinship reports, and genealogy reports to photo albums, timelines, and more—into one continuous document. Family Tree Maker can even generate a table of contents and index for you.

When your book is complete, you can export it as a PDF and share it with family and friends through e-mail or by posting it on a website. Or, you can print it, bind it, and create a unique gift for your family to cherish for generations to come.

Selecting a Book Style

You want to capture your ancestry in a book. But how do you get started? Before you grab a pen and paper or your keyboard, there are a few questions you might want to ask yourself that will simplify the process.

Desktop Book-Building or MyCanvas?

Family Tree Maker includes a desktop book-building tool integrated into the software and gives you access to an online self-publishing service called MyCanvas. Before starting your family history book, you should decide which tool is best for the type of book you're creating. Here's a side-by-side comparison of their features:

- **Text.** The desktop tool handles text like any word processing program. You can choose fonts and formatting, change spacing and margins, and flow text from page to page. MyCanvas also lets you add and format text; however, you cannot flow text from page to page and your font choices are limited.

- **Images.** Both tools let you add photos and record images. However, MyCanvas has photo-editing capabilities so you can crop and resize images, rotate pictures on a page, and even add finishing touches like drop-shadows and borders.

- **Charts and reports.** MyCanvas can generate standard pedigree charts, descendant charts, and timelines. The desktop tool lets you include every chart and report available in Family Tree Maker.

- **Print options.** The desktop tool allows you to print your book on a home printer or export it as a PDF, which you can take to a copy shop to be professionally printed and bound. MyCanvas also allows you to print your book pages at home; however, the quality of the printout will be low. For a fee MyCanvas will professionally print and bind your book and send it to you.

- **Book size.** The desktop tool lets you choose a landscape or portrait layout, and you can include as many pages as you'd like. MyCanvas books are available in 8" x 8", 14" x 11", and 11" x 8 1/2". And while you can include as many pages as you'd like, you'll pay an additional fee for a book with more than twenty pages.

- **Accessibility.** MyCanvas books are stored online so you can work on your project anywhere you have a computer and an Internet connection. You can also allow others to access your book and add their own stories. A book created in Family Tree Maker can only be worked on in the software. However, if you have gathered all the records, photos, and text files you need on your computer, you don't have to worry about uploading these to an online site.

- What type of book do you want to create? A biography? Autobiography? A standard family history? A scrapbook? As you're sorting through material to use, knowing what the final product will be can help you weed out irrelevant information and images.

- Who is your audience? For example, if you're creating a book to be submitted to a local genealogical society, you'll need to plan on including a variety of reports and numerous sources. However, if your book is for your grandchildren, you might want to fill your pages with photos and personal stories.

- Who is your book about? A book that mentions every individual in your tree could be overwhelming for a reader—and take forever to create, depending on the size of your tree. You may want to focus on a specific family line or a certain number of generations.

- What will you do with the book when you're done? If you're planning on having the book printed and bound at a copy shop or publishing company, start looking now to find the company that best fits your needs.

If you're looking for advice on writing your family history, I've found these two books to be helpful: Patricia Law Hatcher's *Producing a Quality Family History* and *Writing Up Your Family History: A Do-It-Yourself Guide* by John Titford.

Preparing Your Tree

Perhaps the best thing you can do to give your book a good start is to make sure that your Family Tree Maker tree is as complete and accurate as possible. Remember, in a book, your research will likely be scrutinized by others. Before I started my book, I took some time to go through my tree with a critical eye and evaluate my information. Here are some steps I took to get my tree in order:

- Review sources. Are facts documented and sourced? Have I checked for inaccurate dates and spelling errors?

- Be consistent when entering data. Are individuals' names spelled the same throughout the tree? Are counties and countries entered for locations (where known)?

- Run the Data Errors report. This showed me which facts had been left blank, and where I had duplicate individuals, inaccurate dates, etc. (for more information, see page 169).

- Identify media items. I made sure any photos and records I was including in the book contained captions, dates, and descriptions.

- Gather additional photos, records, and images. I discovered several photos I hadn't included in my tree but wanted to use in my book. Make sure you scan any photos or records you want to include in the book if you haven't already.

- Create customized reports or charts and save them. Although you can create a chart or report within a book, I saved time by making a list of all the reports I wanted to use and created them beforehand. I also decided to create a custom template for charts so that regardless of the type of chart, they would all have the same boxes, borders, and fonts.

Note: To learn more about how you can make your tree more accurate and error-free, see the Tree Maintenance workflow on page 250.

> **TIP**
> As you sketch out your book, you may want to take advantage of the organizational tool built into Family Tree Maker—the To-Do list. You can use it to detail the research you have left to do, set deadlines for tasks, and track your progress.

Building a Book

You're an expert on your family. You've spent years entering facts, gathering photos, and analyzing records, but you probably haven't given much thought to the actual pieces that go into creating a book. As you get ready to put it all together, consider adding some of these elements to make your family history book more complete and professional.

- **Title page.** A title page is automatically created for your book in Family Tree Maker. However, you might want to add a subtitle, edition number, author names, or images to it (fig. 7-1).

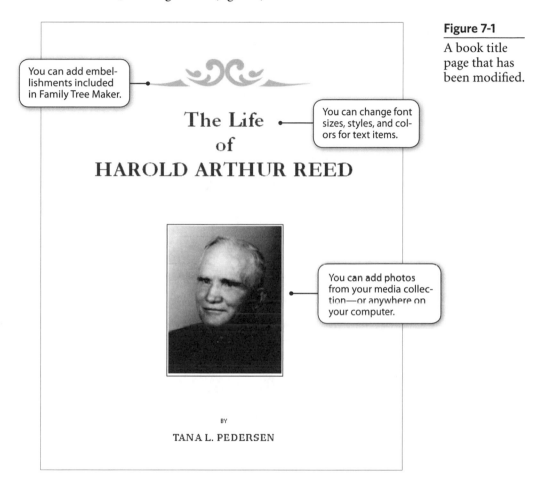

Figure 7-1

A book title page that has been modified.

- **Copyright.** Although you do not have to include a copyright notice in order to be protected from unauthorized usage, you should consider adding this information, especially if you want to submit your book to a library, society, or association.

- **Dedication or Acknowledgments.** A dedication is usually a short inscription dedicating the book to an individual or group. If you have many people who have contributed to your book, you can create an acknowledgments page to thank them.

- **Table of Contents.** In any book, a table of contents is an essential element that helps your readers quickly locate the items they're interested in. Family Tree Maker can automatically generate a table of contents for you (fig. 7-2).

Figure 7-2

A table of contents that has been generated automatically.

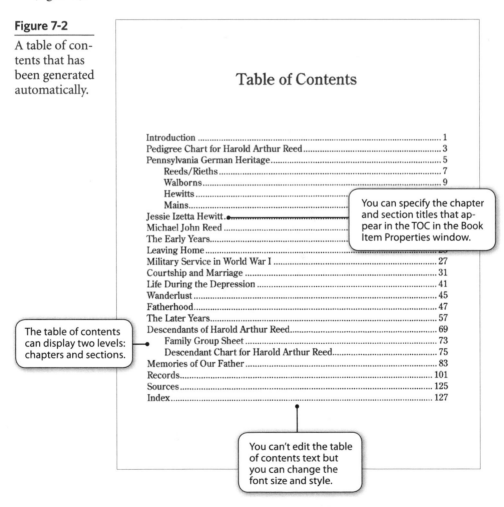

Table of Contents

You can specify the chapter and section titles that appear in the TOC in the Book Item Properties window.

The table of contents can display two levels: chapters and sections.

You can't edit the table of contents text but you can change the font size and style.

- **List of Illustrations.** If you are including photos and records that you want people to be able to find easily, you might want to include a list of their captions and the pages they're located on.

- **Preface.** A preface contains information about you, the author, such as your research methods or your reasons for writing the book.

- **Introduction.** An introduction explains what readers will find in the book and why you've included—and excluded—specific content.

- **Contents.** The contents of your book can include charts, reports, Smart Stories™, timelines (fig. 7-3), photos, record images, and more.

Figure 7-3

A timeline created with Smart Stories™.

TIMELINE

02 Aug 1895	Harold Arthur Reed is born in Haddam, Kansas.
31 Mar 1901	Sister Cora Evelyn Reed is born in Haddam, Kansas.
17 Sep 1903	The Wright Brothers fly the world's first airplane.
04 Jun 1906	Maurine Bobbitt is born in Cleo Springs, Oklahoma.
27 Sep 1908	The Ford Model-T is mass-produced.
1910	The Reed family moves to Elk City, Oklahoma.
1910	Harold leaves home at age 15 to work in the oil fields in California.
28 Jun 1914	World War I begins.
1918	Harold is drafted into the Army and serves as a courier in France.
1920	The Reed family moves to Kokomo, Oklahoma; Harold meets Maurine.
18 Aug 1923	Harold marries Maurine Bobbitt in Beaver County, Oklahoma.
1924	Harold and Maurine move to California looking for work.
24 Apr 1924	Son Donal J. Reed is born in Riverdale, California.
27 Oct 1925	Daughter Patricia Lorraine Reed is born in Santa Clara, California.
02 Apr 1929	Daughter Loretta Beatrice Reed is born in Santa Clara, California.
02 Jun 1929	Father-in-law James C. Bobbitt dies in Balko, Oklahoma.
Oct 1929	The stock market crashes, causing the Great Depression.
1930	Harold works as a farm hand in Oklahoma and Arkansas.
30 Nov 1933	Father Michael John Reed dies in Benton County, Arkansas.
27 Jul 1927	Sister Lela Mae Reed dies in California.
04 Nov 1936	Mother Jessie Izetta Hewitt dies in Balko, Oklahoma.

- **Index.** An index of individuals is automatically created for your book in Family Tree Maker. It lists the names of every individual included in a chart or report and the page numbers where they appear.

Adding Finishing Touches

Your family history book is probably made up of various pieces: ancestor and descendant charts, genealogy reports, imported stories, timelines, photos, and more. After you've added the book's content, you may want to take some time to pull together all the items into a cohesive unit. This section explains how you can organize your book using chapters and page breaks, set up headers and footers, and change margins to give your book a uniform look and feel.

Setting Up Chapters

If your book is very long, you'll want to divide the material into chapters so it is easier to read.

Starting a New Chapter

1. In the book outline select the text item you want to designate as a chapter.

2. Click the **Book Item Properties** button in the book outline toolbar. The Item Properties window opens.

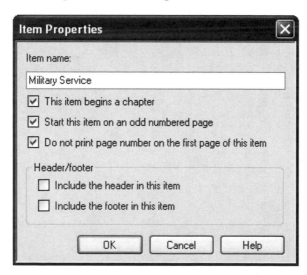

3. Enter a title for the chapter in the **Item name** field. This is the title that will appear in the book's table of contents and can be included in the chapter's headers and footers.

4. Select the **This item begins a chapter** checkbox.

5. Select the **Start this item on an odd numbered page** checkbox if you want this chapter to open on a right-facing page—the customary page for a chapter to begin on. When this option is selected, Family Tree Maker adds blank pages where necessary to make sure the chapter starts on the correct page. These blank pages are not visible in the text editor; you can view them by clicking the **Preview Book** button.

    Note: You might not want to use this option if you're concerned that your book is too long or you're worried about wasting paper.

6. Select the **Do not print page number on the first page of this item** checkbox to prevent a page number from appearing on the chapter's first page—chapter openers typically do not include page numbers.

    Note: Page numbers appear only if you've included them in the book's headers or footers.

Adding Multiple Items to a Chapter

Each chapter can be composed of multiple text items, charts, and/or reports; it's up to you (fig. 7-4). To add a new section to a chapter, add the item to the book outline, then drag it underneath the chapter. In the book outline toolbar, click the **Book Item Properties** button. Then, make sure the **This item begins a chapter** checkbox is *not* selected.

Figure 7-4

This book outline shows a chapter that includes five text items.

Adding Page Breaks

Your readers may find it easier to look at a chart or photocopy an image in your book if the back side of the page is left blank. To do this, select the item in the book outline. Then click the **Book Item Properties** button. Select the **Start this item on an odd numbered page** checkbox. Now, select the following item in the book outline. Click the **Book Item Properties** button and select the **Start this item on an odd numbered page** checkbox.

Setting Up Headers and Footers

Headers and footers are small lines of text at the top and bottom of a page in a book; they help a reader understand where they are within the document. You can choose what information appears in your book's headers and footers (for example, page numbers or chapter titles). Even though you select a header/footer format for an entire book, you can still determine whether specific chapters or sections display them. For example, you may not want to include a header on charts or reports.

> Note: The text editor does not show the changes you make to headers and footers. To see how headers and footers will appear in the book when it's printed, click the Preview Book button.

Setting Up Headers and Footers for a Book

1. Click the **Book Properties** button in the book outline toolbar.

2. Choose a header type from the drop-down list. (Headers are typically the title of a book or chapter, but you can choose to have no header, or a combination of the book title, chapter name, and page number.)

3. Choose a footer type from the drop-down list. (Footers are typically page numbers, but you can choose to have no footer, or a combination of the book title, chapter name, and page number.)

    > Note: If you choose "Book title, chapter name" be aware that if the title and chapter name are both long, some text may be cut off.

Changing Headers and Footers for a Text Item

You can determine whether or not a header and/or footer appears on a specific Text Item. Select the Text Item in the book outline. Then click the **Book Item Properties** button in the book outline toolbar. To hide a header or footer, select/deselect the **Include the header in this item** and **Include the footer in this item** checkboxes.

Changing Footers for a Chart

Family Tree Maker charts have "built-in" footers. When you include a chart in a book, you need to decide whether you want to use these chart-defined footers or the footers that you can change within the book; otherwise you'll have two footers (fig. 7-5). In my book I used the book-defined footers so that my charts would be paginated with the rest of the chapter.

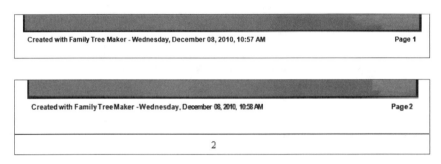

Created with Family Tree Maker - Wednesday, December 08, 2010, 10:57 AM   Page 1

Created with Family Tree Maker - Wednesday, December 08, 2010, 10:58 AM   Page 2

2

Figure 7-5

Chart footers. *Above*, a chart-defined footer; *below*, a chart-defined footer and a book-defined footer.

Changing Headers and Footers for a Report

Family Tree Maker reports have "built-in" headers (the title of the report) and footers. When you include a report in a book, you need to decide whether you want to use these chart-defined headers and footers or the ones that you can change within the book; otherwise you'll have two headers and footers (fig. 7-6).

The Life of Harold Arthur Reed: Introduction
Individual Report for Harold Arthur Reed

Individual Summary: Harold Arthur Reed	
Sex: Male	
Father: Michael John Reed	
Mother: Jessie Izetta Hewitt	

Figure 7-6

Report headers. A report with a chart-defined header and a book-defined header.

In my book I used the book-defined footers so that my charts would be paginated with the rest of the chapter and used the chart-defined headers so the title of the report was included at the top of every report page.

Changing Page Margins

Margins determine how much white space appears on the edges of a page. Unfortunately Family Tree Maker doesn't have one tool that lets you change the margins for an entire book at once. If you want your book to have uniform margins, you'll have to update the margins for each text item, chart, and report separately.

Note: If the book includes headers and footers, make sure margins at the top and bottom of the page have enough room to properly display the text.

> **TIP**
> If you plan on having your book bound, make sure you add an extra ⅛ to ¼ of an inch to the margin on the edge where the book will be bound.

Changing Margins for a Text Item

Select the Text Item in the book outline. In the text editor choose **File>Page Setup**. On the Margins and Paper tab, click the **Margins** up and down arrows to change the margin size. Then click **OK**.

Note: You cannot change the margins for the automatically generated index or table of contents.

Changing Margins for a Chart or Report

Select the chart or report in the book outline. In the chart/report editing toolbar, click the **Page Setup** button. Enter the margin size you want in the appropriate fields and click **OK**.

Previewing and Printing

Before you print a book—at home or at a copy shop—you should preview the document to make sure it looks the way you want it. I like to look for (1) punctuation, grammar, and spelling mistakes, (2) information that is private or concerns living individuals that I need to strip out, and (3) formatting problems such as missing headers/footers and unexpected blank pages. You might also want a friend or family member to look over the document before you call it complete.

To preview a book, click the **Preview Button** underneath the book outline. The Preview window opens (fig. 7-7).

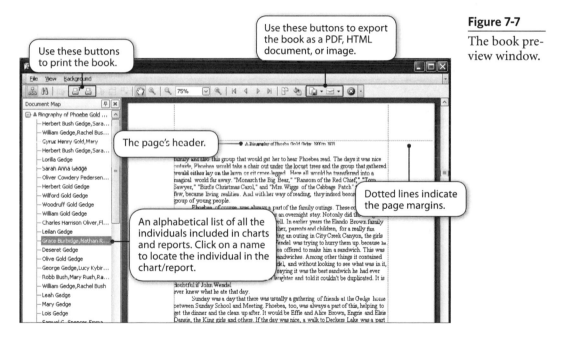

Figure 7-7

The book preview window.

Chapter Eight

Making the Software Work for You

It's easy to get in the habit of opening Family Tree Maker, entering data, and closing the application without really thinking. But if you take a few minutes to customize the workspace or tweak settings that are compatible with how you work, you'll find that you're recording the information that you're interested in, and you're spending less time doing it.

Changing the Workspace Layout

Each workspace has a default layout that shows all the features and options that are available in this area. Depending on what you're trying to do, you may want to display one area of a workspace more than the others. In this task, you'll learn how to rearrange the People workspace, but the process is the same for all workspaces.

The People workspace has four different sections: the Index, the pedigree view, the family group view, and the editing panel. You can resize or hide each section to make room for whatever task you're working on (see fig. 8-1 on the following page).

To hide a panel, simply click the small arrow next to it; click the arrow again to show the panel. To resize a panel, move the pointer to the edge of the panel until you see the resize cursor (two arrows with a line between) and drag the panel until it's the size you want. Figure 8-2 shows the People workspace with the family group view hidden and a smaller Index panel.

To return a panel to its default size and location, place your pointer at the edge of a panel and double-click the mouse.

Figure 8-1

The default layout of the People workspace.

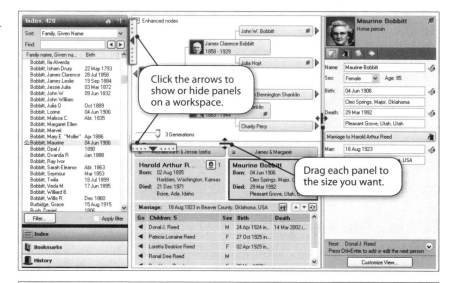

Figure 8-2

The People workspace with the family group view hidden; the index has also been resized.

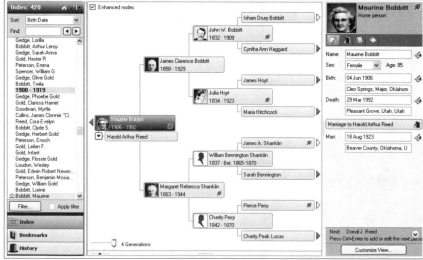

Setting the Default Display of the Editing Panel

The editing panel on the Family tab (fig. 8-3) is where you enter basic information about an individual, such as birth and death dates and places. By default, the editing panel on the Family tab in the People workspace displays these fields: Name, Sex, Birth Date, Birth Place, Death Date, Death Place, Marriage Date, and Marriage Place. You can customize this panel to display the facts you enter most often. For example, if you often enter burial or christening dates, you can add these facts to the editing panel so you can enter the information more easily.

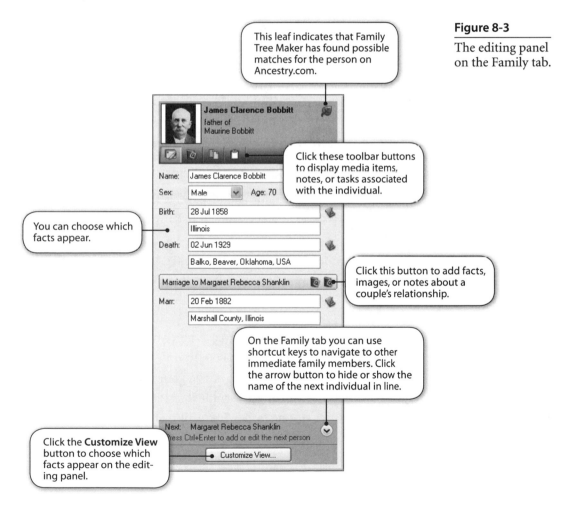

This leaf indicates that Family Tree Maker has found possible matches for the person on Ancestry.com.

Figure 8-3

The editing panel on the Family tab.

Click these toolbar buttons to display media items, notes, or tasks associated with the individual.

You can choose which facts appear.

Click this button to add facts, images, or notes about a couple's relationship.

On the Family tab you can use shortcut keys to navigate to other immediate family members. Click the arrow button to hide or show the name of the next individual in line.

Click the **Customize View** button to choose which facts appear on the editing panel.

1. Go to the Family tab on the People workspace and click **Customize View**. The Customize View window opens.

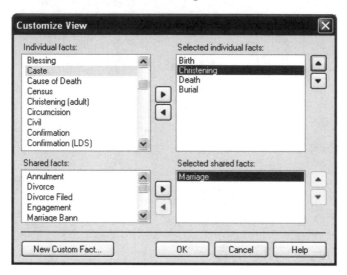

2. In the Individual facts section or the Shared facts section, select the fact you'd like to add to the editing panel; then click the right arrow button to add the fact to a Selected facts section.

3. To change the order in which the fields will display on the panel, select a fact in a Selected facts section and click the up or down arrows on the right side of the window.

4. Click **OK**. The editing panel now includes the selected fields.

Managing Facts

Facts are the essential building blocks of your tree, where you record the details about your family that are important to you. In order to capture the information you care about, you might want to create your own facts. And if you need to make comprehensive changes to your tree, don't worry; you won't have to face the tedium of editing facts person-by-person, Family Tree Maker lets you change facts as a group.

Creating a Custom Fact

Family Tree Maker has a variety of default facts you use when entering information about your family. However, some of the details you might gather don't fit into these defined categories. You could enter this information into a person note for the individual. But before you do, consider making a custom fact. When you add information to an individual as a fact rather than a note, you can assign dates and places and attach sources, and you can include the fact in reports and charts.

I have created several custom facts that I have used for my family. Here are a few suggestions for custom facts you might want to add to your trees:

- Cemetery
- Civil Union
- Clubs and Associations
- Died as Infant
- Godparent
- Hobbies
- Never Had Children

- Number of Children
- Obituary
- Migration
- Moved
- Political Office
- Witness
- Wars

You might also want to create a fact for each specific census year or for specific wars (such as the Civil War, American Revolution, or Korean War). And if you can't remember which facts you've created and which facts came by default, go to the Manage Facts window and select a fact. The software displays the fact labels and whether or not the fact is custom or predefined (fig. 8-4).

Figure 8-4

The "fact type" field shows that the selected fact is a custom fact.

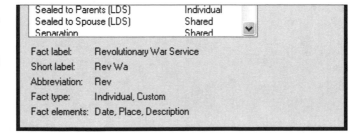

1. Choose **Edit>Manage Facts**. The Manage Facts window opens.

2. Click **New**. The Add Custom Fact window opens.

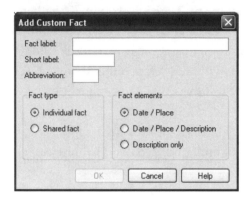

3. Enter information for the fact as necessary:

   • **Fact label.** Enter a name for the fact. This is the name that will appear on the Person tab and in charts and reports.

   • **Short label.** Enter a short name for the fact. This is the label that will appear on the Family tab editing panel; you can enter up to six characters.

   • **Abbreviation.** Enter an abbreviation for the fact. This is the abbreviation that will appear in reports; you can enter up to three characters.

   • **Fact type.** Choose **Individual fact** if the fact applies to only one person, such as birth or death. Choose **Shared fact** if the fact applies to more than one individual, such as marriage or divorce.

   • **Fact elements.** Choose the fields that you want to appear for the fact: Date and Place; Date, Place, and Description; or Description only. For a Cause of Death fact you might want only the Description field; for a Civil War fact you would probably want to use all three fields.

4. Click **OK**.

Deleting a Custom Fact

Although you can't delete the predefined facts included in Family Tree Maker, you can delete any custom facts you've created (or facts that have been imported into your tree).

1. Choose **Edit>Manage Facts**. The Manage Facts window opens.

2. Select the fact your want to delete and click **Delete**. If you attempt to delete a custom fact that is being used still, you will be given the choice to delete the custom fact (and all data contained in the those facts) or move the data to another fact type.

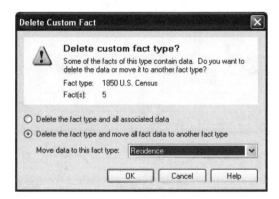

3. Make any necessary changes and click **OK**.

Editing Facts as a Group

If you need to modify the same fact for every person in your tree (for example, you want to make the Social Security Number fact private) it can take a lot of time to access each individual and then update the fact. Instead, you can edit a fact type as a group. Family Tree Maker gives you three ways to group-edit facts: move data from one fact type to another; move data from one field to another (within the same fact); make facts private or public.

I have found group-editing particularly helpful when importing or merging others' trees with my own. One tree included cemetery names in the

Place field of the Burial fact; I keep this information in the Description field. A quick edit and all my facts were back in order. Perhaps you've imported a tree that doesn't match how you've recorded information in yours. For example, you could move all data in a "Job" fact to your "Occupation" fact.

> Note: When you edit a group of facts, you will be prompted to back up your tree. It's always a good idea to back up your tree before making major changes like this.

1. Choose **Edit>Manage Facts** and select the fact type you want to edit.
2. Click **Data Options**. A list appears displaying every individual who has information entered in the selected fact type. You can sort the list by clicking on a column heading.

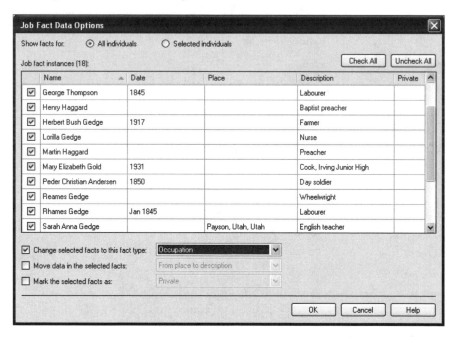

3. If necessary, you can filter the list by clicking **Selected individuals** and choosing a select group of individuals. You can also exclude a specific individual by deselecting the checkbox next to his or her name.

4. Use this chart to determine what to do with the fact; then click **OK**.

To do this	Do this
Move information from the selected fact type to another (for example, you can move data from the Job fact to the Occupation fact)	Select the **Change selected facts to this fact type** checkbox. Then choose the new fact type from the drop-down list.
Move data from one field to another field (within the same fact). You can move text from the Place field to the Description field, the Description field to the Place field, or simply swap the two fields	Select the **Move data in the selected facts** checkbox. Then choose an option from the drop-down list. Note: If the field already contains text, the new information will be added after a forward slash (/). For example, Illinois/ Hart Cemetery.
Change the privacy status of a fact type	Select the **Mark the selected facts as** checkbox. Then choose "Private" or "Not Private" from the drop-down list.

Customizing Historical Timelines

Timelines are a great way to show your family in the context of the world in which they lived. In Family Tree Maker you can view an individual's timeline on his or her Person tab (fig. 8-5) or you can create a Timeline report (see page 155).

Figure 8-5

The timeline on the Person tab.

Family Tree Maker has a database of historical events from all over the world that can be used in an individual's timeline. You can add, edit, or delete events in the database. For example, you might want to add entries that are relevant to your family history, such as international events that caused your ancestors to immigrate, or natural disasters that affected your family.

When you view an individual's timeline, or create a Timeline report, Family Tree Maker chooses which events to include by looking at dates and locations entered for that individual. If an event occurs at any time during the individual's life, it may be displayed in the timeline. For example, if an event begins before an individual was born but continues after the individual was born, it will be in the timeline. Family Tree Maker also includes events that occur in locations listed for an individual.

Adding a New Event

You may find that the database doesn't contain many events that are relevant to a location where your ancestors lived. For example, the paternal side of my family is from Denmark and although the database contains some European events, there aren't any specifically about Denmark or Scandinavia, so I have added some myself.

To add a new event choose **Edit>Manage Historical Events**. Then click the **New** button. Add information about the event as necessary:

- **Event title.** Enter a display name for that event that will appear on the timeline view and Timeline report.

- **Event date.** Enter a date for the event. You can use approximate dates Bef. (before), Aft. (after), or date ranges Bet. (between).

- **Place where event occurred.** Enter the location where the event occurred. This is a display name only and does not need to match a place name in the locations database.

- **Category.** Choose a category from the drop-down list or click **Add** to create a new category. Categories do not reflect where an event occurred; they are geographical groupings to tell Family Tree Maker that people living in these locations should have this event included in their personal timeline. For example, a timeline event about the moon landing would have the category of World History because it is relevant to everyone. But an event about the California Gold Rush might be relevant only to people living in the United States.

Note: If you delete a category, the event will be assigned to the World History category.

- **Description.** If you want to you can also enter a summary of the event (up to 1,000 characters). This summary only appears on the timeline on the Person tab when you select a specific event.

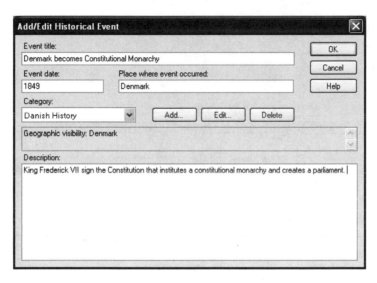

Editing an Event

You can edit events in the historical events database. For example, an event about women's suffrage in New Zealand kept appearing in all my timelines. I didn't want to delete the event, but I didn't want it to display in timelines for my American family members. I changed the event category from "World History" to "Australian History" (which includes New Zealand) and the problem was solved.

To edit an event choose **Edit>Manage Historical Events**. Double-click the event you want to edit or select the event and click the **Edit** button. You can edit the title, date, and category.

Deleting an Event

If you find that a historical event isn't relevant to anyone in your family, you can delete the event. A word of caution though. Historical facts are connected to the software and not to a specific tree. If you delete an event, you won't be able to use it in any of your trees; you would have to reinstall the software to retrieve it.

To delete an event choose **Edit>Manage Historical Events**. Select the event you want to delete and click the **Delete** button.

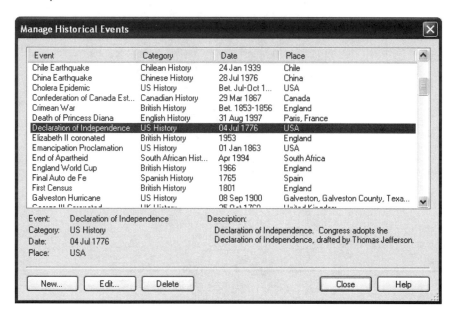

Chapter Nine

Using Family Tree Maker and Ancestry.com Together

Family Tree Maker connects directly to Ancestry.com so you can take advantage of the website's valuable resources—without ever leaving the software. You can access and download your Ancestry Member Trees, receive Ancestry news feeds, get hints about matching records, use the powerful Web Search to merge records into your tree, and more.

Setting Up Web Search

You can't use Family Tree Maker very long without enjoying the benefits of Ancestry Hints and the Web Search—enter a few facts about an individual and before you know it that shaky leaf appears telling you that Family Tree Maker has found a possible match for the individual on Ancestry.com. You can decide whether or not Family Tree Maker searches Ancestry every time you connect to the Internet, determine whether Ancestry Hints include Member Trees in search results, and change the Ancestry website that Family Tree Maker searches.

Automatic Searching: Turning On and Off

Family Tree Maker automatically conducts behind-the-scenes searches when your Internet connection is available. You might want to turn this feature off if you have a large database and your computer seems to be running slowly.

Note: If you turn off this feature, you can still search Ancestry manually by going to the Web Search workspace and entering your own search criteria.

Open the options window by choosing **Tools>Options**; then click the **General** tab. Deselect the **Search online automatically** checkbox.

Excluding Member Trees

Ancestry Member Trees can be a good way to jump-start your research. However, there may come a time when you don't want Member Trees included in Ancestry hints. I like to exclude trees so I know that any hints I receive are for actual records.

Open the options window by choosing **Tools>Options**; then click the **General** tab. Select the **Exclude Ancestry.com Family Trees from automatic search** checkbox.

Web Searching Tips

Family Tree Maker is packed with so many features that it's easy for little options to be overlooked. Here are some of the ways I improve my Web Searching.

- You can open a Web Search result in a separate browser window outside of Family Tree Maker. (I do this so I can look at documents or records before I merge them into my tree.) On the Web Search workspace, click the **Browser Options** button in the browser toolbar. Then choose **Open In New Window**.
- You can enlarge the size of text in the Family Tree Maker Web browser. On the Web Search workspace, click the **Browser Options** button in the browser toolbar. Then choose **Text Size** and select the text size you want.
- You can edit or delete specific Web Merge facts before you merge the information into your tree. In the Search Result Detail panel click the pencil icon to edit a fact or click the red X icon to delete the fact.

Changing the Default Ancestry Website

If necessary, you can change which Ancestry website Family Tree Maker searches automatically—the default is Ancestry.com. For example, if you live in the UK and have a subscription to Ancestry.co.uk, you'll want the software to automatically access this website.

> Note: Although I have had no problems switching back and forth between Ancestry websites, I should mention that when you modify the registry there is the possibility of creating serious problems in your system. Make sure you back up your registry and also understand how to restore the registry if a problem occurs. For information about the registry, go to the Microsoft Knowledge Base at <http://support.microsoft.com>.

1. Before you start, make sure Family Tree Maker is closed.

2. Open the Run window by pressing the **R** key and **Windows** key (the one with the Windows symbol) at the same time. You may also be able to open the Run window by choosing **Run** on the **Start** menu.

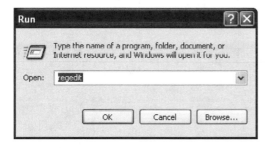

3. To open the Registry Editor, type "regedit" and click **OK**. The Registry Editor opens.

4. Expand the HKEY_LOCAL_MACHINE folder by clicking the plus sign (+) next to it. Then expand each of these subsequent folders: SOFT-WARE, Ancestry.com, Family Tree Maker. (If you're using a 64-bit version of Windows, you will need to expand the Wow6432Node folder after the SOFTWARE folder.)

5. Expand the 20.0 folder and then select the **Run Options** folder.

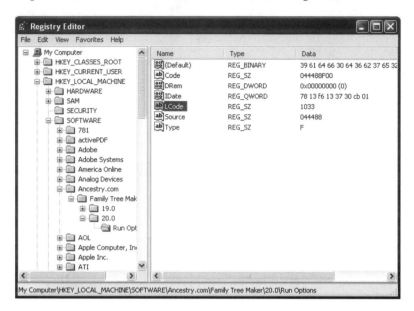

6. In the right panel, double-click "LCode" to open it. The Edit String window opens.

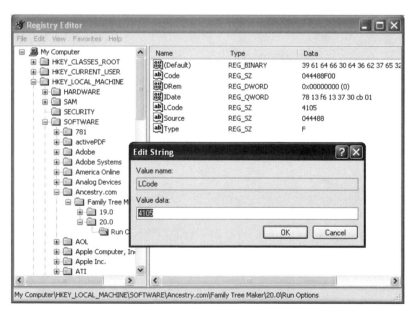

7. In the **Value data** field, enter the code for the appropriate country website and click **OK**.

Country	Website	Country Code
Australia	Ancestry.com.au	3081
Canada	Ancestry.ca	4105
France	Ancestry.fr	1036
Germany	Ancestry.de	1031
United Kingdom	Ancestry.co.uk	2057
United States	Ancestry.com	1033

8. Reopen Family Tree Maker. When you click the Web Search button, the website you have selected will appear.

Downloading Blank Charts and Reports

Family Tree Maker lets you download PDFs of blank pedigree charts, family group sheets, census extraction forms, and research reports—a helpful option that can make your research simpler. You may want to print out copies of the forms and mail them to your relatives so they can confirm birth dates, wedding dates, and other vital statistics from distant branches of your family.

1. Make sure you are connected to the Internet.

2. Go to the **Collection** tab on the Publish workspace.

3. Click **Charts** under Publication Types; then select **Pedigree Chart**.

4. On the right-hand side of the window, click the **Click here** link. A Web browser opens.

5. On the right-hand side of the browser, select the type of chart or report you want. Then click the **Download form** link.

Using the Web Dashboard

One of the Ancestry resources in Family Tree Maker is the Web Dashboard. It gives you quick access to your Ancestry subscription; you can also log in to your account, access your Ancestry Member Trees, view Member Connect activity, and even read a live news feed that tells you the latest news from Ancestry.com and Family Tree Maker (fig. 9-1).

Figure 9-1

The Web Dashboard on the Plan workspace.

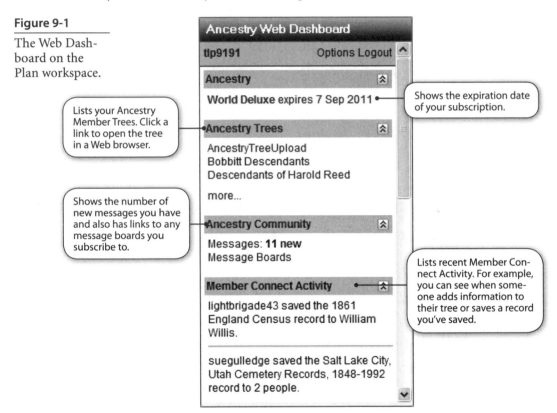

Lists your Ancestry Member Trees. Click a link to open the tree in a Web browser.

Shows the number of new messages you have and also has links to any message boards you subscribe to.

Shows the expiration date of your subscription.

Lists recent Member Connect Activity. For example, you can see when someone adds information to their tree or saves a record you've saved.

To select the information that will appear in the Dashboard (and choose how often the data will be refreshed), go to the Plan workspace and click the **Options** link. Make the selections you want and click **OK**.

Ancestry Member Trees or Family Tree Maker Trees?

Every time I teach a class about Family Tree Maker or go to a family history conference, I am asked the same question, "What is the difference between trees on Ancestry.com and trees in Family Tree Maker?" Here's a short explanation of some of the key differences (and similarities) between the two types of trees:

- **Accessibility.** A Member Tree on Ancestry.com is online and can be accessed anywhere you have a computer and an Internet connection. To use Family Tree Maker, the software must be installed on your computer and the tree saved to its hard drive.

- **Features.** Both trees allow you to add individuals, create relationships, add media items and sources, and attach Ancestry records. However, Family Tree Maker is a more robust and feature-rich product that allows you to delete groups of people, merge duplicate individuals, use source templates, and more.

- **Collaboration.** Because an Ancestry Member Tree is online, other people researching your family can find you and then you through the Ancestry Connection service. If you are using Family Tree Maker and want to share your tree, you'll need to export your file or create a family tree chart and send it to family members.

- **Media.** You can attach photos and documents to both types of trees. However, Family Tree Maker also lets you add audio and video.

- **Charts and reports.** In Ancestry Member Trees you can generate only standard pedigree charts, descendant charts, and timelines (through MyCanvas). Family Tree Maker lets you create a variety of charts and reports in multiple formats.

- **Privacy.** Ancestry Member Trees can be "public" or "private." Public trees can be viewed and searched by all Ancestry members; private trees cannot be viewed by Ancestry members but names, birthplaces, and birth dates will appear in search results so members can see if a tree contains an individual they're interested in. Family Tree Maker trees can only be viewed by someone who has access to your computer.

Family Tree Maker and Ancestry Member Trees

I've kept my family trees in various locations over the years—my first experimental tree on WorldConnect at RootsWeb, a tree for sharing on Ancestry.com, and my main "working" Family Tree Maker database.

I like using Family Tree Maker because entering information is fast and easy, and I can create custom reports that show me statistics about my data or create a beautiful chart for a family member. I also have Member Trees on Ancestry.com. These online trees make it easy for me to show off my latest finds to my family—no matter where they are. And because of my Member Trees, I've been contacted by relatives who have shared stories and photographs I never would have had access to otherwise. Both types of trees are valuable for my research for different reasons. The challenge is figuring out how to use both types of trees together.

Unfortunately, at this time Ancestry.com doesn't have the functionality to sync an online Member Tree with a Family Tree Maker tree—meaning that you can't update one tree and have the other one updated automatically. I will be the first to admit that the ability to transfer information back and forth between each service is essential. But until that time comes (and sooner is better than later!), I hope I can provide with some practical suggestions that will make maintaining both types of trees easier.

Uploading a Tree to Ancestry.com

Uploading a tree from Family Tree Maker to Ancestry.com is simple. You can upload your tree in one step and it will contain not only your dates, names, and places, but all your media items, sources, and Ancestry records too. (For more information on how your Family Tree Maker tree will appear on Ancestry see "What Data Transfers Between Ancestry and Family Tree Maker?" on page 243.)

To upload a tree, click the **Share** button beneath the main toolbar and choose "Upload to Ancestry."

Note: To upload a tree to Ancestry.com, you do not need to be a subscriber, but you do need to register your copy of Family Tree Maker.

Downloading a Tree into Family Tree Maker

If you have an Ancestry Member Tree, you can download the tree into Family Tree Maker and use it to either create a new tree or merge it with your currently open tree. The tree will include the facts, sources, and images you have manually attached to individuals. (For more information on how your Ancestry Member Tree will appear in Family Tree Maker see "What Data Transfers Between Ancestry and Family Tree Maker?" on page 243.)

To download a tree from Ancestry.com, go to the Plan workspace and click the **New Tree** tab. Click **Download a tree from Ancestry**; then select the appropriate tree and click **Download**. (To merge a downloaded tree with your current tree, see "Merging Files" on page 64.)

> Note: In order to download an Ancestry tree, you must be the tree's owner; even if you have been invited to view or edit a tree, you will not be able to download it. If you do find a tree you want to download but don't have rights to it, consider using the Ancestry Connection Service to politely request that the owner download a GEDCOM for you.

Maintaining Trees in Family Tree Maker and on Ancestry

As I mentioned earlier, your Family Tree Maker trees and Ancestry Member Trees do not sync. In other words, when you enter information in one tree, the other tree is not updated automatically. Instead, when you enter information in one tree (regardless of which system you're using) you must enter the information manually into the other tree or follow a process that involves downloading, merging, and possibly even uploading again.

After spending years trying to keep my online tree and Family Tree Maker databases identical, I have decided that the best option is to use one tree as my working or master tree and use the other one for sharing or publishing. I don't maintain both trees at the same level anymore. Instead I add all my new information to my working tree and then periodically (every six months or so) update my other tree.

Should My Working Tree Be on Ancestry or in Family Tree Maker?

Family Tree Maker and Ancestry trees are both great ways to record your family history. Deciding where your working tree will reside is as simple as figuring out what you want to do with your tree.

If your focus is collaborating with family members and you want to be able to invite others to help build and edit your tree, it makes sense to keep your main tree online. If you want to create reports and charts or have access to advanced functionality (such as the ability to merge duplicate individuals), Family Tree Maker is a better option. (For more information about the differences between the two types of trees, see the sidebar on page 239.)

How Do I Transfer My Trees Back and Forth?

If you are using your Ancestry Member Tree as your working tree, you can simply download your tree into Family Tree Maker. You will have the choice to merge the tree with the currently open Family Tree Maker tree or import it as a new tree. If you haven't made any updates or changes to your Family Tree Maker tree, I would recommend that you import it as a new tree and delete your old one. That way you don't have to go through the merging process. (To learn more about merging, see "Merging Files" on page 64.)

If you are using Family Tree Maker as your working tree, you can upload your tree at any time. The first time you do this is easy. The challenge comes when you need to update the tree at a later time. Keep in mind that uploading a tree does *not* replace or overwrite an existing online tree. You will be uploading a completely new tree.

When you upload your tree again, you will have to decide whether to keep both online trees or delete the old one. If you delete the original tree, people you've invited to be part of your tree as guests or editors will be unable to access your new tree and you will have to reinvite them. If you are only collaborating with one or two people, this might not be a problem, but if you have many collaborators this could be problematic. Also, when you delete a tree, you lose any comments that other Ancestry users have posted. If you do delete your old tree, I suggest that you upload the new version first and make sure all your information looks good before deleting the old version.

> **TIP**
>
> You may not realize it, but people recognize your online tree (and trust your work) based on the name of your tree. If you rename your tree every time you upload it, people who are looking for you won't be able to find you. A better option is to use the same name every time but add a date after it. That way others will recognize it and be able to see when it was last updated.

What Data Transfers Between Ancestry and Family Tree Maker?

Because Ancestry.com and Family Tree Maker trees are in different formats, information in trees does not always transfer as you'd expect. This section explains how the data in your Ancestry Member Trees and Family Tree Maker trees transfers back and forth.

Facts

All fact dates, names, and places (including custom and alternate facts) are moved seamlessly between Family Tree Maker and Ancestry trees—with these exceptions:

- Names suffixes such as Jr. and Sr. are not included when you upload your tree from Family Tree Maker; when you download your tree from Ancestry.com suffixes may be duplicated.

- Alternate names or nicknames are transferred between the Also Known As fact (Family Tree Maker) and the Alternates fact (Ancestry.com).

- A cause of death is transferred between the Cause of Death fact description (Family Tree Maker) and the Death description (Ancestry.com).

- Contact information fields (Address, Phone Number, and Email) in Family Tree Maker are not uploaded to Ancestry.com.

- Occupation information is transferred between the Employment fact (Family Tree Maker) and the Occupation fact (Ancestry.com).

- Physical descriptions are transferred between the Physical Description fact (Family Tree Maker) and the Description fact (Ancestry.com).

    You can view facts for a person on the Individuals and Shared Facts panel in Family Tree Maker and on the Vital Information and Facts and Sources tabs on Ancestry (fig. 9-2).

Figure 9-2

Above, facts for an individual in Family Tree Maker; *below*, facts for an individual in an Ancestry Member Tree.

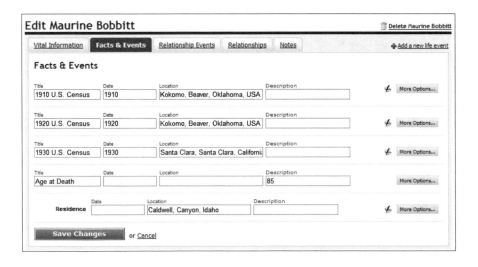

Relationships

When you upload your tree to Ancestry.com, you have the option to privatize living individuals. (To learn how Family Tree Maker calculates living individuals, see the sidebar on page 74.) Here's how a living individual's information is uploaded:

- Given names are replaced with the word "Living."

- Relationships are exported.

- Facts about the individual are not exported.

- Shared facts are not exported, even if the other individual is deceased.

Notes

In Family Tree Maker you can create a variety of notes: person, research, fact, relationship, media, and source citation. On Ancestry.com you can create only person notes (fig. 9-3).

Figure 9-3

Notes for an individual on Ancestry.com.

Here's how notes transfer between trees:

- Person and research notes (Family Tree Maker) are moved to person notes (Ancestry.com). Relationship and media notes (Family Tree Maker) are not uploaded.

- Fact notes (Family Tree Maker) are moved to source citation notes (Ancestry.com).

- Note formatting in Family Tree Maker (such as bold and italicized words) is not included.

Stories

Family Tree Maker and Ancestry.com both allow you to create stories about individuals in your tree.

- A story created on Ancestry.com will transfer into Family Tree Maker as a .htm file, which can be viewed in a Web browser (fig. 9-4). You can't edit the text, but you can copy and paste the information into Family Tree Maker or a word-processing program.

Figure 9-4

An Ancestry story that has been downloaded to Family Tree Maker.

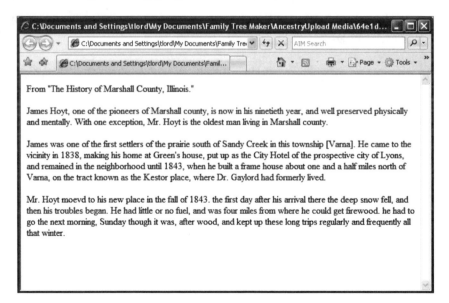

- Smart Stories created in Family Tree Maker will be uploaded as a text (.rtf file). The story can't be viewed within the Ancestry tree but the document can be downloaded. Only Smart Stories attached to individuals are uploaded.

Media Items

Family Tree Maker and Ancestry.com both allow you to attach a variety of media items to your tree. These items are transferred automatically between Family Tree Maker and Ancestry trees with these exceptions:

- Media details such as descriptions and dates are transferred. The name of a media item is moved between the Caption field (Family Tree Maker) and the Picture name field (Ancestry.com). (Media file names are *not* transferred.)

- Audio and video items are not transferred between Family Tree Maker and Ancestry.com.

- Media items attached to relationships (Family Tree Maker) are not transferred.

- Media items attached to sources (Family Tree Maker) are attached to the tree and not a source in Ancestry.com.

- Records on Ancestry.com that you've linked to your Ancestry Member Tree won't be downloaded into Family Tree Maker. You'll need to do this manually. For help see "Record Images on Ancestry.com" on page 248.

Sources

Sources and source citations transfer correctly unless the sources you've created in Family Tree Maker are based on source templates. When these sources are uploaded, details that can't be placed into the standard source fields (such as author, title, and publisher) won't be deleted, but they will be moved to the Notes field.

Places

Place names are transferred correctly. However, if you have entered shortened display names for locations or custom GPS coordinates in Family Tree Maker, they will not be transferred.

Reports, Charts, and Books

Reports, charts, and books cannot be transferred from Family Tree Maker to Ancestry.com.

Record Images on Ancestry.com

When you download a tree from Ancestry.com, source citations include links to records and documents you've found on Ancestry, not the actual record images.

Family Tree Maker can help you download the images so you don't have to re-attach them manually.

To download a single image

If only a few images are missing, you can download them one by one. Go to the Sources workspace in Family Tree Maker and access the source citation with the missing media item. Click the **Media** tab at the bottom of the window and click the **Download Missing Media** button (fig. 9-5). (You can also double-click the source citation and click the **Download Image If Available** button on the Media tab.)

Figure 9-5

The Download Missing Media button on the source citation Media tab.

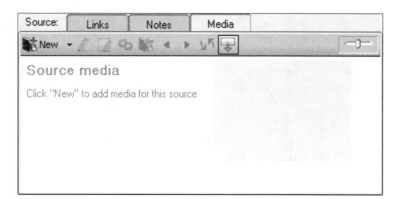

To download multiple images

If your tree included many records and documents, you will want to download all the missing items at one time. Go to the Media workspace in Family Tree Maker and click on the Collection tab's display area. Then press **CTRL+F5**. A progress window shows which images are downloaded.

Chapter Ten

Cleaning Up Your Tree

As your tree expands and the generations build upon each other, you'll notice that you have to create more and more sources and the number of media items you need to keep track of multiplies. And inevitably the more people you add to your tree, the more likely you are to introduce mistakes into your file.

In order to keep my tree as organized and error free as possible, I like to perform some maintenance tasks every month or so. Figure 10-1 on the following page shows the workflow I use. You might want to follow a similar process before you export a tree to give to family members, upload a tree to Ancestry.com, or create charts and family history books.

Note: Some tasks in the workflow are discussed in this guide; all others are covered in the *Companion Guide*.

Cleaning Up Your Sources

When you care about the accuracy of your family history, it's important to do some upkeep on your sources so they are consistent, complete, and ready to be shared.

Figure 10-1

A workflow you can follow to keep your tree organized.

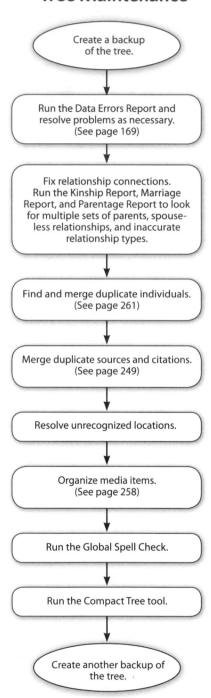

Tree Maintenance

Create a backup of the tree.

Run the Data Errors Report and resolve problems as necessary. (See page 169)

Fix relationship connections. Run the Kinship Report, Marriage Report, and Parentage Report to look for multiple sets of parents, spouse-less relationships, and inaccurate relationship types.

Find and merge duplicate individuals. (See page 261)

Merge duplicate sources and citations. (See page 249)

Resolve unrecognized locations.

Organize media items. (See page 258)

Run the Global Spell Check.

Run the Compact Tree tool.

Create another backup of the tree.

Transferring an Existing Source to a Source Template

Family Tree Maker includes more than 170 source templates based on the QuickCheck models used in Elizabeth Shown Mills's book *Evidence Explained*—the premier reference for citing genealogy sources. A list of these templates can be found in appendix B, "Source Templates."

If you have created your sources using the basic format and now want to use these standardized templates, you don't have to re-create a source; you can map the fields from the original source to fields in the desired template and transfer the contents over automatically.

1. Click the **Sources** button on the main toolbar.

2. In **Source Groups**, double-click the source you want to transfer to a template. The Edit Source window opens.

3. To find the template you want to use, enter keywords in the **Source template** field or click **Change** to select a template from a categorized list. The Change Source Type window opens.

I like to drag the Change Source Type window so that I can also see the Edit Source window. That way I can see the original source and don't have to guess what information appears in each field.

4. Do one of these options:

   • Select **Existing template** to view the fields from the original source. The drop-down lists contain the template fields you can map to.

   • Select **New template** to view the fields available in the template. The drop-down lists contain the original source fields you can map to the new template.

   Note: If your original source includes a source repository but the template does not use the Source repository field, your repository information will be discarded. You might want to add the repository information to the Comments field in the template.

5. For each field, do one of these options:

   • Choose **Discard data** from the drop-down list to leave the field blank.

   • Choose a field to move the contents to. You can map multiple fields to one field.

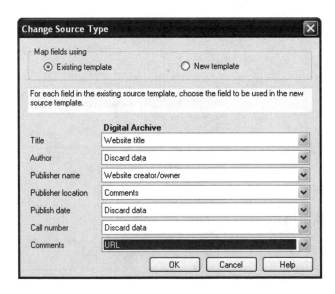

> **TIP**
>
> If you can't decide which field your source information belongs in, map the information to the Comments field; you can copy it to a different field later, if necessary.

6. Click **OK** to return to the Edit Source window. The contents of the original source appear now in the template's fields.

Merging Sources

If you have accidentally created multiple sources for the same database, book, or index, you can merge these sources without losing any information.

1. Choose **Edit>Manage Sources**. The Sources window opens.

2. In the list of sources, select the source that you want to *replace*. You can use the scroll bar to move up and down the list.

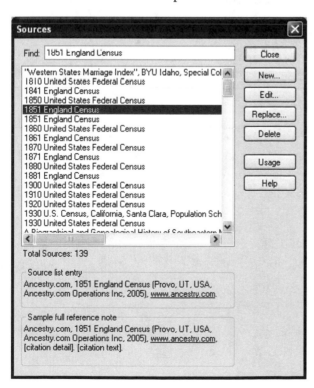

Note: If you want to see which facts are associated with the source before you replace it, click the **Usage** button.

3. Click **Replace**. The Replace Sources window opens.

4. In the list of sources, select the source that you want to *keep*.

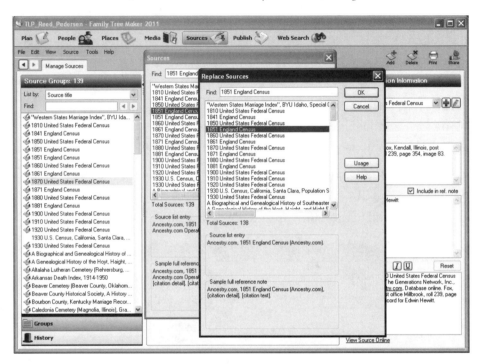

5. Click **OK**. A message asks if you want to replace the source. Click **Yes**. All facts associated with the first source will now be associated with the source you chose to keep. Click **Close**.

Merging Source Citations

If you have duplicate source citations, such as for the same page of a book or the same household in a census, you can merge these source citations without losing any links to individuals or media items you've connected them to.

1. Click the **Sources** button on the main toolbar. Find the source citation you want to replace and select it in the Source Citations list.

2. Choose **Source>Replace Source Citation**. The Find Source Citation window opens.

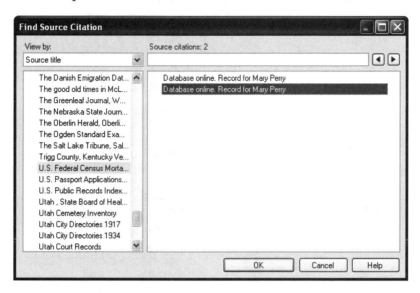

3. In the list of source citations, select the citation that you want to keep. Click **OK**. A message asks if you want to replace the source citation. Click **Yes**. All facts and media items associated with the first source citation will now be associated with the remaining citation.

Sorting Out Sources: Original and Derivative

As you analyze the quality of your sources, you'll want to determine whether they're original or derivative.

- Original sources are just what the name implies—original records (or digital copies of originals) of passenger lists; birth, marriage, and death certificates; censuses, land records, and more.
- Derivative sources are records that have been extracted, transcribed, or translated from the original. For example, a marriage certificate is an original record, but an online index that transcribes the names and dates on the record is a derivative source.

Rating a Source Citation

Family Tree Maker lets you rate the reliability of sources. You can rate each source citation to note both the legibility of the source as well as its potential accuracy (i.e., primary source, secondary source, family legend, etc.).

1. Click the **Sources** button on the main toolbar. Find the source citation you want to rate and select it in the Source Citations list.

2. Click the **Links** tab. If the source citation has more than one individual and/or fact linked to it, select the appropriate person and fact.

3. Click the **Rate the source** icon (a yellow star) in the toolbar. The Rate Source window opens.

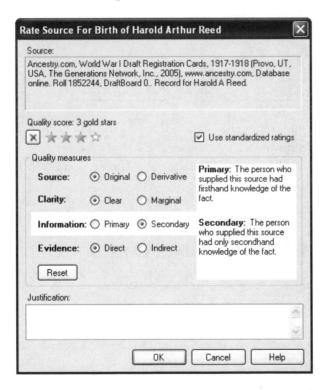

Note: You can click the gray (X) icon or the Reset button to clear the current rating.

Sorting Out Sources: Primary and Secondary

As you're gathering records you'll find two types of sources: primary and secondary.

- Primary sources are documents that were created at the time of the event (or soon after) by someone who had direct knowledge of the event. Examples include birth and death certificates, photographs, diaries, letters, and contemporary newspapers.
- Secondary sources are published works that were created sometime after an event by someone who might not have been personally aware of the event. For example, you might find your grandfather's birthplace listed on a birth certificate (a primary source for birth information) and in a census record (a secondary source for birth information). While both sources are valuable, the primary source (birth certificate) is a more reliable source.

Be aware that records can contain both primary and secondary information. For example, a marriage certificate would be a primary source for a marriage date but a secondary source for a bride's birth date or birthplace.

4. Use this chart to change the source's rating:

To do this	Do this
Rate the source yourself	In the **Quality score** field, click the number of stars you want to assign the source. The more stars you choose, the higher the quality of the source. Note: In the Ratings column, self-rated stars appear in blue.
Use a standardized rating system	Click the **Use standardized ratings** checkbox. Choose how to rate the source: - **Source.** Choose whether the source is an original document or a transcription or translation of the original. - **Clarity.** Choose the legibility of the source. - **Information.** Choose whether this information comes from primary or secondary sources. - **Evidence.** Choose whether the source states a fact or requires additional evidence. Note: In the Ratings column, standardized stars appear in gold.

5. If necessary, you can add additional comments about your ratings in the **Justification** field.

6. Click **OK**. You can see the rating on the Links tab.

   Note: You can also see a source citation's rating in the People workspace. Click the **Person** tab; then select the sourced fact in the Individual and Shared Facts section. The rating appears on the Sources tab in the editing panel.

Keeping Your Media Files Organized

I love organizing. My bookshelves at home are sorted by genre. The shirts hanging in my closet are grouped together based on color (and style). And the obsession doesn't stop there. I'm always looking for new ways to put my family history in order, especially my media items.

Utilizing Media Categories

When I first started using Family Tree Maker, I didn't bother doing much with my media items. I was just happy if they were in my tree and linked to the right people. But as my family tree grew larger and I added hundreds and then thousands of items, I realized I needed a system. I started taking advantage of the ability to assign multiple categories to each item. Family Tree Maker comes with some default categories and I created a few of my own:

- Audio
- Censuses
- Documents
- Letters and Correspondence
- Maps
- Newspapers
- Photos — Family Homes
- Photos — General
- Photos — Heirlooms

- Photos — Locations
- Photos — Portraits
- Photos — Weddings
- Records — Birth, Marriage, Death
- Records — Church
- Records — Immigration/Emigration
- Records — Military
- Research Guides
- Signatures

- Slideshows
- Tombstones

- Video
- Categories for family surnames

To add a new media category, go to the Media workspace and click the **Edit** button in the media editing panel. In the Categorize Media window, click the **Add** button, enter a name for the category, and click **OK**. (You can also select a category and click **Edit** to change a category's name.)

Viewing Uncategorized Media Items

Because I rely on categories to organize and sort my media, I check my media collection periodically to make sure I've assigned a category to each item I've added to my tree.

To view media items that are not assigned to categories, go to the Media workspace. In the Groups panel, choose "Media category" from the **List by** drop-down list. Then click the "Uncategorized" link at the bottom of the list. The display area shows thumbnails of the uncategorized items.

Labeling Media Items

After I got my media categories working the way I wanted, the next step I took was to create a labeling system. My goals were (1) to be able to quickly identify all the items for a specific individual (Family Tree Maker takes care of that by letting me attach media items to specific people), (2) to group media items together by type (media categories help with this), and (3) to display my media items in an order that I found helpful.

Family Tree Maker lets you choose whether your media collection will be sorted by captions (entered in the software) or by file names. My media files were already named in a way that matched all the other genealogy files on my computer (surname, first name, description of image or document, date) so I didn't want to change the file names. The only problem was, this system wouldn't permit me to display images in the order I wanted in Family Tree Maker—scrolling through hundreds of images with labels that start with Pedersen was not appealing. I decided to utilize media captions to label photos, records, and documents.

Instead of different types of records being labeled differently for each individual, every record now has a caption consisting of a grouping and a name (some examples are: Death certificate – Herbert Gedge, Obituary – Harold A. Reed, Tombstone – Lorine Bobbitt). You could also add captions or file names so that every item related to a specific person appears together; for example, Harold A. Reed - Marriage certificate, Harold A Reed - Obituary, Harold A. Reed - WWI Draft registration).

When it comes to organizing media items, one question I hear often is, "Can I sort my media items by date?" The answer is, yes and no. Unfortunately, the date you enter for a media item as part of its media details isn't used for any kind of sorting or identification. If you want to use dates to sort your media items, you'll need to make the date the first part of your caption or file name; for example, "1972 Obituary – Harold A. Reed". Keep in mind though, Family Tree Maker sorts items numerically, not by date. So 2 August 1865 would appear after 1 August 2010 or even 1995. If you decide to incorporate dates in your labels, I recommend that you only use years.

Unlinking a Media Item from an Individual

If you find that you've linked a media item to the wrong individual (or wrong source), you can unlink the media item in a couple different ways.

- On the People workspace, access an individual's Person tab. Then click the **Media** tab at the bottom of the window. Click the media item you want to detach and click the broken link icon in the media toolbar. Click **Yes** to unlink the item.

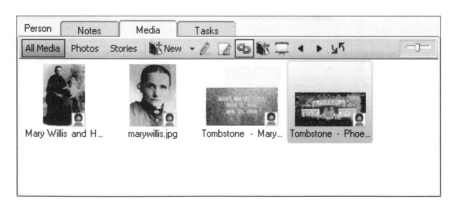

- On the Media workspace, click the media item you want and then click the **Detail** tab. On the Links tab at the bottom of the window you'll see all the individuals the media item is linked to. Select the individual and click the broken link icon in the media toolbar. Click **Yes** to unlink the item.

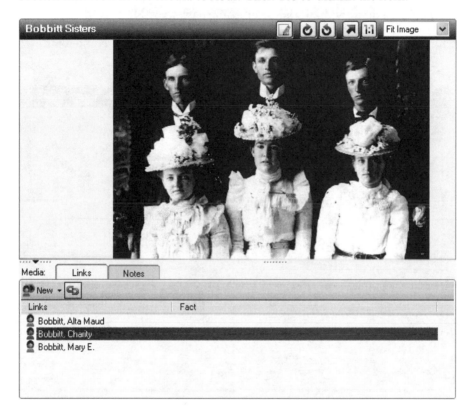

Creating a List of Duplicate Individuals

Family Tree Maker 2011 contains a great new feature to prevent duplication of individuals. When you enter new family members, Family Tree Maker analyzes the information and alerts you if it believes the individual already exists in your tree. In spite of this, you may still get duplicate individuals in your tree, especially if you're adding a lot of new information to your tree or merging a family member's file with yours.

Luckily Family Tree Maker has a tool that can quickly compare names, birth and death dates, places attached to facts, and parents' names and then create a list of individuals who could possibly match each other. Because I don't always have time to compare all the suggested duplicates at once, I sometimes create a saved list of individuals that I can come back to at a later time.

1. Choose **Edit>Find Duplicate People**. The Find Duplicate People window opens.

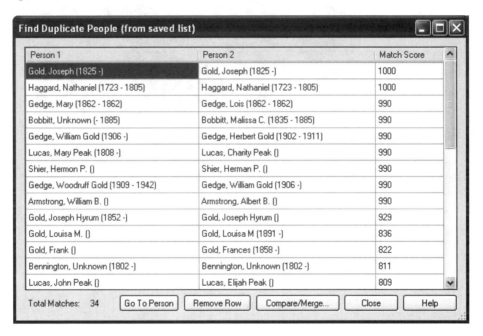

2. If you see individuals who are not duplicates, such as brothers who have similar names, you can take them off the list by selecting one of the individuals and clicking **Remove Row**.

3. If you want to merge a pair of individuals (or just compare the two), select one of the individuals and click **Compare/Merge**. The Individual Merge window opens.

> **TIP**
>
> If you want to be able to see the individuals in relation to other people in your family tree or want to compare the individuals more thoroughly, click the **Go To Person** button. Family Tree Maker will display the selected individual in the People workspace.

4. When you are finished making changes, click **Close**. You will be asked whether you want to save the list; click **Yes**.

5. When you want to access the list again, choose **Edit>Find Duplicate People**. Then click **Load Saved List** to view your saved list or click **Perform Matching Again** to start over.

Deleting a Group of Individuals

You're probably familiar with the process of deleting a specific individual. But occasionally you may need to delete a group of people from your tree. For example, you might receive a file from a family member that contains a branch you aren't related to or that you don't want to keep in your tree.

To delete a group of individuals, you first need to display them in a tree chart; this feature works on every chart so you can choose the chart that best displays the individuals you want to remove from your tree. However, the Extended Family chart can display every individual in your tree and is generally the best chart to use.

> **TIP**
>
> Instead of deleting a group of individuals, you might want to leave them in your tree and detach them from the people they're linked to. That way if you ever find a connection, you can simply reattach this branch to the appropriate member of your family, and you won't have to re-enter any information.

Warning: Deleting individuals from a tree is permanent. You should create a backup of your tree before proceeding.

1. Go to the **Collection** tab on the Publish workspace.

2. Select the individual whom you want to be the focus of the chart in the mini-navigation pedigree tree or click the **Index of Individuals** button and choose a person.

3. Double-click the chart that will best display the group of people you want to delete. (The Extended Family Chart can be useful because it can display specific individuals or every individual in your tree.) Don't worry if individuals you don't want to delete appear in the chart; you can use the selection tools to further refine your choices.

4. To select specific individuals or groups to delete, right-click an individual's name in the chart. A drop-down list lets you choose specific groups to include (e.g., ancestors, descendants, individuals of the same generation). For more information on selecting people in charts, choose **Help>Help for Family Tree Maker**.

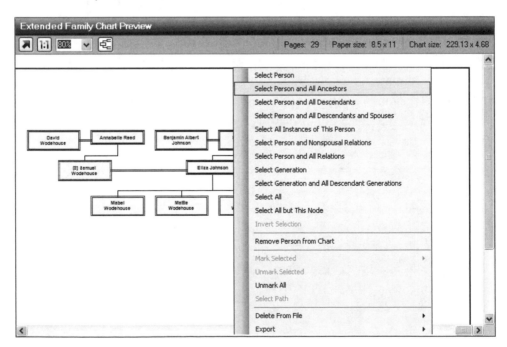

5. After you have selected the group of individuals you want to delete, right-click one of the highlighted boxes and choose **Delete from File>Selected Persons** from the drop-down list. (You can also delete every person displayed in a chart by right-clicking the chart and choosing **Delete from File>All Persons in Chart** from the drop-down list.) The Delete Selected Persons window opens.

6. If you want to further refine the list of people to be deleted, click **Select** to open the Filter Individuals window (for help selecting individuals, see "Selecting a Group of Individuals" on page 46).

7. Click **OK** to delete the individuals.

   Note: Because Family Tree Maker contains a variety of charts and there are multiple ways to select individuals within these charts, this task includes only basic instructions. I recommend experimenting with various charts until you find the method that works for you.

Removing an Unknown Spouse

When you delete a marriage for a couple or detach individuals who are in a relationship, you might see that an individual is now linked to an unknown spouse (fig. 10-2).

Figure 10-2

A spouseless relationship or unknown spouse.

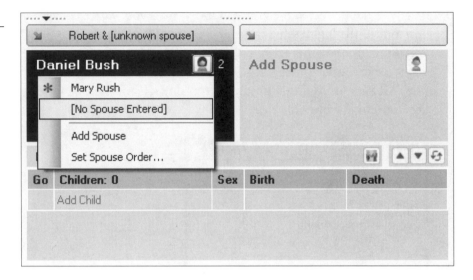

It's easy to get rid of this "phantom" spouse. Go to the People workspace and select the individual with the unknown spouse. Then choose **Person>Attach/Detach Person>Detach Selected Person**. When prompted to select a family to detach the individual from, choose the family with no spouse entered and click **OK**. When you view the spouse list again, the unknown spouse should be gone.

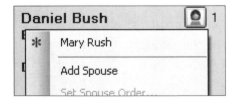

Making Global Changes

Have you ever entered important information in a note but you can't remember whom it was attached to? Or have you accidentally spelled an ancestor's name incorrectly throughout your tree? I make these types of mistakes on a regular basis. Luckily Family Tree Maker has a Find and Replace tool that lets you search for specific terms and names in facts, individual notes, media captions and descriptions, to-do tasks, and sources. In addition to searching, the tool also lets you replace any incorrect terms.

In my tree, I have a tendency to transpose the I and E in my great-grandfather's name, making him Neils instead of Niels. Instead of sifting through every fact, source, and media item for the incorrect spelling, I used the Find and Replace tool to find the mistake and correct it.

Note: If your search term includes a date, keep in mind that text in Date fields cannot be searched. A date shows up in search results only if it appears in the Description field or in a note, source, or media item.

1. Choose **Edit>Find and Replace** and enter the term(s) you want to search for in the **Find** field and change the search options, as necessary. You can choose how exact you want the search to be and which software elements to search. In this situation I want to search all elements because I am looking for a misspelled name. If you know the term you're looking for is in a source or a note, you can select only that option.

TIP

You can search using wildcards if you are unsure of the exact word or phrase you're looking for. Use an asterisk to represent up to six characters. For example, a search for "fran*" will return matches such as Fran, Franny, Frank, Frannie, and Frankie. Use a question mark to replace a single character. For example, a search for "Hans?n" will return matches such as Hansen and Hanson.

---

2. Click the **Find** button. The window expands to show the first item that matches your search.

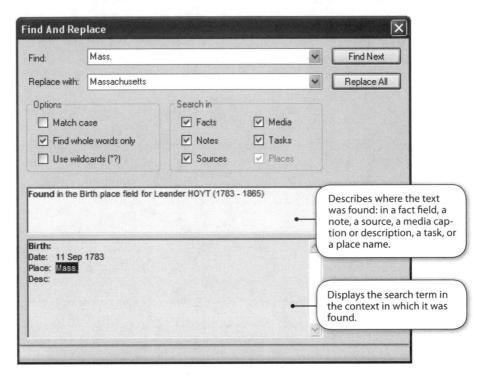

Describes where the text was found: in a fact field, a note, a source, a media caption or description, a task, or a place name.

Displays the search term in the context in which it was found.

3. If you want to open the record or workspace where the search term is used, click the **Go To** button. If you want to replace the term, enter a new term in the **Replace with** field and click the **Replace** button.

4. To find the next matching term, click **Find Next**. Continue searching and replacing terms, as necessary.

Note: Although you can replace all matching text by clicking the **Replace All** button, I recommend viewing each search result individually. For example, if I had chosen "Replace All" when replacing my great-grandfather's name, it would have changed a record transcription in a source citation. This is an instance in which I wanted to keep the name as it was. If you do use the Replace All functionality, you should back up your file first because you cannot undo this change.

Appendix A
Keyboard Shortcuts

You may prefer to use the keyboard instead of the mouse when you're entering information in Family Tree Maker. This appendix lists some of the most commonly used keyboard shortcuts and options.

Navigation

Task	Windows	Mac OS
Go back to the previous window	ALT+left arrow	⌥+left arrow
Go forward to a window you've already accessed	ALT+right arrow	⌥+right arrow
Open the Plan workspace	ALT, V, A or CTRL+1	⌘+1
Open the People workspace	ALT, V, P or CTRL+2	⌘+2
Open the Places workspace	ALT, V, C or CTRL+3	⌘+3
Open the Media workspace	ALT, V, M or CTRL+4	⌘+4
Open the Sources workspace	ALT, V, S or CTRL+5	⌘+5
Open the Publish workspace	ALT, V, U or CTRL+6	⌘+6
Open the Web Search workspace	ALT, V, W or CTRL+7	⌘+7

Working in Trees

Task	Windows	Mac OS
Open a new tree file	CTRL+O	⌘+O
Close Family Tree Maker	ALT+F4	⌘+Q
Undo a change	CTRL+Z	⌘+Z
Go to home person (People workspace)	CTRL+Home	⇧+⌘+H
Use the Find and Replace tool	CTRL+F	⌘+F
Bookmark an individual	CTRL+B	⇧+⌘+B
Open the Date Calculator	CTRL+D	⌘+D
Access the index of individuals (People workspace)	F2	⌘+F2
Add a media item (Media workspace)	CTRL+M	^+⌘+M
Add a source citation	CTRL+S	⌘+S

Working with Text

Task	Windows	Mac OS
Highlight the character right of the cursor	SHIFT+right arrow	⇧+right arrow
Highlight the character left of the cursor	SHIFT+left arrow	⇧+left arrow
Highlight an entire word right of the cursor	CTRL+SHIFT+right arrow	^+⇧+right arrow
Highlight the entire word left of the cursor	CTRL+SHIFT+left arrow	^+⇧+left arrow
Highlight an entire line	SHIFT+End	⇧+End

Task	Windows	Mac OS
Highlight a paragraph one line at a time	SHIFT+down arrow	⇧+down arrow
Highlight all lines above the cursor	CTRL+SHIFT+home	^+⇧+Home
Copy text	CTRL+C	⌘+C
Cut text	CTRL+X	⌘+X
Paste text	CTRL+V	⌘+V
Delete highlighted text	CTRL+Delete	⌘+Delete

Appendix B
Source Templates

Family Tree Maker includes more than 170 source templates based on the Quick-Check models used in Elizabeth Shown Mills's book *Evidence Explained*—the premier reference for citing genealogy sources. Source templates take the guesswork out of citing facts: no more wasted time entering irrelevant information; no more hoping that you've captured the right data; and no more wondering whether other family members will be able to follow your research paths. And templates also ensure that your sources are consistent.

This appendix lists all the source templates that are available, organized by source group and category.

Archives and Artifacts

Category	Templates
Archived Material	Artifact
	Digital Archive
	Manuscript Record by Collection
	Manuscript Record by Document
	Manuscript Record by Series
	Personal Bible
	Portrait
	Research Report
	Unpublished Narrative
	Vertical File

Category	Templates
Preservation Film	FHL-GSU Preservation Film
	In-House Film
Private Holdings	Artifact
	Diary or Journal
	Family Bible Records
	Family Chart or Group Sheet
	Historic Letter
	Interview Tape and Transcript
	Legal Document—Unrecorded Family Copy
	Personal Correspondence
	Personal E-mail
	Research Report
	Tradition, Recorded
	Firsthand Knowledge

Business and Institutional Records

Category	Templates
Corporate Records	Bound Volume
	Document—Loose Record
	Extract Supplied by Staff
	Microfilm
	Online Database
	Online Image
Lineage Society Records	Application File
	Online Database
Organizational Records	Archived In-House
	Archived Off-Site
Professional Reports	Genetic Testing
	Historical Research—Corporate
	Historical Research—Online
School Records	Administrative Material
	Student Transcript

Cemetery Records

Category	Templates
Cemetery Office Records	Personally Used
	Supplied by Staff
	Online Image
	Preservation Film, FHL-GSU
Grave Markers	Rural Location
	Urban Location
	Online Image
Memorial Plaques	Memorial Plaque
Derivatives	Cemetery Abstract—Vertical File
	Cemetery Abstract—Card File
	Online Database

Census Records

Category	Templates
Original Manuscripts	Local Copy—United States Federal Census
	National Archives Copy
Digital Images	CD/DVD—United States
	Online Archive—France
	Online Archive—United Kingdom and Wales
	Online Commercial Site—Generic by Census Year and Location
	Online Commercial Site—Generic by Census Year
	Population Schedule—U.S., 1790-1840 by Census Year and Location
	Population Schedule—U.S., 1790-1840 by Census Year
	Population Schedule—U.S., 1850-70 by Census Year and Location
	Population Schedule—U.S., 1850-70 by Census Year
	Population Schedule—U.S., 1850-60 Slaves by Census Year and Location
	Population Schedule—U.S., 1850-60 Slaves by Census Year
	Population Schedule—U.S., 1880-1930 by Census Year and Location
	Population Schedule—U.S., 1880-1930 by Census Year

Category	Templates
Microfilm	Native American Tribal Census
	Non-population Schedule—NARA Film
	Non-population Schedule—FHL-GSU Film
	Non-population Schedule—UNC Film
	Population Schedule—U.S., 1790–1840 by Census Year and Location
	Population Schedule—U.S., 1790–1840 by Census Year
	Population Schedule—U.S., 1850–70 by Census Year and Location
	Population Schedule—U.S., 1850–70 by Census Year
	Population Schedule—U.S., 1850–60 Slaves by Census Year and Location
	Population Schedule—U.S., 1850–60 Slaves by Census Year
	Population Schedule—U.S., 1880–1930 by Census Year and Location
	Population Schedule—U.S., 1880–1930 by Census Year
	Population Schedule—U.S. State-Level Copy: In-House Film
	State-Sponsored Census—FHL-GSU Preservation Film
Derivatives	Database, CD/DVD
	Database, Online
	SOUNDEX and Miracode, Microfilm
	Statistical Database, Online, User-Defined Report

Church Records

Category	Templates
Church Books	Named Volume—Held by Church
	Numbered Volume—Held by Church
	Named Volume—Archived Off-Site
	Numbered Volume—Archived Off-Site
Image Copies	Digitized Online
	Microfilm—FHL-GSU Preservation Copy
	Microfilm—LDS Records at the FHL
	Microfilm—Publication
Derivatives	Church-Issued Certificate
	Church Record Book, Recopied
	Church Records Database, Online

Local and State Records—Courts and Governance

Category	Templates
Original Records	Local—Case File
	Local—Record Book
	Local—Case File, Archived Off-Site
	Local—Record Book, Archived Off-Site
	State Level—Appeals Court Record Book
	State Level—Legislative Petitions and Files
Image Copies	CD/DVD
	Microfilm—Archival Preservation Copy
	Microfilm—FHL-GSU Preservation Copy
	Online Image
Derivatives	Database Online

Local and State Records—Registrations, Rolls, and Vital Records

Category	Templates
Local Records	File Item
	File Moved to State Archives
	Registers—Named Volume
	Registers—Numbered Volume
	Vital Records Certificate
	Vital Records Register
	Vital Records, Amended
	Vital Records, Delayed
State-Level Records	Miscellaneous Files
	Vital Records Certificate
	Vital Records Register
	Vital Records, Amended

Local and State Records—Property and Probate

Category	Templates
Original Records	Local—Case File
	Local—Registers
	Local—Tract (Plat) Book
	State Level—Land-Grant Registers
	State Level—Land Warrants, Loose
Image Copies	CD/DVD
	Microfilm
	Online
Derivatives	Abstracts, Online
	Database, Online

National Government Records

Category	Templates
Original Materials (United States)	Audio Recordings—National Archives
	Manuscript—Library of Congress
	Manuscript—National Archives
	Manuscript—National Archives, Regional
	Map—National Archives
	Photograph—Library of Congress
	Railroad Retirement Board Pension File
	Social Security Administration Forms SS-5
Databases	CD-ROM Publication
	Database Online—National Archives (Australia)
	Database Online—National Archives (Canada)
	Database Online—National Archives (United Kingdom)
	Database Online—National Archives (United States)
	Database Online—Generic (any country; any online database)
	Database Online—Social Security Death Index

Category	Templates
Image Copies	NARA Microfilm—NARA-Style Citation
	NARA Microfilm—Publications-Style Citation
Images Online	Online Image—Library of Congress
	Online Image—National Archives (U.S.)
	Online Image—Patent and Trademark Office (U.S.)

Publications—Books, CDs, DVDs, Maps, Leaflets, and Videos

Category	Templates
Print Publications	Book—Basic Format
	Book—Chapter
	Book—Edited
	Book—Multi-volume Set
	Book—Reprint
	Book—Revised Edition
	Leaflet
	Map
Electronic Publications	Audio book
	CD/DVD Book—Text
	Video
	Website as Book
Image Copies	CD/DVD Publication
	Microfilm—FHL-GSU Preservation Copy
	Microfilm Publication
	Online Publication

Publications—Legal Works and Government Documents

Category	Templates
Book—Basic Format	Book—Basic Format
Legal Reference Works	Case Reporter—Series Named for Editor Case Reporter—Standardized Series Codes and Statutes, Online—State Database Codes and Statutes, Online—United States Code Slip Law—Federal Statutes—Federal Statutes—State
Printed Government Documents	Congressional Records—Citing Volume from Title Page Congressional Records—Traditional Academic Style Congressional Records—Online Images National Archives (U.S.) Guides—Descriptive Pamphlet, Online National Archives (U.S.) Guides—Preliminary Inventory, Microfilmed

Publications—Periodicals, Broadcasts, and Web Miscellanea

Category	Templates
Periodicals	Journal Article—Print Edition Journal Article—Online Archive of Print Journal Journal Article—Online Journal Magazine Article—Print Edition Magazine Article—Online Reprints, Random Title Newsletter Article—Print Edition Newspaper Article—Print Edition Newspaper Article—Print Edition by Location Newspaper Article—Print Edition by Newspaper Name Newspaper Article—Online Archive by Author Name Newspaper Article—Online Archive by Newspaper Name
Broadcasts and Web Miscellanea	Blog Discussion Forum or List Podcast Radio or Television Clip

Index

About the Author

Tana L. Pedersen

Tana has been writing and editing in the technology industry for almost fifteen years. She has earned several awards for her writing, including the Distinguished Technical Communication award from the Society for Technical Communication. Tana is author of *The Companion Guide to Family Tree Maker 2011*, five editions of *The Official Guide to Family Tree Maker*, and co-author of *The Official Guide to RootsWeb.com*.

Photo by Braden Lord